Andrew,

Enjoy the book!

Advance Praise for *The Collaborative Organization*

At TELUS, we believe passionately that our culture is key to sustaining our competitive advantage and that open and clear communication fosters meaningful engagement and spirited collaboration. This book guides organizations on how to properly implement collaboration tools and strategies to obtain that competitive advantage.

—Darren Entwistle, CEO, TELUS

Yum! Brands recognized early on that using social platforms designed for collaboration and integrated into employee work environments was non-negotiable. Jacob's book is a must read for leaders of organizations who also recognize that employee collaboration is not an option but a requirement to succeed in today's world.

—Dickie Oliver, VP Global IT, Yum! Brands

ManpowerGroup recognizes that in the Human Age, it is people that power the world of work and people are capable of much more when they collaborate to achieve their goals. Jacob's book provides an excellent overview for other companies that recognize the power of collaboration in the workplace.

—Denis Edwards, Senior Vice President,
Global Chief Information Officer, ManpowerGroup

Many organizations have lots of people disconnected in different silos, and these folks know a lot and could get lots more done if they had a way to "connect the dots." *The Collaborative Organization* helps you get that done, talking seriously about the culture of collaboration, useful tools, and realistic advice about overcoming organizational barriers.

—Craig Newmark, Founder of craigslist and craigconnects

Everyone knows that the future of work is engaged employees who collaborate to get things done but struggle to figure out how to get there. Jacob's book is a valuable strategic guide to help leaders deploy emerging collaboration technologies and strategies to "get there."

—Jonathan Becher, Chief Marketing Officer, SAP

New social and collaborative tools are causing an industry shift to the social enterprise, changing not only the way people work but also the way businesses engage with and delight their customers. Morgan has created a comprehensive strategic guide to help ensure these new tools and strategies succeed within the enterprise. A valuable resource for executives and decision makers.

—**Derek Burney, Corporate Vice President, Microsoft**

There are many collaboration resources that talk about the value of collaboration and why it's important. But I've found only one resource which actually walks leaders of organizations through how to deploy collaborative tools and strategies effectively. That resource is this book.

—**Parker Harris, EVP and Cofounder, Salesforce.com**

Social behavior is not new. What's new today is the emergence of platforms to allow communities to come together, to share ideas, expertise, and a sense of purpose and trust. Jacob's book provides the roadmap for how to build this kind of a collaborative organization.

—**Alistair Rennie, General Manager, Social Business, IBM**

At AVG Technologies, our employees are very dispersed geographically and heavily rely on tools for employee collaboration and engagement. Developing strategies for collaboration and figuring out which tools to use can oftentimes feel like trying to shoot a moving target. Jacob Morgan helps take the guesswork out of the process, so businesses can harness collaboration in ways that truly empower employees, customers, and the organization as a whole.

—**JR Smith, CEO, AVG Technologies**

Organizations cannot succeed without engaging their employees and connecting them to each other and to the information they need to get their jobs done. Leaders cannot succeed in building this type of a collaborative organization without this book.

—**Ben Haines, CIO, Pabst Brewing Company**

Morgan covers all aspects of emergent collaboration from understanding through implementation. This book provides much-needed knowledge at a time when collaboration is coming to the forefront of business.

—**Jason Sharpe, GM Collaboration, Knowledge & Intelligence, Telstra**

Jacob understands that it is not about the technology; it is about the people. If you have employees, this book will help you set the strategic foundation needed to engage your employees and foster collaboration so that the right information gets to the right people at the right time.

—**Walton Smith, Principal, Booz Allen Hamilton**

The
Collaborative
ORGANIZATION

A Strategic Guide to Solving Your Internal Business Challenges Using Emerging Social and Collaborative Tools

JACOB MORGAN

New York Chicago San Francisco Lisbon London
Madrid Mexico City Milan New Delhi San Juan
Seoul Singapore Sydney Toronto

To my friends and family and Blake,
who always encourages and supports me,
my Bashert.

The **McGraw·Hill** Companies

1 2 3 4 5 6 7 8 9 0   DOC/DOC 1 8 7 6 5 4 3 2

ISBN   978-0-07-178230-2
MHID   0-07-178230-3

e-ISBN 978-0-07-178231-9
e-MHID 0-07-178231-1

McGraw-Hill books are available at special quantity discounts to use as premiums and sales promotions or for use in corporate training programs. To contact a representative, please e-mail us at bulksales@mcgraw-hill.com.

This book is printed on acid-free paper.

Library of Congress Cataloging-in-Publication Data
Morgan, Jacob.
 The collaborative organization : a strategic guide to solving your internal business challenges using emerging social and collaborative tools / Jacob Morgan. — 1
        p. cm.
 Includes index.
 ISBN 978-0-07-178230-2 (alk. paper) — ISBN 0-07-178230-3 (alk. paper)
 1. Corporate culture. 2. Cooperation. I. Title.
 HD58.7.M675   2012
 658.4'012—dc23

                                                    2012000525

contents

foreword

The problem is not new. You run an organization with many
people, all working for some common goals: *your* goals. You tell
them what you want done and give them the time and money to do it.
Sounds simple enough, but it never is. They complain to you that they
don't know where to find the information they need to get their jobs
done. You know of experts in the company who can help them, but
they can't find the experts without your help. Over time you lose a few
good employees, some of whom were experts. Some retire, and some
find other jobs, and you wonder how much knowledge just walked out
the door.

Now let's look at this from the perspective of one of the many workers
in your organization. Let's assume that she knows her job and how it fits
with the organization's goals. Yet she doesn't know who else she should
be working with when facing a problem that might have already been
solved. She wonders, Where is that presentation that was written by the
guy who left the company last month? Someone said it was a really good
presentation. Maybe it's in some folder somewhere. After searching for
25 minutes, she finds the wrong version of the presentation and a ton of
other files that could have helped her last week. Frustrating.

This is not a new problem, and despite the progression from paper-
file cabinets to intranets, it still has not been solved. Getting things
done requires coordination, which incurs *high coordination* costs.
Those costs include management, infrastructure, and meetings—
many meetings. Ask anyone who works in a large corporation what
it's like to get stuff done, and you wonder if the megacorporate model

makes sense. Short of rebuilding the entire model of a workplace from scratch, there are ways to address the coordination problem and create a workplace that actually works. This underlies the goals of the Enterprise 2.0 movement, a revolution in the way people work together for common productive goals. The revolution is based on a simple observation: The Internet succeeded at bringing people together in ways that were unimaginable 25 years ago. Why can't the *intra*net do the same thing for my company?

Creating a socially effective workplace is not a simple task. Jacob Morgan explains in this book why this is so and what you can do about it. He studied the problem and spoke to many people who have succeeded and failed at tackling this issue. Let me preface his book with a few thoughts.

1. The problem is old, but the current approach to it is new, and it's worth understanding what is new about Enterprise 2.0.

2. The fallacy in using Enterprise 2.0 is thinking that there is one solution or approach you should take. It's worth understanding why thinking this way is a prelude to disaster.

3. Getting perspectives on your company's problems is essential. It's worth understanding and accepting the fact that you will need help.

What's New?

Technology and behaviors are at the core of the collaboration problem. Technology is always new and changing; behaviors, however, not so much. Herein lies the promise and challenge of Enterprise 2.0. Managing knowledge as an asset used to be the role of a corporate librarian, and those librarians lived in the world of paper files. Do you remember the rows and columns of dusty cabinets, shelves of neatly bound journals, and tables for research? If you were working in a corporation in the 1980s or 1990s, you probably do. If you walk into the back office of most doctors' offices and hospitals, you'll still see these things. For many companies, these file cabinets have been replaced with an intranet file system. An improvement? Mostly yes.

The age of digital information makes it much easier to store and access information, but it also makes it much easier to overwhelm seekers with too much information, much of it wrong, obsolete, or irrelevant. The intranet is mostly helpful, but sometimes it is too helpful. Sure, you can get the file in a snap, but it can take hours to find the right file.

One of the great changes taking place in the world is that information is becoming abundant and accessible. You don't need to know all that much anymore. All you need is a smartphone and Wikipedia, and you can get hold of information very quickly and nearly everywhere. Not that long ago, people would hoard information, hoping they would gain competitive leverage over others if they preserved secrets. These days, it's increasingly difficult to have any secrets.

When the workers in an old-style corporation acquired information, they would store it in their files in case it might be helpful in the future. Much like a precious gem or a rare resource, wealth is the reward of those who hold on to it. Information used to be treated like precious gems and hoarded. But in an age in which information is abundant, hoarding it is futile. In fact, it is counterproductive. Sharing the information widely gives you a better chance of making that information useful to you and to others.

What About Enterprise 2.0 Is for You?

Let me debunk a myth. When you think about how Enterprise 2.0 applies to you, you'll find that there is no single experience of Enterprise 2.0 — there is *your* Enterprise 2.0. Every company comes to its Enterprise 2.0 projects with a unique set of needs and resources, much the way every person's journey toward health (e.g., dieting, addiction recovery, or consolation) is unique. We talk about the journey in generalized terms, since it is easier to convey that way. Similarly, each company faces its own set of challenges when considering how it can foster emergent collaboration within the corporation. Yet the Enterprise 2.0 conversation is generalized into patterns.

The challenge you'll face is that many people engage in doublespeak: They tell you that everything is important and everything has to be considered first. Few engage in doublelisten, where they listen carefully for your unique needs and pay careful attention to how their advice might apply to your unique situation. Thus, you have to approach the generic Enterprise 2.0 conversation with some healthy skepticism about how the patterns affect your company.

Indeed, all organizations face similar challenges. They all wonder where to share information so that it can be found. They all wonder how to connect the people in their companies in efficient and effective ways. They all want to capture and leverage information and wisdom for competitive advantage. Yet when you get into the details, you find that nobody's problems are exactly the same. Many companies have a graveyard of partial solutions they have tried. Most Enterprise 2.0 projects will face friction, and in many cases downright resistance, coming from different places in the company. This makes your journey unique.

When a company starts an Enterprise 2.0 project by following the patterns set by another company, you know one thing for certain: It is starting with the solution, not the problem. Since every company faces its own journey, it can (and should) be inspired by other companies' successes. But it will need to chart its own path based on its own starting point. This means that books, blogs, and general presentations about Enterprise 2.0 are informative and inspirational, but alone are not actionable. It is much like trying to get in shape by watching other people exercise.

What You Need to Get Started on Your Path to Success

Let me suggest a simple process to help you get started:

1. **Understand the issues.** You will be on the right path by reading this book. The goal here is to help you see the game board

and understand how the pieces move. You'll learn some strategies about various stages of the process from the masters.

2. **Measure and test what is going on in your company.** Your
exploration into transforming and improving your company
needs to start from facts—not just any facts, but *your* facts.
Explore and understand before you introduce a new
understanding.

3. **Get help.** It's very hard to fix these problems on your own. If
companies were able to fix themselves, they would have done
it already. Much as people who need to lose weight consult
with dietitians and personal trainers, companies need to seek
the advice of experts or they will yo-yo back to their old habits.

They say it's difficult to find good help these days. One of the ways
you know you have good helpers is to see them in action and hear what
others say about them. I've been inspired by what I have seen Jacob
and Chess Media Group do with real organizations that faced real (and
unique) challenges. You'll find the insights from their experience and
explorations inspirational and educational.

Gil Yehuda

acknowledgments

Putting a collaboration book together requires just that, collaboration. There are many people who have supported me and the work that I have done over the years. I've also learned a great deal from these same people.

Connie Chan, thank you for being the best business partner that anyone could ask for and a great friend. Gil Yehuda, thanks for always sharing your wisdom, humor, and insight with me; it's always a pleasure to be in your company. Don Tapscott, thanks for helping pioneer the world of emergent collaboration and for contributing your wisdom and ideas to this book. Andrew McAfee, your work in 2006 is a big part of what inspired me to get involved in this type of work. I always learn from you.

All the guest contributors to the book, you helped make this book what it is and I couldn't have done it without you. This includes Adam Metz; you've been a great friend, supporter, and neighbor and helped make this book possible. To all the amazing leaders, executives, and visionaries who endorsed the book, your words have been an extremely valuable source of inspiration and encouragement.

Carl Frappaolo, thanks for always sharing your insight with me and for encouraging me to push forward with my ideas even when I wasn't sure where they were going to go. Charlie H. Green, you truly are a trusted advisor and a source of inspiration. Karthik Chakkarapani, you helped me to think more strategically and critically about many of the concepts and applications in this book—thank you! Paul Greenberg, thanks for being an early supporter of mine.

To all our Chess Media Group clients, thanks for believing in us and working with us.

I also want to thank our absolutely amazing designer at Chess, Pita, who helped with many of the images in the book.

Mark Fidelman, thanks for all your support and words of wisdom. I'm looking forward to reading your upcoming book. Lyle Fong, you've been a good friend and I always look forward to our engaging conversations.

I know the book is vendor agnostic but I do owe a thank you to the collaboration vendors who help move this industry forward and who helped support the book, especially Moxie Software, Salesforce, Box, Harmon.ie, Microsoft, Avectra, and NewsGator.

Finally I want to thank the team at McGraw-Hill who worked so hard to make this book come to life and everyone else who has supported me over the years and has encouraged and taught me.

introduction

By the time you are reading this book I will be 28 years old. This means that although I understand how business was conducted before emergent social and collaborative technologies existed, I never worked for any organization that wasn't using these types of technologies. In fact, it's safe to say that I don't know what it's like to do business without using emergent social and collaborative technologies and strategies. This is why this book is worth your time.

I was born in a social, collaborative, and digital world. Chess Media Group, the management consultancy and strategic advisory firm that I run, was built on and is still operating because of emergent social and collaborative tools, and we're just a small shop based in San Francisco and Vancouver.

We have all heard about how social media tools such as Twitter, Facebook, and blogs are changing the ways in which organizations communicate and collaborate with customers. In fact, I'm sure many of you are already using customer-facing tools at your organizations. There are plenty of case studies, stories, and examples of this that can be found all over the web; try googling "Social Media Case Studies" and see what happens. It is important to use these tools to engage with and collaborate with customers; however, organizations need to change and evolve from the inside out, and that means starting with the employees.

What about using similar concepts and ideas for collaboration within organizations among the employees?

This book was not written to convince organizations or individuals why emergent collaboration is important; thousands of pages in other books are devoted to that topic. This means that I'm not going to devote several chapters to background information about how the world is changing or the ways in which organizations need to adapt. There are plenty of books that provide excellent overviews of the emergent collaborative landscape and how we got to where we are today. This book is written for those who already know that emergent collaboration should be a critical investment for an organization and those who realize that it's time to act to make this happen.

What I believe is lacking are resources for organizations that can guide them and provide strategic advice on how they can use emergent collaborative software and strategies behind their firewalls and among employees to solve business problems and unearth opportunities. That is why this book was written.

I have spent the last few years working with and researching organizations that are using these new tools and strategies internally. However, I felt that there were a lot of questions not being addressed, such as how budgets are being allocated, how success is being measured, and what tools are being used and why. This led my company, Chess Media Group, to conduct an industrywide survey on the current state of emergent collaborative technologies and strategies. The data from that survey are used throughout the book as supporting material.

The survey Chess Media Group conducted included responses from 234 individuals around the world who are involved in emergent collaboration at their organizations. The responses came from smaller companies with under 1,000 employees and large companies with over 100,000 employees. Responsibilities varied from midlevel to C-level employees and encompassed various industries and geographies around the world.

You will notice that almost all the chapters feature a guest contributor. I was careful to make sure that the contributors weren't vendors or consultants but people who are actually "doing" these things full time at their companies. These contributors are actual practitioners who are implementing collaborative tools and strategies for their organizations. Their contributions add another layer of depth to the book. You will get insights, ideas, and advice directly from people who are doing this at some of the world's largest and most recognized companies. Most of the chapters also have a section titled "Summary and Action Items" at the end with some suggestions and recommendations for taking the necessary steps to progress toward achieving your goals.

The purpose of this book is to act as a guide for executives, decision makers, and those involved with collaborative initiatives at their organizations. I'll admit that writing the book was daunting because as a single individual in an emerging and evolving space, I by no means had answers to all the questions. However, I knew that these questions and topics needed to be addressed, so I made sure to try to provide the answers to the best of my ability. I hope this book can be used not only as an industry resource but also as a stepping-stone to help further the necessary education and resource base we need for organizations to succeed in an increasingly collaborative world.

When you think about the amount of time people spend at work, you start to realize what a tremendous impact our work lives have on our personal lives. I believe that the business world needs to and will change to become more collaborative. I believe that successful organizations will be composed of employees who trust and inspire one another, and I believe that organizations are going to have to support their employees with new strategies and technologies to enable this to happen. In effect I believe that the business world is starting to change and will never be the same. Imagine an organization in which employees feel fulfilled and happy with their jobs, their stress is reduced, they trust their managers and peers, and they feel as though they are a part of something great.

Organizations are composed of three types of broad communities.

External communities are made up of customers (this is where you typically hear about social CRM, social media, or the social customer); hybrid communities are made of partners and suppliers (or perhaps certain types of customers); and internal communities are composed of employees who make up the organization. You may have heard of the terms *enterprise social software, Enterprise 2.0, emergent collaborative software*, or the ever popular *social business*. These different terms all refer to an organization's ability to leverage new strategies and technologies to solve business problems, whether those problems involve customers, partners/suppliers, or employee facing. Instead of worrying about the different buzzwords, let's focus on understanding the type of community we are going to be discussing, and that is the internal, or employee, community.

Collaborative organizations can help make the world a better place. Imagine employees who are more productive at work, are happier, and feel more fulfilled and inspired with the work they do. This doesn't just impact their lives at work, but it also impacts their lives at home. These employees will have more time to spend with family, less stress (which hopefully causes fewer arguments), and an overall improved quality of life.

Although collaboration alone isn't enough to make this happen, I believe it is a big step in the right direction. I do my best to discuss not only the hard benefits and strategic aspects of emergent collaboration but the soft benefits and real human aspects of emergent collaboration as well.

The book is broken down into three sections, and those who know chess will be familiar with the section titles: "The Opening," "The Middle Game," and "The End Game." The opening focuses on organizations that are just getting started with their emergent collaboration initiatives. I cover things such as business drivers, case studies, evaluating risk, and having the right people involved. The middle game is for organizations that are more involved in their collaborative efforts and perhaps are already deploying solutions. This section covers things such as evaluating vendors, developing a strategy, dealing with resistance, rolling out a platform, and developing governance. Finally, we have the end game, which is about sustaining and maintaining these initiatives in the long term. Here I discuss things such as measuring success, sustaining adoption, and the future of emergent collaboration.

Things such as web conferencing and telephony systems are not addressed here. When I use the terms *enterprise collaborative software*, *Enterprise 2.0*, and *emergent collaborative software or tools*, what I'm specifically referring to are a new class of collaboration tools that have many of the features and functionality of the consumer-grade social network–type tools and platforms that are being leveraged within organizations. These tools come in many different shapes, sizes, prices, and features. What they all have in common is that they are emergent, they are social, and they are collaborative.

part one

THE OPENING

one

A Tale of
Two Changes

The last few years have seen the emergence of consumer and enterprise social and collaborative platforms. We've seen new agencies and analyst firms emerge and have also seen a flurry of new terms and buzzwords swarming the Internet like angry bees. Terms such as *social customer relationship management (SCRM), social business, Enterprise 2.0, social media,* and *social customer* are unavoidable. They all mean different things to different people. I can't tell you how many times I hear these terms used interchangeably at conferences and events, and I bet you are also having a hard time keeping up with the latest jargon. In fact, it has become such a problem that when writing this book I wasn't even sure how to refer to it.

I settled on using the term *emergent collaboration* because *emergent* means "becoming visible or being noticed" and *collaboration* means "working with someone to create something or achieve a goal." This sums up exactly what this book and this business evolution are about: new ways of working with people to create things and solve problems.

Social business has become a popular term. However, many executives and decision makers I have spoken with shy away from the term *social* because it is overused and has become synonymous with fun and time-wasting applications such as Facebook and Twitter instead of being associated with something that can provide real business value to an organization, such as collaboration. If the term *social business* works for you, go for it but understand which type of community you are referring to (internal, external, or hybrid, discussed in the Introduction). I have found that *social* doesn't inherently convey any type of business value, whereas *collaboration* does; I like to joke that social is what happens when you remove the business value from collaboration.

One thing you will come to realize by reading this book is that none of the terms really matter; after all, it's not how you define something but how you actually implement it that really matters. Truth be told, it's easy to get lost in the jargon, the products, and the ideas that are making the rounds across the Internet. However, I believe that everything we are seeing today in the social and collaborative circles can be attributed to two key changes in the world: culture and technology.

Culture (or as Gil Yehuda Likes to Say, Observable Behaviors)

It's a bit weird to think that just a few years ago many of the tools and platforms we use regularly today didn't exist. What did we do before Facebook, Yelp, Wikipedia, and Foursquare? How did we find, communicate, and share information with one another?

Over the last five to seven years we have become much more comfortable sharing information publicly. Facebook allows us to share our hobbies and interests, Twitter lets us share our thoughts and ideas, Flickr gives us the power to share images, and platforms such as Foursquare allow users to share their physical locations. Yes, the world has become much more public. In fact, it is becoming hard to distinguish between our personal and professional lives. The time we spend on our personal lives and the time we spend on our professional lives are blurring. We frequently see employees take their work home with them or get things done from the road. It seems that we are always "connected" to the digital world. Not that long ago we had to make an effort to get connected; now we have to make an effort to get disconnected, and aside from moving to a remote location in the wilderness or cutting off the power to our houses, we don't have many other options (even cutting off the power won't prevent you from getting Wi-Fi at the café just around the corner).

One of my greatest passions is traveling, and a few years ago I spent a month in China traveling all over the country to some of the large cities and remote villages. I was amazed at my ability to stay connected in virtually any location. This connectivity is virtually all we need to get our jobs done and manage many aspects of our lives.

Ten years ago if people would have told me (or you) that so much of our personal information would be online for the world to see, I would have told them they were nuts! Now look at where we are today. The Internet and social media have permeated every facet of our daily lives (at work and at home) from how we consume news and information, to how we communicate with one another, to how we share and create content.

As someone who has grown up using these tools and technologies I don't remember what it was like to conduct business when these platforms did not exist. In fact, my company, Chess Media Group, was built using these social and collaborative technologies; virtually nothing we did would be considered traditional. Younger generations are going to be even more fluent with and accustomed to using these tools and technologies as part of their everyday lives, and that includes time spent at work.

I always try to imagine my little brother Josh (born in 1992) working at a company that doesn't use emergent collaboration platforms, and I don't see how he would be able to get his job done. I was born in a digital world, but my little brother might as well have been born with a computer in his hands.

As the years go by, we are going to see this trend increase with younger generations entering the workforce and with our comfort with and fluency in social and collaborative technologies increasing. This isn't a question of if but a question of when, and I think the when has already happened.

The big challenge we see, however, is that there is a large gap between how social tools are being used by customers and how they are being used by organizations internally. If you think about it, popular social media tools and platforms are now commonplace in our everyday personal lives, yet these tools and strategies are years behind inside organizations. We are gradually starting to see that gap close as more companies are starting to realize the immense value of connecting their employees and information.

Technology

There have been quite a few technological advances over the last few years, and in the social and collaborative software space we have seen the rise of platforms such as Twitter, Facebook, LinkedIn, and Foursquare, among others. We have companies developing products that can scour the web for any and every relevant conversation about a brand, product, competitor, service, or company and deliver those searches in a neat little dashboard. There are other companies that allow organizations to develop active and thriving communities for both customers and employees that allow for two-way communication and collaboration, and we are starting to see effective data integration of traditional and social data into single systems. The way we communicate and share information with one another, with customers, and with employees has changed dramatically, and these technological advances are the enablers that are making it happen.

Together these changes we are seeing in culture and technology are propelling our world into a more connected and collaborative existence. People are now accustomed to interacting and collaborating with one another through social and collaborative platforms and are bringing these habits and methods with them into the workplace.

The challenge for organizations today is finding a way to continue doing business and improving the way they do business, but in the context of the ways in which these two changes are affecting them.

Emergent Collaboration Is Not Social Media

Platforms such as Twitter and Facebook are now virtually mainstream, but aside from the technological differences between these consumer platforms and emergent enterprise platforms, there are some very different business dynamics. It's important to understand these business dynamics, so let's take a look at them.

Money

In general, with social media we can do pretty much what we want the way we want to do it; there aren't really any restrictions on how we can use these tools. This is not true in the workplace, and the fact that employees get paid to do work by the organization creates a very different dynamic. Organizations want to make sure that employees aren't wasting time with pointless activities when they should be working.

Legacy Systems and Multiple Data Sources

In most enterprises there are a plethora of technology solutions and data sources that all need to be weaved together to provide content and context to the employees. This is not something we need to worry about in the consumer social media world, but it's a challenge for many organizations today. These technology solutions are often outdated as well.

Team Dynamics

Hierarchies exist, and they will most likely continue to exist in the foreseeable future. This means that employees don't operate alone and that their actions affect others around them for better or for worse. In the social media world we often operate as individuals, but in the enterprise we work as teams.

Trust

Trust is a very important dynamic within the enterprise, and unfortunately, it's something that many companies struggle to create among their employees. Without trust it's very hard for employees to collaborate with one another and share information.

Workflows

Employees today all have a way they do things; this includes everything from creating proposals to following up on customer service requests.

Emergent collaboration affects these workflows (one hopes for the better) and augments the way employees do what they do in the workplace.

This is discussed more fully in Chapter 4, but it should be noted here that these are very real and different dynamics that affect emergent collaboration within the enterprise. There are perhaps other factors at play here that are specific to each and every organization, but the point remains the same: Emergent collaboration in the workplace is not the same as social media.

Summary and Action Items

Although it is possible to get swept away in the terms, definitions, concepts, and ideas that are being thrown around, the key thing here to remember is that everything we are seeing can be boiled down to culture and technology. These two things are the drivers for everything "social" and "collaborative" that we are seeing today:

- Look at how culture and technology at your organization have changed over the last few years (or how they have changed at various companies you have been with).

- Try to understand what causes these changes and what the results of these changes are. Where do you think things are headed?

To help us understand more about how culture and technology are affecting our work, let's hear what Augie Ray, the executive director of community and collaboration at the USAA, has to say.

It is vital for business decision makers to realize the accelerating pace of change that is occurring in technology, human behavior, and business culture; moreover, it is important to recognize that these three things do not move evenly but in fits and starts. An idea that is supported only by innovative technology but that fails to fit either current consumer behavior or organizational culture is doomed to fail. Conversely, an organization that waits until technology, behavior, and culture are comfortably and adequately evolved can miss out on opportunities. A couple of examples help convey the importance of timing.

Back in 1997, the site sixdegrees.com was launched to allow Internet users to discover how connected they are to one another. It was an early precursor to LinkedIn and Facebook, but rather than enjoy the success of those social networking sites, sixdegrees.com shuttered in 2001. It was the right technology and the right idea, but human behavior was not prepared—people had not yet adopted the Internet into their lives sufficiently, nor were they prepared to share that much information so openly.

Another example is Napster, a file-sharing site that was shut down by court order in 2001 because of rampant copyright infringement. (It has since reopened as a legal music sub-scription service.) Before being closed, Napster had 25 million users and 80 million songs. In this case, the technology and human behavior were ready but the business culture was not. Even now, 10 years later, record companies and the Recording Industry Association of America (RIAA) struggle with intellectual property (IP) issues, but the industry has since embraced the online distribution of music.

Bringing an idea to market before technology, behavior, and the business culture are prepared is dangerous, but so is waiting too long. Blockbuster was considered a model of innovation in the 1980s and 1990s, when its scale and ability to customize a store to its neighborhood squeezed out smaller mom-and-pop video stores. But it waited too long to waive onerous late fees and adopt new technologies such as online streaming and kiosks. As Netflix approached 23 million subscribers in the United States and Canada and Redbox opened more than 20,000 kiosks, Blockbuster shrank from 4,000 stores to fewer than 2,000 before declaring bankruptcy in 2010. In this case, technology and consumer behavior evolved more rapidly than did Blockbuster's corporate culture, resulting in a disastrous business outcome.

Technology, behavior, and corporate culture have never moved more quickly. Moore's law, which was described in 1965 and has proved remarkably accurate, states that computing power doubles every two years. The same could be said of ideas, with the half-life of ideas growing ever shorter. For more than 50 years, the big three U.S. automakers were able to hold on to their preeminent collective market share until oil crises and competitive imports fundamentally changed the domestic auto market in the 1970s. Compare that to MySpace, which went from being the most popular and innovative social site to being an also-ran behind Facebook in just two years.

With the pace of change increasing and the risks of moving too fast or too slow never greater, the ability to have employees collaborate effectively regardless of space, time, language, and other impediments is no longer just a competitive advantage—it is vital. Collaborating effectively inside and outside the organization is the only way to ensure that the enterprise and the employees are prepared for rapid changes in technology, human behavior, and business culture.

---

two

The First Step to Recovery Is Admitting You Have a Problem

Have you ever thought about what collaboration actually means? Perhaps this sounds like a silly question, but I'm often surprised by the responses I get. Quite simply, collaboration is defined as working with someone (or multiple people) to create something or achieve a goal. That's the definition, but what does collaboration actually allow employees to do?

In 1977 T. J. Allen wrote *Managing the Flow of Technology*, and one of the things that he was able to show was that when people work more than 30 meters apart, the likelihood for collaboration and communication falls off dramatically (see Figure 2.1). In fact, if employees are more than 30 meters apart they might as well be across town!

So the most important thing collaboration enables employees to do is form bonds and connections with one another, in effect building relationships. These relationships and the engaged employees are what lead to ideas and discoveries within organizations. The more employees can share, communicate, collaborate, and engage with one another, the greater the flow of ideas is. These ideas can be new revenue-generating opportunities, cost-cutting strategies, recommendations for productivity enhancement, improvements in product development, and almost anything else.

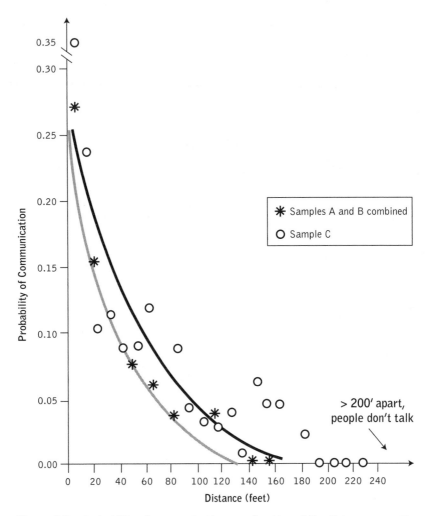

Figure 2.1 Probability of communication as a function of the distance separating pairs of people

Source: Professors John Carroll and Li Tao, *Managerial Psychology,* Massachusetts Institute of Technology: MIT OpenCouseWare, Fall 2006, http://ocw.mit.edu, accessed January 19, 2012. Used by permission of MIT OCW.

To understand this better, we need to look at strong and weak ties. Strong ties exist with people whom you know well and with whom you engage frequently, such as friends. Weak ties exist with people whom you don't know well and with whom you don't engage frequently; one might call them acquaintances.

In 1973 the sociologist Mark Granovetter published a paper titled "The Strength of Weak Ties" in which he asserts the value of weak ties as bridges that are valuable for the dissemination of information. In fact, Granovetter states, "all bridges are weak ties." Strong ties exist in limited numbers because they require effort to maintain; weak ties require far less effort, which means there can be many of these bridges.

Two people with strong ties to each other also typically know many of the same people, and so there is a strong overlap. Thus, if Tim and Erica have a strong tie and Tim needs to find or get access to information he can't find by asking people he knows, it's likely that Erica will not be able to help him since their friends overlap. But if Tim has a weak tie with Peter, Tim now has a bridge to Peter's network (whose members are most likely strangers to Tim) and gains access to a new group of people who are likely to be able to help.

Emergent collaboration solutions allow the creation of strong ties, but more important, they allow for the creation of weak ties, or bridges, within organizations. These bridges allow employees to get access to information and people within a larger network instead of simply relying on the people they know. LinkedIn, Facebook, Twitter, and blogs are great examples of consumer-grade applications that are extremely effective at allowing people to build weak ties. On a trip to Dubai a few years ago I was able to sit down with a senior-level manager at Nestlé because of a weak tie I had with him through LinkedIn. The first large client Chess Media Group worked with came as a result of a weak tie formed through my blog.

Examples of weak ties are easily seen in people's personal lives. How many times have you met acquaintances you have later been able to call on for favors? Perhaps you asked them for introductions in companies, invitations to exclusive events, or discount offers for products. We form weak ties regularly at conferences, by meeting friends of friends, by going to parties, or pretty much by doing anything social where there are people outside our network.

Internally, these weak ties are easy to build through rich profiles that allow employees to discover coworkers by posting status updates or sharing information, by blogging internally, by submitting ideas publicly, or simply by asking and/or answering questions via an emergent collaboration platform.

As Andrew McAfee clearly wrote in one of his articles, which can be accessed at http://andrewmcafee.org/2007/10/the_ties_that_find/:

> Strong ties are unlikely to be bridges between networks, while weak ties are good bridges. Bridges help solve problems, gather information, and import unfamiliar ideas. They help get work done quicker and better. The ideal network for a knowledge worker probably consists of a core of strong ties and a large periphery of weak ones. Because weak ties by definition don't require a lot of effort to maintain, there's no reason not to form a lot of them (as long as they don't come at the expense of strong ties).

The key is that weak ties are important to build bridges to connect your organization, and emergent collaboration is the best way to do it.

The success of any enterprise collaboration initiative doesn't begin with technology or with the desire to find the coolest new shiny object; in fact, that's probably the shortest route to failure. Enterprise collaboration begins with a specific business driver or problem that the organization is looking to solve. Not every organization is going to invest in emergent collaboration for the same reasons, and that is as it should be. Specific and unique business problems occur behind the walls of each organization around the world. However, based on the research Chess Media Group has conducted, we can identify some of the common business drivers of these emergent collaboration initiatives within organizations regardless of company size, verticality, or geographic location.

Figure 2.2 breaks down all the Enterprise 2.0 business drivers for organizations.

Chess Media Group has a full report (which can be found on the Chess Media Group website under "resources") that discusses these findings in more detail, but in the figure one can see that the top five business drivers for organizations are (survey participants were able to select more than one response):

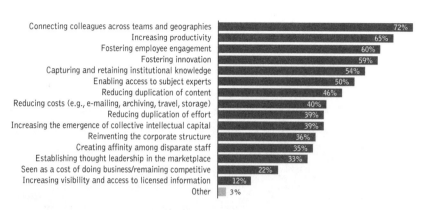

Figure 2.2   Enterprise 2.0 business drivers

- Connecting colleagues across teams and geographies
- Increasing productivity
- Fostering employee engagement
- Fostering innovation
- Capturing and retaining institutional knowledge

As competitive pressures increase and organizations continue to grow and expand while dealing with macroeconomic factors (e.g., a sluggish economy), it becomes increasingly apparent why this route toward a more collaborative organization becomes a focal point for many organizations. These emergent collaborative tools serve as the connective fibers that keep employees connected to one another. Employees today are working from multiple physical locations, on multiple devices, and often with other employees they have never met. It's also not uncommon for organizations to have "offices" with only one or two people in those locations. Organizations need a way to connect all those employees to allow them to collaborate and share information. The reality is that an organization is no longer limited to a physical structure or proximity; an organization is now limited only by its ability to connect employees and information together.

By far, the number one business driver for most organizations is being able to connect colleagues across teams and geographies, and this should come as no surprise. Companies of all shapes and sizes have employees based in multiple physical locations and working remotely; this is now commonplace. The ability to keep employees connected is not something that legacy systems and e-mail platforms can do effectively or perhaps at all.

Almost all the organizations surveyed stated that their business drivers fell into one of the categories listed in Figure 2.2. However, if your business drivers are not listed there, that's not a problem. The important thing is not to match your business drivers with the figure but to identify what those drivers are. It's crucial to understand your business drivers so that you understand *why* this should be an area of investment, which will in turn lead to *how* these tools should be deployed and *how* the strategies are developed. Once the business problem is identified, use cases from those business problems can be developed and expounded on. We will take a look at the various categories of emergent collaborative technologies in Chapter 6, where we will also look at the specific business drivers for each type of solution.

As was mentioned earlier, collaboration isn't new. Employees have collaborated for many years via phone, e-mail, in-person discussions, letters, carrier pigeons, and other media. In fact, collaboration has been around since the first two humans grunted at each other while planning their next kill for sustenance.

If collaboration has already been enabled in other ways, why bother investing in collaboration via emergent collaborative software? Why do organizations need to connect their employees via internal social networks, wikis, or workspaces when they can just e-mail one another or call one another on the phone? Ed Coleman, the CEO of Unisys, put it best when he said, "Sharpening our organization's communications capabilities, creating greater transparency, and improving access to our intellectual assets [people] could only increase our flexibility and responsiveness."

There are several unique benefits that are not realized via other means of collaboration, including the following:

- Knowledge sharing and transfer

- Alignment

- Identifying subject matter experts
- Thinking out loud
- Listening
- Cross-department, cross-company, and cross-boundary communication
- Collective intelligence and memory
- Inspiring employees and building trust
- Identifying new opportunities and ideas

Knowledge Sharing and Transfer

There are two types of knowledge that need to be shared and transferred at organizations: new knowledge and old knowledge. The concepts are exactly what they sound like: Old knowledge refers to knowledge that already exists within the organization, and new knowledge refers to knowledge that is created within the organization, perhaps new ways of doing things.

At your company, if you want to share information or transfer knowledge, how do you do it? Most likely your organization is using a legacy intranet system that basically acts as a massive warehouse for information. Employees attempt to search for and find the information they need. If an employee wants to edit that information (assuming he or she has permission to do so) or update it, it is usually necessary to download it, make the edits, and re-upload it. Even then it becomes a bit tedious for multiple people to collaborate on a document or a piece of information. Chances are, your organization also uses e-mail as a way to share information. E-mail has become the de facto chat messaging program in many companies. Employees send an e-mail and then instantly get a response. That's not e-mail, that's instant messaging, and it needs to stop. Atos Origin, a global information technology (IT) services company with around 80,000 employees, pledged in 2011 that within three years it planned to be a zero e-mail company. The CEO, Thierry Breton, said: "The volume of e-mails we send and receive is unsustainable for business. Managers spend between 5 and

20 hours a week reading and writing e-mails . . . e-mail is on the way out as the best way to run a company and do business."

Does this mean that e-mail is evil or that a massive war should be waged against it? Although many would say yes, I say absolutely not.

E-mail was meant for asynchronous communication, and sometimes using it does make sense. However, e-mail shouldn't be used for everything and should be integrated into other existing flows of work. Even though e-mail was meant for asynchronous communication, what do we do? We stare at our inboxes and our phones, waiting for new messages. In fact, I can't tell you how many times I have watched people walk into poles, walls, and other people because they were checking and responding to e-mails. Technology is supposed to support us and do what we tell it to do. Instead we have the opposite: Technology tells us what to do and when to use it.

Sharing knowledge and information in this way is very inefficient. Using e-mail causes problems with versioning, content duplication, reaching the right people, and locating the proper information later, among a host of other annoying problems.

Emergent collaborative platforms not only allow employees to store and share information; more important, those platforms allow them to collaborate on that information without ever sending an e-mail. Institutional knowledge is something that exists within every organization yet is one of the hardest things to share.

The federal government predicts that there will be around 500,000 new employees joining its organizations over the next 10 years. The problem is that organizations such as the federal government don't have a way to transfer knowledge from more established employees (who may be on their way out of the organization) to new employees. If you have been at an organization for many years, chances are that you know quite well how things work. You know where to find the right people and the right information. But how do you transfer that knowledge and information to someone who just joined your organization, and how can you do it at scale? That is not something that e-mail and legacy intranet systems do. Legacy systems allow for virtually no communication or actual collaboration, and e-mail does a mediocre job of communication at best.

Vistaprint had a problem a few years ago when it started growing and needed to hire and onboard new employees quickly. Through the use of wikis they were able to decrease their onboarding time for new engineers by almost 50 percent. Wikis were used to store the more relevant and up-to-date information for training new employees, which was maintained and edited by a collective group, thus helping ensure the quality of the information. This is something e-mail and traditional legacy systems cannot do.

Alignment

One of the things many organizations have trouble with is alignment both from a cultural and from a business standpoint. This might be the result of a physically distributed organization or perhaps an enterprise that has acquired another company or several companies. The larger an organization grows and the more distributed it becomes, the harder it is to make sure that there is alignment across the organization. How can an organization make sure that the same processes are being applied in the United States as are being applied in Denmark? How does the marketing team in Sweden make sure it has the information that a team in Japan has? Making sure that the organization as a whole is on the same page is no doubt a challenge.

Emergent collaborative solutions allow companies to organize their teams, departments, and employees in a way that allows all the right people to see the relevant information. Employees then have the ability to provide feedback and collaborate on that information seamlessly.

I had a conversation with an executive at a midsize consulting firm who told me that his company had just gone through a series of acquisitions of smaller companies. Each company had its own processes, culture, resources, and way of doing things. Those acquired entities had little communication with one another. That meant that there was a lot of content duplication, misaligned services and processes, and confusion among employees, along with a general sense of chaos. Effectively deploying tools and strategies can help ensure that an organization can align itself in all the relevant and required areas at scale. This is something that no other technology is capable of doing.

Subject Matter Expertise

Let's assume that you are working on an international marketing project. You are based in the United States but want to find someone at your company who is familiar with overseas rules and regulations. Or perhaps you want to get in touch with someone who is in charge of a particular product launch. How would you go about finding this person? Most employees would send out an e-mail asking for help; those employees would then send out their own e-mails and so on and so forth until the e-mail finally reached the right person. Elementary school kids used to play a similar game called telephone. We've grown up, and so should our businesses.

The tools and platforms available today make it much easier to find subject matter experts by letting employees develop rich profiles, thus allowing them to specify what it is their expertise is in. Employees are also often able to tag their colleagues with keywords and phrases, making it easier for other employees to find them when searching for a relevant person. Furthermore, many of these platforms also allow for companywide communication via status updates to the organization. These status updates can be used for a variety of things, including asking a community who is the best person to help out on a project or task. Basically, what all this means is that if an employee is looking for someone, he or she should have no problem finding that person and won't have to ask or e-mail anyone else about it.

Thinking Out Loud

This is not something I typically hear many people talk about, but I believe that is an oversight. I believe one of the ways people learn from themselves and from others is by thinking out loud. This allows coworkers and colleagues to see the thought process around how certain decisions are made within organizations. I know many of us have that little internal voice we hear when working on something, especially if it's an exciting project. I'm sure many of you often talk to yourselves out loud. You are not the only one who can benefit from that little voice inside your head. I guarantee that you have several colleagues who could learn from you by tapping into your thought process, and you could learn from them. For example, let's say you want to develop a business model for something you are working on. You can share your thought processes publicly as you begin to crank out ideas. Other employees will then be able to provide you with feedback and their own ideas, which you may be able to incorporate into your model. This ability to think out loud was never possible before.

Listening

Pick up any social media book today, and chances are that you will read about how listening to customers is perhaps the single most important thing any company can do today. I believe the same thing is true within the enterprise. One of the complaints I have heard from executives at organizations is that they have trouble following what is going on at the ground floor of their companies. Deploying enterprise collaboration platforms helps solve that problem by allowing employees to understand what is happening within their departments and across the enterprise. Keeping an eye on the things that matter to you is crucial for making sure you are always able to contribute when needed while staying up to date on the things that matter to you.

Cross-Department, Cross-Company, and Cross-Boundary Communication

In most organizations today information doesn't flow organically; in fact, it often doesn't flow much at all. Employees in a particular department usually keep to themselves. This means that if you are in the marketing department or the product development department, you're probably not going to be speaking with or reaching out to anyone from the IT or sales department. This is unfortunate because often employees in other departments have information that can benefit you in whatever you and your team are doing.

In a midsize medical association I wrote a case study on, I learned how one department was able to share its experience in developing and advertising mobile apps with another department. That other department applied similar ideas and thus far has generated over $50,000 in additional revenue that would not have been generated otherwise. This resulted from sharing some experiences for mobile apps.

This type of collaboration isn't crucial only between departments but also across dispersed geographic areas, for example, two marketing teams: one based in San Francisco and the other based in Dubai.

Collaboration tools ensure that communication flows throughout the organization, and that information can be shared between departments, across the organization as a whole, or through any type of organizational silos that exist within the enterprise.

This is a key benefit noticed by a 1,500-person department in Penn State University called Penn State Outreach. Through the use of collaborative tools supported by strategies, Penn State was able to improve collaboration across the organization and break down the silos it was plagued with (more on this is covered in Chapter 3).

Collective Intelligence and Memory

Lew Platt, the former CEO of Hewlett-Packard, once said, "If HP knew what HP knows, we would be three times more productive." Collective intelligence refers to the ability of an organization to use the wisdom of its employees to make business decisions. This premise means that better, more accurate decisions can be made. Let's say that an executive at your company says that she wants a new product developed in three months. Employees from different departments and business units can share their ideas and feedback on whether this is feasible. Perhaps the marketing team is not able to meet the deadline because of a conference it is planning, or perhaps the product team is already swamped with projects. The same idea can be applied for budget estimates for projects. Being able to leverage the knowledge of a collective is more accurate and far more powerful than leveraging the knowledge of just a few.

Chances are that your employees can solve virtually any problem or answer any question you throw at them. This works on a collective basis, not on an individual basis.

The concept of collective memory is quite powerful. Being able to capture and access the information your employees have even when they are not there physically or perhaps no longer are working there is a very powerful thing. One employee can remember and know only so much.

Building Trust and Inspiring Employees

This is a unique benefit of emergent collaboration that I do not hear discussed often. So much of our attention is focused on productivity, integration, workflows, and technology that we forget to step back and take a look at the human side of all this. The way we build trust inside our organizations is not that dissimilar to the way organizations build trust with customers through social media channels. Often the easiest way to start trusting someone is by finding something you have in common with each other. In his presentations and his book *Start with Why*, Simon Sinek states that when we surround ourselves with people who believe what we believe, trust emerges. Emergent collaboration makes this possible by allowing employees to share basic profile information (for example, who else lives in my city or works in my department); this is deepened by interactions, shared content, and development of communities of interest (groups of people with similar interests and/or beliefs). Sure, trust is largely a cultural thing, but deploying an emergent collaboration solution should be a message to the employees and in fact an impetus to build a culture of trust and collaboration.

Inspiration is something we don't hear about nearly enough these days. I recently read an article in the *New York Times** written by Teresa Amabile, a professor at Harvard Business School, and Steven Kramer, an independent researcher, the authors of *The Progress Principle*, which cited some interesting statistics:

---

* http://www.nytimes.com/2011/09/04/opinion/sunday/do-happier-people-work-harder.html.

Culture
of
Trust
✗

- Americans feel worse about their jobs—and work environments—than ever before.
- Gallup estimates the cost of America's disengagement crisis at a staggering $300 billion in lost productivity annually.
- Inner work life has a profound impact on workers' creativity, productivity, commitment, and collegiality.
- Employees are far more likely to have new ideas on days when they feel happy.
- Of all the events that engage people at work, the single most important—by far—is simply making progress in meaningful work.
- Ninety-five percent of the surveyed managers failed to recognize that progress in meaningful work is the primary motivator, well ahead of traditional incentives such as raises and bonuses.

What does this mean? It means that organizations have an amazing opportunity to learn about and inspire their employees in ways that were never possible before. The same concept of listening to our customers on social channels can and should be applied to listening to our employees via our internal collaboration platforms. By using these new technologies we can find out what really makes our employees tick, what they care about, what they are passionate about, what they are unhappy about, and why they get up in the morning. I feel that this fundamental human aspect of collaboration inside organizations is being diminished, and that needs to stop. Employees should feel fulfilled and inspired with the work that they do and collaborative organizations can make that happen. A midlevel employee at a large company told me that when he goes to work, he is reminded of that scene from *The Matrix* in which humans are used as batteries to power the machine world. What a terrible way for anyone to feel!

New Opportunities and Ideation

How does your organization come up with new ideas or identify new opportunities? Chances are that specific teams within departments or groups of executives get together to discuss these topics. However, every employee in your organization should be empowered to share his or her ideas and help discover opportunities. Why should this be limited?

Many organizations struggle to empower their employees to develop and create new ideas that they can share within the organization. In effect, the voice of the employee is lost inside many enterprises. Being able to empower the employees to share ideas and opinions in a public way allows an organization as a whole to develop new ideas while exploring potential new opportunities.

Océ, a 21,000-employee global printing company, is a classic example of this. After Océ deployed a series of collaborative tools, employees started to contribute ideas for how the company could improve and cut costs. One of those ideas involved encouraging truck drivers to fill up with gas at local stations instead of near the highways, where gas was more expensive. As a result of implementing this idea, Océ as an organization was able to save 800,000 euros annually (read the full case study in Chapter 3).

Now that we have looked at some of the business drivers and benefits of emergent collaboration, how do organizations map out their business problems and tie them to specific actions or outcomes? I believe that one effective way to do this is to follow a framework that was inspired by a friend and company advisor, Gil Yehuda (see Figure 2.3).

The framework works like this:

- Identify the overall business problem or problems you are looking to solve; there will most likely be several.

- Narrow down the business problem into specific use cases; each business problem will have multiple use cases.

Figure 2.3 Solution mapping process
© 2012 Chess Media Group

- Model the situation that needs to present itself for that use case to be applicable.
- Understand and clarify the action you would like to see take place.
- State the desired result.

Let's see what going through this framework actually looks like, starting with identifying the business problem.

Business Problem

There is a lack of collaboration among employees that causes employees to work in silos. As an organization, we want to empower our employees to communicate and share their ideas, work, and information with one another.

Use Case 1

An employee wishes to distribute a document among coworkers so that they can share, make changes to, or edit the document.

Situation

The employee has a document that he or she wishes to share with relevant coworkers to solicit feedback and get additional ideas. The document the employee seeks to share is either complete or not complete and requires additional editing from coworkers.

Expected Action of the Platform

An employee uploads a document and has the ability to tag that document so that it can be easily retrieved or searched for. The platform recommends additional tags that might be relevant for the document that is uploaded and allows the employee to accept or reject those additional recommended tags. Other employees are able to open the document directly from the same platform and make any edits or changes they would like. Those changes and additions are tracked, saved, and versioned. Employees are also able to leave comments, thoughts, or ideas on the document for others to see. Once changes, comments, or edits are made, the relevant employees should receive a notification letting them know that a change has occurred. Employees are also able to search for this document by using tags, the title of the document, or keywords within the document.

Desired Result

The document can be developed in a collaborative way, and this will reduce duplication of content and the use of e-mail. The document is easily accessible and easily located by employees looking for it.

Use Case 2

An employee wishes to find a subject matter expert on a particular topic.

Situation

The employee is working on a project and realizes that he or she can use additional insight and ideas on a particular part of the project in which the employee is not proficient. For example, an employee working on a marketing project is seeking help with understanding international law and regulations.

Expected Action of the Platform

Employees within the organization have a rich profile with relevant and updated contact information. The profile also lists areas where the employee self-identifies as being a subject matter expert. Other employees can add additional tags and categories where they feel their colleagues have strong subject matter expertise. These rich profiles will pull information from an existing directory so that employees do not need to duplicate information that already exists. Employees will then be able to do a search within the organization, and a list of relevant suggested employees will be returned. The employee will be able to see the profiles of individuals who match the search query and will be able to send them a private message if necessary.

Desired Result

Employees in the organization will know who to go to for information or help with something or will be able to find the right person to go to.

This is one method, and I'm sure there are dozens of others. I have found that going down this road is effective not only for the key stakeholders in the organization but also for the vendors you are most likely going to be evaluating. Walking through this process clearly helps people understand what the business problem is, which use cases fall under that business problem, in what situation that use case applies, what the desired action that is required to help with that use case is, and what the desired end result is. How you go about this doesn't really matter as long as you are able to address these key questions (and perhaps others that you might have in mind as well).

Most organizations don't typically go through and define every single use case, but it's important to get together some of the major use cases for various business units or teams that are going to be using emergent collaboration solutions. Your organization may be surprised to find how many additional use cases emerge in the future that you didn't think about while strategizing.

Summary and Action Items

Emergent collaboration starts with being able to identify business drivers (or problems). This has nothing to do with going after the next cool thing. Emergent collaboration solutions provide benefits and value that other forms of collaboration do not. After understanding the business drivers, it's crucial to map them to specific desired states; this can be done by using the solution mapping process:

- Either in small groups or individually, make a list of your Enterprise 2.0 business drivers and prioritize them. Try to think of a few examples and real-life scenarios for each of these business drivers to add context. You may also want to conduct an employee survey to find out what the most important or desired initiative at your organization should be.

- Go through the unique benefits section and list what you believe the most relevant benefits are to you. Is there something missing that you wish to add? Again, try to come up with some real-life situations or scenarios in which you believe a particular benefit will be applicable and/or relevant.
- Walk through the solution mapping process either in teams or individually to understand how to move from a business problem to a desired result.

There are many business drivers and unique benefits of deploying emergent collaborative solutions in organizations. To explore some of these even further, I asked Oscar Berg to share some of his insights and ideas. Oscar is the future office evangelist at Tieto, an IT services and product engineering company with over 18,000 employees around the world.

More and more organizations turn their eyes to knowledge work as they experience diminishing returns from their efforts to optimize transformational and transactional processes. When they do, it is likely they will first look at how they can improve task efficiency as a means to improve knowledge worker productivity.

One global organization does this by trying to reduce the completion time for the tasks that are most frequently performed on their intranet, such as finding a person or a location. These are tasks that can quite easily be defined and measured. The organization has estimated that just the task of finding and opening a file shared on the intranet costs about 2 million euros per 1,000 employees a year and that this cost can be reduced by 1.2 million euros simply by improving the usability of the intranet. Such numbers catch the attention of most executives, and rightly so.

Although a lot can be gained by improving the efficiency of knowledge work, focusing too hard on optimizing existing tasks and practices can make organizations miss out on opportunities to improve their responsiveness, decision making, and ability to innovate as an organization. Such opportunities can come from tasks and practices for which there is little or no support today simply because there haven't been any technologies that support them well enough. But things change, and new technologies emerge all the time. In today's highly competitive business environment organizations can't afford not to investigate and evaluate new technologies that could have the potential to solve problems or create opportunities they are not yet aware of.

The organization in this example chose only to consider tasks that were already supported by the existing intranet in its optimization effort. Tasks such as sharing information with anyone who might have a need for it were missing simply because they were not supported by the current intranet. Employees could share information in a file either by uploading it to a shared space or by e-mailing it as an attachment to a specified list of receivers, with the latter probably being the more common practice. But they could not share a file with anyone who might have use for it without knowing who it might be in advance. Now, what is the problem with not supporting such a task?

In a less connected and rapidly changing business environment in which each business unit or team could do well on its own and that was good enough to be successful, there was no problem. Today the problem is huge; an organization's responsiveness, decision making, and ability to innovate are seriously hampered when information cannot be rapidly shared across all structures with anyone who might need it. It is more than likely that the information shared in e-mail attachments or uploaded to shared spaces that only a few select users can access is of interest and useful to other people within the organization as well. It's not just that they can't find or access the information; they don't know that it exists in the first place.

It is easy to fall into the trap of trying to improve only tasks and practices that are already supported and can be easily measured. Although the indirect costs resulting from informa-tion lock-in are easy to reason about and understand, they are hard to estimate and translate into monetary figures that would make an executive raise an eyebrow. To make it even harder, the remedy is also to be found in introducing new practices, not just improving those which already exist. That requires a significant dose of creativity and curiosity in addition to optimization skills. Curious and creative organizations are continuously exploring new technologies such as social software, hoping to become aware of—and address—problems and opportunities they were not aware of before. They are well on their way to unlocking their information silos by introducing new practices enabled by technologies such as microblogging, RSS [Rich Site Summary], social filtering, activity feeds, and other technologies that are emerging as this is being written.

three

Walk a Mile
in Their Shoes

This chapter will discuss several case studies from organizations that vary in industry focus and company size. The case studies will give readers an idea of the unique business problems that organizations are faced with and how new enterprise collaboration tools and strategies can help solve those problems. The case studies here are shortened versions of longer and more in-depth cases. Although many other examples are discussed throughout the book, I wanted to devote a section to more in-depth explanations.

Pennsylvania State University

Pennsylvania State University was founded in 1855 and currently is home to around 40,000 students. The university employs around 22,000 people, 1,500 of whom are part of the Penn State Outreach department, the group that made the investment in enterprise collaboration.

What Were the Business Problems?

In 2005 Penn State Outreach conducted an employee survey and found the following:

- Employees felt isolated and were geographically dispersed.

- Employees didn't have the information they needed to get their jobs done.
- Employees weren't aware of how their jobs affected the rest of the organization.

- The executive team was unaware of what was happening at the ground level of the organization.
- Communication was inefficient, and collaboration was virtually nonexistent.
- Employees had no voice within the company.

The organization agreed that all these things had resulted in missed opportunities, poor decision making, and extra spending.

What Was Done to Solve the Problems?

To solve these problems Penn State deployed a collaboration platform, ThoughtFarmer, which is described by its parent company OpenRoad as a social intranet software platform. As a part of the deployment, Bevin (the woman responsible for the initiative) met with all the upper-level managers to convey the business problem and the proposed solution. It was important to get their buy-in and support. Once this was done, volunteers were recruited to help move things into action.

Volunteers were solicited in five areas:

- Content
- Multimedia
- Policy
- Evangelists
- Data/analytics

The volunteers were shown the ThoughtFarmer platform and were asked to help with creating, fixing, and curating content. Although no formal tools were developed, these evangelists had access to links and to information that was shared actively throughout the group. One thing to note is that the value of this initiative was conveyed from an individual level, not from a company level. This meant that employees weren't told that "this is how Penn State will benefit as a result of you using this"; they were told that "this is how *you* will benefit." The actual jobs of the evangelists never changed; what did change was *where* the jobs were done.

Some optional training classes were offered to employees, but nothing was forced, thus creating what Bevin likes to call a "seeded organic approach." Penn State made the necessary resources available to interested employees, but again, nothing was forced on them.

No formal standardization process was ever developed; instead, activity on the platform was monitored and employees were coached and encouraged on things they could do to improve their use of the platform. For example, if an employee put information in a certain area and Bevin or her team thought it could be better served somewhere else, she would nudge or suggest to the employee to move the information by saying something like "Let's try doing it like this" (or would move it herself with the permission of the employee). This approach was always cooperative and not forceful. Bevin and her team also kept an eye out for duplicate information by monitoring the activity streams. Old information was also crawled, and relevant links were added in the older content when relevant.

Today the intranet serves a few key purposes:

- It is used to communicate and push information and collaborate on that information.
- Departments put out forms or common things that they use, and others comment on things to be changed.
- Project teams share files and meeting minutes.

The ThoughtFarmer deployment at Penn State Outreach currently includes the following feature set:

- Rich profiles
- Activity streams/status updates
- Shared calendaring
- Embedding of tools in media (YouTube embedder)

- Private groups and workspaces
- Sharing of and collaboration on documents

The Results

At least 75 percent of the employees use the intranet at least once a week and more frequently when new projects are being worked on. It was anticipated that the implementation and adoption of the intranet would take 3 to 5 years, but it actually took around 1.5 to 2 years. It's important to note that there was never an in-depth strategy for all this.

Instead of going with a pilot program, Penn State University chose to go all-in for a few reasons. The first was that a small team was perceived as an "elite" team and was less likely to be listened to. There was already a shadow story that only certain people were able to participate in the interesting projects, and it was necessary to counter that with broad participation to avoid misperceptions within the organization. Penn State also believed there had to be a certain user base to help move the project forward. Social networks in general depend on scale, which means that if you have only a small number of people using something, the value is greatly diminished because the scale is not there.

ThoughtFarmer was purchased on a licensed (with 2,000 seats) model, not an annual per user model. This meant that Penn State had an up-front annual cost of $80,000 for the first year. Around $50,000 was directly related to technology costs, and around $30,000 was directly related to human capital costs. Since the platform is licensed, Penn State pays an annual maintenance fee of around $8,000 plus the cost of a part-time employee to manage the system in any subsequent years. As far as financial numbers regarding how much was saved or earned, I was told that this is not being measured at this time. The funding for the platform came from eliminating an annual event that Penn State hosted for employees. That event involved only around 500 employees, and the decision was made to take the money for engaging one-third of the employee base and invest it in a digital way to engage 100 percent of the employees.

As of now, the anecdotal evidence suggests that the problems are being solved and Penn State is happy and satisfied with the investment. I asked if there were any horror stories that Penn State wished to share with me, and not to my surprise, they didn't have any.

Océ

Océ is a copying and printing company with its international head-quarters in the Netherlands. Océ has just over 21,000 employees from around the world.

What Were the Business Problems?

The recession was a crucial factor in propelling this initiative at Océ. As a result of the economy, Océ had a very small budget to improve communications within the company. They had to take a big step back to look at ways to improve innovation, collaboration, and knowledge sharing across the entire organization; that was not an easy task. The challenge was that Océ needed something very low-cost but also powerful. Everything was very isolated, and information was very siloed. People were not talking to one another, and they all kept to themselves. Sharing and collaborating over organizational entities was not easy.

What Was Done to Solve the Problems?

Océ implemented a series of collaborative platforms and solutions, including the following:

- A Wiki that was implemented in 2006 was used as a tool to process information, mainly by the research and development (R&D) department.
- Internal blogs that were started in 2008 were used for thought leadership, knowledge sharing, and subject matter expertise.
- Océ TV, which was launched in 2008, included an internal video platform that was used to share news, announcements, updates, and communications from the senior team.

- Microblogging (Yammer, begun at the end of 2008) was used for announcing company updates, asking questions, sharing content, and sharing information on projects.
- Social bookmarking, which was initiated in 2009, was used to store, share, and save relevant and interesting information.

Unlike Penn State University, Océ took the piloted approach to enterprise collaboration by starting these initiatives in the R&D department and then growing them from there. Océ believes that it's always important to justify the business case for everything that it does. In the case of the wiki, Océ had a problem housing and organizing project information. The wiki didn't solve that problem, but it did solve the problem of managing process information, which became the use case for having the wiki and thus the catalyst for getting it created.

Despite all this, there needed to be some sort of force of influence to propel all those efforts within Océ. Thankfully, Jan and Samuel (two of the evangelists for the initiative) had two key areas of influence, and for lack of a better phrase, they worked the system. It's actually quite an interesting strategy. Their two key areas of influence were as follows:

1. A steering committee for the intranet was formed:
    - Both Samuel and Jan are on the committee.
    - They already had a vision and an idea of where they wanted to go.
    - Budget disappeared because of the recession, and so they went with free tools.
2. Jan works in the corporate communications department:
    - He developed the communications plan.
    - He selected the tools: "These are the tools corporate communications is going to use."
    - Department managers approved it.

It was very difficult to coordinate work between the IT department and the business units, but they were able to manage it. With Samuel working in the IT department and Jan in corporate communications, they were able to work together to make it happen. When Jan ran into IT issues, he brought in Samuel to support him, and vice versa. Together Jan and Samuel brought a great mix of business and IT.

Traditionally, employees were not encouraged to ask questions or be open about personal doubts and ideas. Employees were often perceived as being weak if they had doubts about something, and as a result, they refrained from asking questions or challenging ideas, especially in a collaboration platform among their peers and colleagues. They overcame this culture of closed communication by leading by example. This meant a few things. The first is that Samuel and Jan had to show their peers that other organizations have successfully adopted an open culture of sharing ideas and expressing doubts and uncertainties. The second is that Samuel and Jan had to "walk the talk" and lead by example. They had to ask questions and openly express their doubts, uncertainties, and need for help.

The Results

As a result of Océ's use of collaborative tools (supported of course by strategies), there were several noticeable benefits. The most visible change was that Océ suddenly saw horizontal communications lines open up across various silos. Within those new communications lines, Océ witnessed idea sharing, collaboration, and employees talking and working with one another more efficiently. Overall, employees at Océ were surprised at the ease of use of the Enterprise 2.0 (E2.0) tools that were deployed. The traditional model required that the IT department get involved with a new tool or technology deployment. However, this has changed, and it's now quite easy (and quick) for employees to do something such as set up a blog in around two minutes without the involvement of IT. Employee use of Yammer was the biggest shock at Océ. Through the tool, employees who had never met were helping one another in a meaningful way.

From a communications standpoint, employees became much less dependent on the corporate communications department to communicate with one another. Employees could now do things on their own and didn't need to rely as much on the IT department to facilitate communication. There was also far more company feedback than there previously had been. People were now sharing information and receiving feedback. This again was a result of employees supporting their own communications needs.

There was also a strong financial impact. Océ had an annual intranet deployment budget of around 350,000 euros, which it was able to reduce to approximately 5,000 to 10,000 euros, resulting in cost savings of around 340,000 euros annually. Océ realized that the intranet was not a critical business tool and was able to replace a lot of what the intranet did and stored with free tools. As a result of the recession, Océ had to look at where it could cut costs, and the intranet was one those areas. Océ stopped all intranet change requests and halted any external hires required to support the intranet (it's interesting to note that Océ also cut back on travel costs and replaced travel with WebEx meetings and e-training).

The current intranet still exists; it's going to stay the way it is. The support team for the intranet platform used to include a program manager, a roll-out manager, a project leader, and a technical team; all those roles were eliminated since the intranet was now in "maintenance"-only mode. Océ stuck to free tools, which required fewer people to manage and very low (if any) development costs. The intranet still gets around 1.5 to 2 million page views a month, but it is no longer seen as a critical tool. Instead, the budget goes toward projects such as enterprise resource planning (ERP).

Océ is a great example of how an enterprise company can reduce costs by implementing an E2.0 strategy within the organization. Following is my favorite financial impact story.

The chief financial officer (CFO) at Océ had his own ideation blog where employees contributed around 60 ideas over time. One of the ideas involved incentivizing delivery employees who were driving leased cars to use gas stations in local towns instead of filling up on the highway. The idea behind this was that gas was cheaper in local towns than it was at gas stations near the highways. The idea was implemented, and employees who filled up at local gas stations were incentivized and rewarded. The financial impact of the idea was a cost saving of over 800,000 euros a year. Océ TV saved the company approximately 40,000 euros annually because the employees could now make their own videos (with simple cameras) and upload them instead of incurring professional video development costs.

Océ has embarked on an interesting Enterprise 2.0 journey, and although it is not currently where it wants to be, the company has certainly learned a lot along the way. Over the course of the last few years one of the most valuable lessons learned is that technology is interesting and great but Enterprise 2.0 is really not about the technology. It's about the concepts and the people; the technology simply enables things to happen. Océ also realized that pilot programs are effective and help justify the case for E2.0.

Focusing on trying to persuade people to use a particular technology has also proved to be a bit of a waste of time. As Océ realized, the best approach is to explain to employees how to use a new type of technology and the benefits of doing so. However, if an employee doesn't understand or refuses to use a new tool or platform, there should be no hard feelings. There are always going to be early adopters and laggards. The hope is that in around six months or a year after initial deployment, employees who initially didn't want to adopt new tools will start using the new tools and technologies.

Océ also learned that having IT and business units working together is a powerful combination and can prove to be extremely convincing for senior-level management. Having people from both IT and business units work together provides a much better perspective on what can be done and what needs to be done. Enterprise 2.0 does not fall under IT or communications at Océ; it's somewhere in between. Like most companies, Océ believes that it is very important for employees to be able to try new things. Océ always had an understanding that some things would work and some wouldn't. There is nothing wrong with that, and companies shouldn't be scared to experiment.

Finally, Océ realized that money was never an issue with Enterprise 2.0; the issue was organizational. Océ never had any money for E2.0 initiatives, yet that never stopped them. The biggest obstacle is overcoming organizational challenges.

I asked Océ to tell me the worst horror story with anything related to its E2.0 initiatives. Perhaps there was an angry employee bashing the company internally, a security hack, or a leak of some type of secret information. Océ's response to this question was, "We have had no issues with anyone trying to harm the brand, any security issues, or any type of information leaks; we have had no incidents."

FSG: Social Impact Consultants

FSG is a nonprofit consulting firm specializing in strategy, evaluation, and research that was founded in 2000 as Foundation Strategy Group and has experienced a decade of global social impact. Today FSG has around 80 employees. This case study was put together after extensive interviews with Carl Frappaolo, the director of knowledge management. FSG is a much smaller company than the others in these case studies, and that is why I wanted it here: to show that emergent collaboration isn't just for companies with thousands of employees. I should also point out that at the time of this writing the implementations were just a few months in.

What Were the Business Problems or Drivers?

The main reason FSG invested in collaborative technologies was growth. FSG was growing very quickly and realized that knowledge sharing and collaboration under the old model didn't scale very well. They went from one geographic location to three and then to four, with a commensurate uptake in work experience and employees. As they expanded, there was a realization that collaboration via e-mail and the shared drive was starting to show cracks from stress. They relied heavily on traditional systems such as the phone, e-mail, and the memory of employees. Someone might ask or pose the question in an e-mail— "Did we ever do this type of project in this geographic area?"—and employees would remember and answer.

New employees in particular had trouble knowing who to go to with questions or where to go to find information. Employees could spend too much time searching for information. This often took up the valuable time of the most-senior consultants, and the question they kept asking was, Is this the best use of our time? The interesting thing is that for FSG the business driver wasn't really dollars and cents, cost savings, and profitability, but a desire to grow and have greater impact and thus for newer employees to become productive more quickly.

The final business driver was to allow communities of interest and communities of practice to organize together and share information in a dynamic, asynchronous, and flexible way.

What Was Done to Solve the Problems?

This was a very top-down initiative for FSG; in fact, most of the senior leadership team was behind it. But there was a grassroots, albeit less formal, push in this direction as well. There was a fair amount of renegade and rogue use of collaboration and Enterprise 2.0 technologies. They were not official or widely deployed, but teams and individuals were using them. For example, Dropbox, Basecamp, and Google were already being used by teams and individuals. Each employee also had his or her own taxonomy and approach to file management and organization on the individual computer drives. It was very autonomous. The senior team didn't have a problem with this because it helped the employees get their jobs done. However, they realized that what was being done was not in the best interest of the entire organization. These pockets of emergent collaboration were not strategic, and so the process needed to be centralized.

Over the years, employees became used to their own routines or approaches to getting work done, and those approaches became almost second nature to them. It's not that there is resistance to the actual change imposed by a centralized and formal approach to knowledge management; it is a matter of having to consciously remind themselves that there are new tools and technologies. It's a bit like having a particular route that you take to work all the time. You know that route so well that you can travel it blindfolded and don't have to think about. Now, all of a sudden, someone is asking you to take a new route to get to work. The second nature concept immediately goes away, and you have to be much more conscientious of the turns you take. Eventually you make it to where you need to go, but you get lost a few times along the way. It's going to take time before you get used to the new route, and the same thing is true for new tools and technologies.

Breaking down the autonomy isn't easy. It's tricky because the entrepreneurial and creative spirit that comes with it needs to be preserved. Furthermore, FSG leverages a culture composed of more carrots than sticks. At FSG, one of the best ways to encourage individuals to accept change and break away from the comfort of established routines is to show employees that there are better ways to do things. Employees need to understand why using the new tools and technologies is good for them individually as well as why it's good for everyone as a company. Value added, both personally and collectively, will drive change.

Employees aren't forced to use anything. Instead, they are shown what they can get from the new tools that they don't get from the existing ways of doing things.

The Results

FSG found that one of the big value statements for employees is that they can leave behind their work and others will find it instead of colleagues having to contact or e-mail anyone looking for information. For example, if someone wants to know if anyone did a project with the AIDS epidemic in Africa, there is a way to check that.

One of the big changes at FSG associated with this initiative was the creation of a new department called knowledge management (KM) and the staffing of it at the director level. Earlier approaches included part-time employees and staffing the role at a more junior level. In addition to the KM director, there are local representatives of the knowledge management team in each office on a part-time basis (one or two hours a week). FSG periodically meets as a team to discuss what's going on in the company, but each of the team members has another "full-time" role to fulfill as well. It's a great approach because these individuals bring an on-the-ground real-world perspective to the discussion.

Less formally, FSG also has KM (knowledge management) evangelists. Some of them are on the knowledge management team, and some are simply consultants and other staff members who "get it." These evangelists share their experiences, tips, and ideas and encourage others to use the new technologies. They exist at various levels. For example, there are at least two managing directors who are very supportive of the initiative and act as senior-level sponsors.

Employees, especially in the communities of practice, are definitely using these tools; they are putting content in central libraries and commenting on information and on other comments. Some are creating small projects within the collaborative sites and managing them there. The rate at which work product is being reused is going up, and employees are remembering that they can access a search tool to look at precedent work products. These tools are making it faster, simpler, and, they hope, more nimble to collaborate and to do so in a fashion that leaves behind a record, so to speak, of that collaboration so that it can be "discovered" and repurposed.

These are some of the tools being used:

Salesforce. This is being used for account management: who the clients are, who the prospects are, who the company is selling to, and what stage that is in.

Central desktop. This is a collaboration hub and content management system. In time it will also be a project management system.

The technology cost is in the low tens of thousands of dollars for two years but will most likey increase in the future as the company considers additional integrations and customizations. Annual labor-hour costs run in the range of $150,000 to $200,000.

The biggest lesson learned was that no matter how prepared you think you are or how diligent you are, there are always going to be surprises. FSG thought it gave a very comprehensive list of use cases to the solution providers it evaluated, but once they deployed, plenty of other case studies came up. Even in known situations there will be glitches and bugs. There is a big difference between a controlled environment and a live environment. The other lesson learned was that the absorption and adoption rate is very different from person to person.

The platform absolutely has to be intuitive. The days of expecting users to go through weeks of training are over.

TELUS

TELUS is a national telecommunications company based in Canada with over 35,000 employees.

What Were the Business Problems or Drivers?

The driving forces behind emergent collaboration at TELUS were threefold: overall employee engagement, its Customers First program, and its Work Styles program.

Emergent collaboration was seen as a way to help improve an already impressive level of engagement at the company. TELUS defines engagement as being a genuine connection between its employees and the company and it wants employees to come to work feeling inspired and fulfilled by the work that they do. Engagement is measured easily and regularly by asking employees how they feel about working at TELUS through routine Pulsecheck surveys.

On the customer front, TELUS has developed the Likelihood to Recommend (L2R) model, which is essentially a net-promoter score. The model asks customers if they would recommend TELUS to their friends or family members. Customers First was launched to help TELUS become the "best in class" in terms of the likelihood to recommend customer metrics. The tagline of the Customers First program is "Promise Made—Promise Kept."

Work Styles, introduced in 2007 and launched nationally in 2009, is an enterprisewide program that supports team members, in eligible roles, to work when and where they are most effective—at home, in the office, or in an alternate location. Work today is more collaborative and mobile than it has ever been and TELUS's Work Styles program combines human resources, IT, and real estate to embrace this changing nature of work. More than half of the TELUS team is remote-work enabled and this future friendly approach to work enhances productivity and reduces environmental impact. By 2015, TELUS plans to have 30 percent of team members working from within TELUS buildings (resident workers); 40 percent of team members working on a mobile basis (mobile workers); and 30 percent of team members working from home on a full-time basis (at-home workers). TELUS listened to what their employees were asking for, which was a more flexible work-life relationship.

A strong link exists between employee engagement and customer satisfaction. At TELUS a "three legs to the stool" concept has been introduced to support organizational enhancements. These legs include an open leadership framework, a connected learning model, and emergent collaboration technologies. Notice that the focus is on collaboration as opposed to being "social."

What Was Done to Solve the Problem?

The early stages of this initiative began in 2009 with the concept of "Learning 2.0," which sought to empower team members to learn and share with and from each other. The theory behind Learning 2.0 is that learning is not merely an event; it is a continuous, connected, and collaborative process bound by formal, informal, and social learning modalities. These initiatives mainly came from the bottom up, but senior-level leaders are directly involved in discussions about improving collaboration and employee engagement. The formal program for emergent collaboration began in 2010.

The first introduction to emergent collaboration technology came when a Confluence Wiki license was purchased to get the ball rolling. This became the corporate standardized wiki and blog platform, later dubbed "Habitat Collaboration" (named after their existing intranet, which was called Habitat). Eventually Confluence was connected and integrated to the existing intranet. This and all emergent collaborative technologies launched since are referred to as "Habitat Social," the umbrella brand for all learning, social networking, and collaborative tools and technologies. There were additional deployments of collaborative technologies at about the same time, but Habitat Social has now become the de facto place for collaboration to occur.

TELUS also developed their own "Enterprise 2.0 Adoption Council," where anyone can join biweekly calls every Friday from 8 to 10 a.m. to discuss new tools, idea, and strategies for collaboration.

One of the big challenges at TELUS, as with any other large company, is balancing the need for hierarchical leadership with the desire for flexible leadership styles. Managers and leaders need emergent collaboration tools to help lead their teams, and a big part of being able to make that happen is leadership DNA. Leaders need to understand whether they have a more "command and control" or "cultivate and coordinate" mindset. Are they open and compassionate toward their employees? If not, these are opportunities for improvement.

As an organization, TELUS needed to be aligned toward a unified goal of collaboration, and change management had to be addressed on three levels: for managers and leaders of the organization, for existing employees, and for new employees who were just joining the organization.

TELUS developed an internal way of classifying the enterprisewide behavior model. TELUS used to be what they call "tight-tight," meaning employees were tight on clarity and understanding of what the future of the company and their roles looked like (a good thing), but they were also tight on empowerment, meaning that team members did not feel empowered and engaged with TELUS. Those who work at TELUS need to feel as though they have a voice that can be heard. The opportunity here was to switch from being a tight-tight company to a tight-loose company where employees felt empowered, fulfilled, inspired, and engaged at work. Decisions at TELUS should not just be made by a few select people. Team members needed to be more engaged and given the opportunity to explore ideas before execution occurred.

As an organization, TELUS wanted to augment the physical water cooler and add the virtual water cooler. This became evident even with the switching of department names. For example, "enterprise learning services" became "learning and collaboration."

TELUS is more interested in an evolution, not a revolution.

TELUS has deployed a robust and integrated technology stack, shown in Figure 3.1, which depicts a timeline of implementing various collaborative tools and technologies.

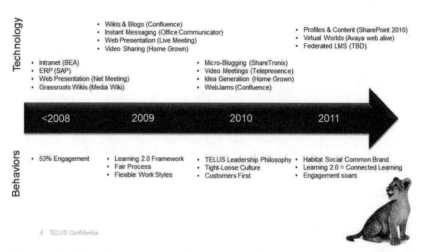

Figure 3.1 TELUS technology and behaviors timeline

Notice that TELUS broke down this timeline not just by technologies but also by behaviors, a crucial component that many organizations forget to consider.

TELUS has done quite a bit in just four short years. The list of technologies adopted has included everything from Cisco Telepresence to Micro-blogging to virtual worlds. The beauty of all this is that it integrated within singular navigation that looks like a navigation bar that hovers above various employee collaboration technologies (see Figure 3.2).

As you can see in the figure, Dan is able to access everything he needs to get his job done by clicking on the navigation bar seen at the top. This particular screenshot shows a profile page built on top of Sharepoint 2010. TELUS does not have a "field of dreams" mentality in which they build things and hope people will come. This all had to be built into the team member flow of work.

As previously mentioned, obstacles had to be overcome on three levels: managers and leaders, existing employees, and new employees.

Figure 3.2 TELUS Habitat Social employee page

A corporate program was developed for managers and leaders at TELUS called "Leading Your Team: The Fundamentals." This program included formal classes and informal opportunities, such as webinars, book chapters, leader highlights, and virtual and in-person chats, for leaders to learn how to become more collaborative while using new tools to help them lead. Additionally, every year an event called the Senior Leadership Forum (SLF) is held for 600 members of the leadership team (directors and above), where specific strategic themes are discussed for three full days. SLF helps to ensure that leaders are aligned, and it gives them the opportunity to build bonds with each other as well as to discuss any issues or ideas that need to be addressed. This event helps to show leaders that collaboration is not just encouraged, but expected. The most recent SLF was focused on three themes: customers first, quality, and collaboration. The fact that the third theme was entirely about collaboration shows how seriously TELUS is taking this enhanced strategic direction. For existing employees, numerous resources were made available for their education and training. When "Habitat Social" was launched, a 17-minute introductory eLearning course was developed to help guide employees through the platform and to understand the value of using it. Yes, formal learning was being used to teach social learning. Regular monthly sessions called "Lead and Grow" were (and still are) run. These 45- to 60-minute sessions address what it means to collaborate at TELUS. These sessions also help employees understand what opportunities exist within the organization and how they can take advantage of those opportunities. Many self-help resources, tutorials, and one-on-one mentoring programs were also put into place so that employees were able to get access to all the resources they needed. TELUS also did something quite unique, which was to develop a type of collaborative starter kit. This is an internal site that employees can access to help them learn about what tools to use for various situations and for various roles.

When employees access the site they can answer a series of questions, and based on their responses they are given options for what and/or how they can proceed to use the company tools to become more collaborative and engaged. The site also lets employees sort and filter information based on certain attributes. For example, employees can access the site and sort through technologies and tips based on their role within the organization, how much time they have to devote to these new tools, how skilled they are at using these tools, or they can even sort by a specific tool. This means that an employee can access the site, tell the platform that he is a "beginner" when it comes to these new tools, and then the platform will provide recommendations for how he can advance.

Finally, TELUS launched a program called "A Day in the Life." Ten employees participated in candid video interviews in which they talked about how emergent collaboration tools and platforms are helping them to solve problems within the organization and how these tools are affecting such things as the way they work and their career development. In other words, TELUS took advantage of storytelling from multiple team members' perspectives.

TELUS employs over 35,000 team members, so it is hiring constantly. In order to accommodate the new strategic collaborative direction for

TELUS, the entire induction program was reworked. It used to be just a two-day class that employees sat in on. Now, new employees are taken through a 90-day collaboration scavenger hunt that educates them on what it means to be collaborative at TELUS. In fact, employees even get access to a special collaborative portal so that they can engage with their fellow workers who are also going to be starting to work at TELUS. These new team members get something called "Passport," which is almost like a Foursquare-type concept where employees receive a badge or a "stamp" for every action that they complete on the collaborative platform. At the end of 90 days, employees get a certificate that they can proudly display. They are now accustomed to using the tools at TELUS to collaborate effectively and to be part of the TELUS team.

What Were the Results?

TELUS team members have told the organization that it is much easier for them to find people and information. In fact, over 70 percent of all team members have seen an improvement in their performance. Learning has also been democratized, meaning that employees are helping to share and educate each other. For example, an employee who might have a solution to a problem or process can simply post a video of the solution, which can then be accessed by other employees. Team members creating their own user guides on some internal products is actually quite popular within TELUS. This means that everyone at TELUS is always learning and always teaching; it's a perpetually learning organization fueled by its team members. Team members are also able to share their opinions, and overall they feel more fulfilled and empowered at work. Finally, communication has also become much more horizontal instead of being strictly vertical.

Rather than hiring new employees to take on roles to support collaboration and engagement, TELUS instead distributed these tasks and responsibilities among the existing workforce who already oversaw or were involved in related areas. The results?

- 750 videos were uploaded
- Over 40 percent were actively participating in social/collaborative learning

- Over 60,000 pages of content were created and over 20,000 comments were posted on blogs and wikis
- 14,000 employees were microblogging
- There were 25,000 original posts and over 100,000 comments

The most obvious example of impact comes in the form of employee engagement. As of 2011, engagement of its 35,000+ team members rose from 53 percent to 70 percent, an outstanding 17 percentage point increase.

The business value of their strategy is evident. Employee engagement is way up, the company is rallying around their Customers First program, and financial results have improved year over year. The organization has clearly set itself up for additional successes in the coming years as a result of their emergent collaboration strategies.

TELUS likes to think of itself as a company in "perpetual beta"; in fact, this is how TELUS believes emergent collaboration should be thought of. In the future TELUS is hoping to get more involved with gamification and badging for employees. TELUS is also looking at business simulations, where high performers or managers can test out ideas in a controlled environment to see how those ideas play. TELUS wants to get more involved with ideation in terms of being able to make various ideas play out as well. Currently team members submit ideas and give them a "thumbs up" (or "down") through a pilot system known as iThink, but the company wants to do a better job of seeing these ideas through from conception to development utilizing collective intelligence and crowdsourcing.

Lessons Learned

TELUS learned a few key lessons during their four-year journey:

1. The journey never ends; it's a continuous evolution of collaboration.

2. It's important to be "technology agnostic"; don't pick solutions because you have a relationship with them; pick them because they are the best solution for your business.

3. Perseverance is crucial, there is no giving up; this is an evolution that will happen.

4. Executive support and buy-in are essential.

5. Champions and early adopters need to get involved during the early stages.

6. Just because someone isn't participating right away doesn't mean they aren't learning. Organizations should remember that lurking is learning. It's OK if employees aren't on-board from the get-go.

7. The behavior change must be treated with equal vigor as the technology rollout.

What Worked and What Didn't—Do You Have Any Horror/Success Stories?

In the beginning, a micro-blogging company that TELUS piloted was overexuberant in its marketing and was essentially spamming employees. Executives and employees would be repetitively e-mailed to invite colleagues to join the platform and e-mails were bombarding everyone. Eventually TELUS went in a different direction, which sent a confusing message to executives because TELUS's internal marketing practices were the exact opposite of what this vendor was doing.

Over the past few years, TELUS also tried some marketing techniques internally that didn't work out as anticipated. A site called "*what if*" was created to show potential scenarios of what TELUS could look like if it became more collaborative. Videos, discussion forums, and content were all populated on the site but nobody actually participated, in part due to the unclear name of the site itself. This project didn't have the impact that TELUS thought it would.

Elizabeth Glaser Pediatric AIDS Foundation

The Elizabeth Glaser Pediatric AIDS Foundation is a nonprofit organization dedicated to preventing pediatric HIV infection and eliminating pediatric AIDS through research, advocacy, and prevention, care, and treatment programs. Founded in 1988, the organization works in 17 countries around the world and has more than 1,500 employees.

What Were the Business Problems?

The foundation was looking to keep doing what it was doing, but more efficiently. There is a lot of knowledge for employees to share with one another but no way to share it. Glaser needed to make sure that information actually flowed from organization to organization around its locations in 17 countries. This was traditionally done via e-mail or care packages with large quantities of printed documents. Information flowed from the top down but rarely from the bottom up, and that was a problem. For example, the proposal development team had a very hard time gathering necessary information from various countries and departments because this was mainly done via e-mail. Glaser was also not able to find and share emerging best practices at a country level. This was becoming increasingly more important as Glaser grew from around 200 employees in 2006 to over 1,500 in 2011. This growth was largely fueled by PEPFAR, a bill President George W. Bush put into action that provided more funding to organizations such as Glaser.

Along with this growth came the requirement to become more "professional," which meant developing and sharing policies and standards.

What Was Done to Solve the Problems?

Glaser put together a knowledge management task force and then surveyed the members to find the most useful solution to the problem of collaboration and knowledge sharing. This task force was composed of various departments and employees in different countries. This was a collaborative effort with both IT and business units involved.

Glaser originally started on SharePoint 2007, but there were a number of problems: It was not easy to use and was overly complex. The different departments couldn't own their own pieces of content in their areas and would always run into problems and bugs. Furthermore, there were big accessibility issues in Africa, where Glaser has a very large presence. As many companies, including Glaser, have discovered, SharePoint is a good system if you have a solid IT team in place to handle it.

Instead, the foundation opted to go with a platform called Interact Intranet.

The Results

Channels of information are starting to open, but the big change is that employees are now identifying collaboration as something that needs to be done; this was not a conversation that Glaser was having even a few years ago. People are starting to think about different ways to share information with one another. The country offices are siloed to a certain extent. Employees who are entry-level still don't feel comfortable engaging with senior-level employees, for example, by commenting on an executive blog, but that is slowly changing. Thus, there is still a status gap between employees. Ideally, the foundation also wants to move from letting the experts give advice to allowing everyone to give advice with the experts listening and providing additional insight and feedback.

The two big changes were the creation of a governance committee and the knowledge management task force.

The governance committee is a group composed of the chief operating officer (COO) and a few of the vice presidents from each division; they meet once a month to discuss things relating to the intranet and to address day-to-day issues that come up, such as deciding whether spin-off entities that might need access to certain pieces of information should have access to the entire corporate system.

The knowledge management task force came into being to redesign the intranet. Since that was completed, the task force is no longer active, but many of those people are now content managers for their respective groups at various locations. One full-time consultant was hired who helps the content managers get their information up and running and who also helps with training and organization.

Within IT, the program innovation and policy, and the communications team, there are one or two people specifically devoted to emergent collaboration. These employees do things such as participating in the conversations and groups, helping organize information, and managing content and the knowledge base. On the IT side these employees are mainly tasked with stabilizing the platform, conducting internal demonstrations, and doing project management work. The model Glaser is eventually going for is to have one content owner in each country (curating and developing a taxonomy that makes sense).

Until now the foundation has mainly been doing a lot of online demos for groups of 10 to 12 people. Some on-site training has also been done. The challenge is training and educating many of the overseas employees. It's much easier to do training in the United States than it is in countries in Africa. Glaser also started a weekly e-mail newsletter that goes out every Friday that highlights a few new things that go up on the new intranet, includes a list of people on the core emergent collaboration team, shares some usage statistics, and provides some general and insightful information about the platform. Some video interviews were put together in which employees talked about how they use the new platform in their daily work.

The current biggest obstacle is accessibility in countries, such as those in Africa, where connection is inconsistent. The foundation installed network optimizers that help speed up application-to-application connectivity (not Internet speed). This is where mobile is seriously going to come into play as many employees do use smartphones. A fully mobile version of the collaboration platform that is compatible on all devices has not been implemented, but that was scheduled to change by the start of 2012.

Before the platform went live, a lot of advanced promotion was done in the form of announcements, newsletters, and word of mouth.

Currently, 28 to 29 percent of the employee base has accessed the site at some point and around 15 percent of the global workforce is using it regularly. The platform has been live for around four months.

Some countries are mandating the use of these tools in their offices. The COO also feels very strongly that this should be a required tool for employees to use, which means that it might be mandated in the near future. Many of the VPs at Glaser also support doing this. Discussions about incorporating collaboration into employee reviews have also been addressed, but nothing formal has been put in place.

Employees are now able to get access to information that they didn't have access to before, such as policies and procedure manuals, which previously existed only in print and were outdated. Staff profiles, pictures, and bios are now accessible to everyone so that employees can build communities of interest, something that was not possible before. This is helping build trust within the organization.

Information is now being shared more openly without fear of horrible consequences or reprimands. Employees are opening up to one another and bringing the human aspects back to the enterprise. The senior leadership team also started blogging, which has helped the company become more transparent. Overall, the exchange of ideas has seen a huge improvement.

Like many companies today, Glaser is not measuring success by dollars and cents but by overall company morale improvement and anecdotal evidence from employees who are telling the company that they are now able to do their jobs better.

For the first year technology costs were under $50,000, and ongoing costs after that were under $40,000. The cost of hiring one full-time employee was $60,000 to $80,000. Aside from that, most of the other responsibilities are shared among existing staff.

Summary and Action Items

You are not alone in seeking to invest in these emergent tools and strategies. Many other companies have already made these investments, and they have a lot of insight and ideas that they can share. These are just a handful of some of the case studies that can be found online today. Here are some suggestions:

- After going through the case studies, ask yourself if you would have done anything differently and why. Did you agree with what the companies mentioned in this chapter did?

- Do you see any similarities or practical applications between what these companies did and what is going on at your organization?

- Are there any other examples or stories that you know of that you think would be relevant and want to share with your team? Start a collection of these case studies, examples, and stories so that you can share them with your colleagues. I have started one at http://www.jmorganmarketing.com/collection-enterprise-2–0-case-studies-examples/.

Now I'd like to introduce Bert Sandie, who is the director of technical excellence at Electronic Arts, Inc. Bert has been instrumental in driving the strategy of emergent collaboration at EA, and he and his team have learned a lot along the way.

One of the major challenges for companies that are deploying social software is to persuade employees to fill in their social profiles with additional details to augment the default information. In companies that have more than 500 employees across multiple offices, it is difficult to visit each employee to convince him or her in a face-to-face conversation, so what are the options? And why do we need more than the default information?

We must also take into consideration that in multinational companies, the privacy laws in many countries allow only a small set of information to be included in a default social profile, and so employees need to opt in via an online waiver to add/display information such as their pictures, birthdays, interests, and hobbies.

Over the last two years, our experiences at EA with the adoption of social profiles have found success through a few key learnings:

- Look for many different avenues to encourage and entice employees to complete their profiles. We send all new employees an e-mail to join, run different contests with prizes every year, and use leaders/executives as role models, showing they have joined.

- Integrate the social profiles into applications that employees use. We have integrated the profiles into our corporate intranet and our global knowledge-sharing solution and have made the social profiles the default company directory.
- Augment social profiles with additional data fields that are useful to your business. We have fields such as discipline expertise, technical skills, gamer IDs, and content contributed to our knowledge-sharing solution that all create a value proposition.
- Provide an enterprise search solution that is fast, is easy to use, and accurately finds employees based on search criteria and intuitive filtering.

---

four

Risky Business

There are risks associated with any business or IT investment an organization makes. In fact, there are risks involved with pretty much anything people do in their daily lives: risks from going outside, risks from eating at a restaurant, and risks from crossing the street. The point is that risks aren't new for anyone, whether an individual or a corporation, so let's not be surprised or intimidated by the fact that a whole chapter of this book is devoted to risk. In case you were wondering, I am not really a Tom Cruise fan, but the title of one of his movies made for a great chapter title.

All good chess players understand the risks of the moves they make on the board and the consequences that can result. However, chess players also have plans in place for what to do if those risks are taken advantage of by their opponents.

Two general categories of risks will be looked at here: the risks of not investing in emergent collaboration tools and strategies and the risks of investing in those tools and strategies. Let's start with some of the risks of not making the investment.

Decreased Productivity and Wasting Time

E-mail does not work as a sustainable collaboration platform, because employees are spending time answering e-mails and searching for information instead of being able to get work done. Butler Group, an IT research group, found that 25 percent of employees' time at work is spent searching for information needed to get their tasks done. Butler Group also found that over 50 percent of staff costs are allocated to employees performing "information work." The amount of time, money, and resources allocated for employees to find information to complete their tasks is huge.

Inability to Stay Competitive

As competitive pressures continue to increase, innovation becomes more crucial to the success of an organization. Deploying emergent collaboration platforms helps organizations surface new ideas and opportunities that can improve business performance, lead to new products or services, and cut costs. Not investing in these tools and strategies when the competition is doing it means that the organization will be inferior, at least when it comes to innovation. This is a risk that organizations cannot afford to take.

Loss of Existing Talent and Inability to Recruit New Talent

As the new workforce enters the market, organizations that do not adopt emergent collaboration solutions will be perceived as old-fashioned, not innovative, and not accommodating. This will result in great difficulty for an organization in acquiring new top talent and retaining existing top talent, especially when other organizations are making these investments. Most people don't want to work for an organization that isn't perceived as innovative, cutting-edge, and exciting.

Death of the Serendipity Effect

Serendipity basically refers to finding something or making something happen by chance (or by accident) or unexpectedly. Some of the greatest opportunities I have seen come out of organizations that deploy emergent collaboration solutions have been serendipitous. Organizations never know when an employee idea will result in a new opportunity, whether it is a revenue-generating or a cost-cutting opportunity. Although serendipity in and of itself is not a business use case for emergent collaboration, it is definitely a benefit. Think of how many opportunities might come about if you allow your employees to ask questions of one another or solicit feedback on ideas. Lowe's experienced this firsthand when an employee shared an idea internally for a demo she had been doing to market a product (she was showing the ease of cleaning paint from a Teflon tray). The employee shared her idea because she was trying to get more inventory of the product, since it had been selling out. However, when other employees at other stores began replicating her demo, they too began selling out of the product, generating over $1 million in revenue for just one product in a short time.

Not investing in these tools and strategies completely kills the possibility of this type of serendipity.

Employees Who Are Not Empowered or Engaged

Employees are the greatest asset of any company, and all smart companies know this. If employees are the greatest asset a company possesses, it is crucial to make sure that they have the tools they need to get their jobs done effectively and easily. Not investing in these tools may lead to disengaged employees and lower company morale. Employees want to stay competitive and relevant, and that is not possible in an organization that does not invest in these emergent collaborative tools and strategies.

This is perhaps one of the greatest problems plaguing organizations today. Recently, BlessingWhite, a leading consultancy and research firm focused on employee engagement and leadership development, released an interesting report on employee engagement called the "Employee Engagement Report 2011." That report included responses from almost 11,000 individuals from North America, India, Europe,

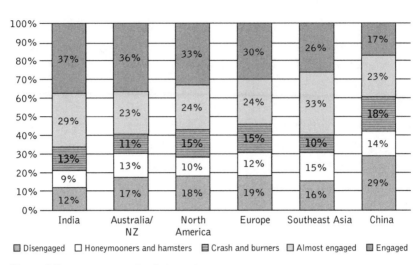

Figure 4.1 Engagement levels by region

Southeast Asia, Australia/New Zealand, and China. The key findings were shocking, but the one that is most relevant to this book is that fewer than one in three employees worldwide (31 percent) is engaged. Nearly one in five (17 percent) is actually disengaged. These numbers are broken down by region in Figure 4.1.

A study done by Gallup toward the end of 2011 also showed that the majority of American workers were not engaged in their jobs (google "Gallup employee engagement 2011" to find the report). Gallup stated, "Seventy-one percent of American workers are 'not engaged' or 'actively disengaged' in their work, meaning they are emotionally disconnected from their workplaces and are less likely to be productive."

Lack of Security

Employees can deploy any emergent tool and platform they want, and the organization will never know about it. This means that many data silos, information leaks, and risks can occur. Investing in these tools and supporting employees will allow organizations to maintain the sense of security they need by giving employees a place to share information and collaborate in a company-sponsored and -supported place.

Inability to Work Effectively

Now more than ever we are seeing a blurring of personal life and work
life. As the work and personal lives of employees begin to converge,
it becomes more important to invest in tools that allow employees to
work and collaborate remotely and across multiple devices, locations,
and platforms. Employees need to be able to access the information
they need any time they need it and anywhere they need to access
it from. Employees don't need more restrictions for how they communicate and collaborate; they need more support to make these
things easier.

Inability to Capture, Retain, and Transfer Knowledge

As knowledge and information are being shared across the enterprise,
there needs to be a way to capture the knowledge. Currently, many
organizations suffer from a "death of knowledge," meaning that once
something is shared or discussed, it dies because the information and
knowledge have nowhere to live and there is no way for other employees
to access them later.

Let's take a look at some of the risks associated with deploying
emergent collaboration solutions and how to deal with those risks.
Understanding these risks is key to making sure that when they do
present themselves, a solution is in place to help resolve them. The
supply chain uses a framework called Failure Mode and Effects
Analysis that we will explore here as it is simple to understand yet is an
effective method for thinking about and mitigating risk.

Before we start to look at how to evaluate and prioritize risk, let's
explore some of the common risks we hear about today and how to
respond to them. Keep in mind that these may or may not be considered risks for your organization but are nonetheless common. The
goal here is not to argue about risks but to have a discussion about them
that leads to a working solution.

Confidential Information Being Leaked or the Wrong Information Being Shared Internally

What is to stop an employee from getting access to information and then making it public for the world to see? What if employees start sharing information that is just plain wrong internally?

The Response

The reality here is that one doesn't really have anything to do with the other. Right now at your company if employees want to share confidential information, they can and chances are that you will never know about it. However, deploying these tools will allow your employees to identify and share the occurrences of information leakage quickly if they occur. I have not seen any examples of how deploying these tools has fostered or allowed information leakages to happen across any of the organizations I have been working with or researching, and I don't know anyone who has.

As far as sharing the wrong information goes, what is to stop employees from having discussions at the water cooler in which one employee has the wrong information and starts to share it? What about sharing the wrong information via e-mail? In those situations there is nothing you can do. However, if employees are sharing information via an emergent collaboration platform, others can quickly see and correct any type of misinformation that is being spread or shared. Thus, in effect, deploying these tools helps mitigate these risks. Also, if an employee posts inappropriate content, the community is able to resolve or fix these issues quickly.

Employees Post Inappropriate or Rude Content

What if an employee hates the company and starts saying negative things about it for everyone to see?

The Response

Neither I nor anyone I have spoken to can recall any instances of this. One of the main reasons is lack of anonymity. You wouldn't go to a party where many people know you are hanging out and walk up to someone and slap that person in the face. Similarly, you wouldn't post inappropriate content or harass colleagues at work. There is no hiding here. When you post and share content, everyone knows who the poster of that content is. This lack of anonymity is a great deterrent to this type of behavior.

Employees Don't Use the Tools

Let's say we deploy something and nobody uses it. In that case we have ended up spending a lot of money for nothing.

The Response

This is a legitimate risk. In fact, this is where most organizations have the greatest difficulty. However, it is where the strategy portion comes into play. If you simply deploy a tool and expect that your employees will use it, chances are that this is a very real risk with which you will be faced. The best way to make sure this doesn't happen is by being able to show and provide value clearly to your employees. This needs to be integrated into the way the employees do their jobs, and every new employee should receive training in the new systems. For organizations that look at deploying these tools as an evolution of how they do business, this risk is never real because it's not seen as a trial, a pilot, a test, or a short-term project. Many organizations simply say, "This is how we are doing things moving forward," and that's all there is to it. This topic is discussed throughout the book.

Loss of Internal Control

We spend a lot of time and money making sure that the content we create and share internally is done in a certain way.

The Response

I understand why control is a sticking point for many companies. However, this idea of control within the enterprise is a bit of a myth and, if you ask me, a fruitless task. The reason is quite simple: Employees don't need to rely on organizations to supply them with tools and technologies anymore. The same discussion and analogy can be drawn between customer-facing social platforms. The issue when social media first became popular was, "Why do I want to use social tools and technologies? I'm going to lose control." However, the reality is that if your customers want to say something about or share something about you, they are going to do it regardless of what you think or do. You might as well be there to engage with your customers and see what they are saying about you and be able to respond.

The same is true internally. This barrier to entry has been eliminated to the point where all the employees in any company can access and start their own collaborative workspace where they can share and control the information in a way that makes sense for them. The idea of control within the organization is dead. Instead of organizations trying to impose this control while forcing employees to do what they are going to do anyway, they should be thinking of ways to empower and support their employees to help them do their jobs more effectively.

I'm sure you and the members of your team can think of plenty of other risks. However, instead of coming up with these lists and including them here, let's take a look at a simple framework for evaluating and dealing with these risks.

The best way to go through this is in small teams, preferably teams that are going to be overseeing this enterprise collaboration initiative. Order some lunch and huddle up in the conference room for a few hours.

In Figure 4.2 you will notice that the risks are written out at the top. I have included two risks for illustrative purposes, but you are going to have far more than two. The first risk is for enterprise collaboration, and the second deals more with customer-facing social and collaborative strategies to show that you can also use this for customer-facing strategies. Keep in mind that the numbers here are made up.

Once you have the risks written out at the top, the next step is to understand the severity of those risks. This doesn't need to be an exact scientific number, only something that will help you gauge and understand how risks compare with one another. The next step is to

	Risk 1: Employees Don't Use Tools	Risk 2: Negative Customer Feedback
Severity (1–10)	8	6
Probability of occurrence (1–10)	4	3
Probability of early detection (1–10)	7	4
Priority index	**224** (8 x 4 x 7)	**72** (6 x 3 x 4)
Recommended action	Develop education and training program	Develop plan for response
Responsibility	CIO and HR teams	CMO and PR teams

Based on failure mode and effects analysis. Values are for illustration purposes only.

Figure 4.2   Framework for evaluating risk
© 2011 Chess Media Group

figure out how likely it is that your organization will detect the risk. If your employees aren't adopting the tools that your organization is providing and you are doing a good job at monitoring employee feedback and participation, the chances of detecting that risk are quite high. However, if you adopt an "if we built it, they will come" mentality, the chances of being able to detect those risks early are quite low. Finally, you want to multiply the three numbers together to get the total priority index number. Now you want to include what the recommended action is for mitigating that risk as well as whose responsibility it is to perform that action. If you can be specific with job titles or personnel names here, do it; you want to avoid ambiguity.

Do this for all the risks you are able to identify and prioritize the risks with the highest severity numbers first. You don't need to tackle all the risks at once; perhaps you can do only 5 or 10 at a time. The important thing is to understand what the risks are and how you can mitigate them when they happen.

It's important to note that in all the case studies I have written, in all the companies I have worked with, and in all the companies I have researched, I have not found horror stories about companies that implemented these initiatives only to find that something terrible happened. Andrew McAfee, the author of *Enterprise 2.0*, also has not heard any horror stories.

It is important to say something about unknown risks. Since these risks are indeed unknown, not a lot of planning can be done. The key thing with unknown risks is being able to spot them early, which is exactly what emergent collaborative solutions allow you to do. As employees communicate and collaborate, it becomes much easier to spot mistakes, pieces of misinformation, and other inaccuracies. One of the common risks organizations prioritize is security, and that is quite understandable.

The interesting thing is that deploying emergent collaborative solutions actually improves security. Think about it. If someone does something to harm the company, the chances are that you will find out about it late or perhaps not at all. Now you have the ability to see exactly what is going on within your company. Furthermore, as was mentioned above, the community acts as a collective security system that can quickly identify risks and help correct risks.

I have found that if organizations truly want to stunt emergent collaboration initiatives, this is quite easy to do. It's possible to make a list of risks that is several pages long, but at the end of the day, I would argue, the same can be done for phone systems, e-mail, and many other things. In fact, if organizations truly want to avoid all these risks, I suggest eliminating the use of computers altogether and, while we're at it, the use of phones.

For some reason, when discussions about emergent collaboration come up, we assume that humans are no longer evolved beings capable of rational thought with the ability to distinguish right from wrong. We have trusted employees with e-mail, with phone systems, with using the Internet, and with USB drives. Why should we assume that emergent collaboration platforms are going to drive employees to act like a bunch of cavemen wreaking havoc within the organization?

The answer is that we shouldn't, and if you don't trust your employees to use these tools, you need to do a better job of hiring employees you trust.

Thus far we have talked about risks as they pertain to the organization as a whole, but risks also exist for the employees who are going to be using the new tools. Think about this as an employee at a large organization. Do you really want to share what you're working on and what you're doing with the rest of the organization? I guarantee that many employees prefer not to share their information with anyone else.

Let's take a look at some of the employee-specific risks.

Sharing Information That Others Can Take Credit For

In many organizations lack of trust is a huge barrier that needs to be overcome; employees don't always want to share what they are working on or what they have developed because anyone can see that information and subsequently use it and repurpose it. This is especially true in highly competitive organizations that reward employees on the basis of how they perform in relation to their peers. It's similar to the way college students are graded on a bell curve in relation to one another. In this scenario you wouldn't want to post your notes and reading information for everyone else to see, especially when you are going to be evaluated against those individuals.

How to Deal with This

This problem comes down to trust. If employees cannot trust one another and their managers, they clearly will not want to collaborate with one another. One of the best ways to break down this risk is by shifting the focus of the organization from one of internal competition to one of internal collaboration. This means changing the way employees are evaluated and having managers (and evangelists) lead by example.

Getting Overloaded with Information

Going from a scenario of limited access to people and information to one in which you can access anyone and anything is a big shift.

Employees may get overwhelmed by the new tools and the amount of information they can access and receive.

How to Deal with This

This is a very common risk, and it's one of the most prevalent forms of resistance from employees. The best way to overcome this risk is by educating and showing employees that emergent collaboration platforms can help minimize the information with which they are bombarded. A decrease in e-mail along with filters that allow employees to select the information they want to follow ensures that employees see only the information that is relevant to them. It's also important to convey that emergent collaboration isn't meant to be used as an additional tool or platform for employees but should be looked at as the door to the organization where almost all work can get done. The ability of emergent collaboration platforms to integrate other technology solutions is a powerful feature that can help make sure this is all integrated into the existing flow of work.

The Second Nature Problem

Employees usually have a certain way they like to get things done. In fact, if you talk to some of your employees, you will find that they can accomplish some of their tasks blindfolded because they are so used to their routine and process. I discuss this in other sections of the book and call it the second nature problem. For employees to go from a routine way of doing something to using a new technology is a difficult change. Inevitably, there will be a period in which it may take employees longer to accomplish a task as they learn how to use the new platform. In a competitive landscape in which employees are already hard pressed for time, this may cause stress and a quick impulse to abandon the use of these new tools.

How to Deal with This

The best way to position these tools is not as alternative routes to doing things but as shortcuts and easier and more efficient ways to get things done. Simply telling employees that a new method exists will get you nowhere. However, communicating to employees that their lives will become easier as a result of using these tools will help overcome this risk. A part of the solution will require education and training and, of course, time. Encouragement and suggestions are also a great method to get past this. For example, if you see that an employee sends a mass e-mail to a group, you can suggest that the employee post the message to a designated group workspace on the platform. Alternatively, you can post the message there yourself and direct other employees there to find the information. This effect of gently nudging employees has been used effectively at several companies, including Penn State University.

Negative Perception in the Eyes of Colleagues

Employees who spend too much time sharing and interacting on emergent collaboration platforms may be perceived as poor workers who spend their time engaging instead of actually working. After all, if you're working, you shouldn't have time to post messages and share content.

How to Deal with This

Again, this stems from focusing the messaging and culture of the organization on collaboration. Employees need to be encouraged to engage with one another and share information, and this has to be communicated clearly by the senior executive team. Remember, ideas come as a result of engagement, communication, and collaboration. Leading by example is also a great strategy here. Océ is a company that faced this situation. At Océ employees were seen as weak or stupid if they publicly asked questions or asked for help. However, once the leaders of their collaboration effort put themselves out there and led by example, others began to follow.

The best way to find out about other risks that your employees might be faced with is simply to ask them. Anonymous surveys or discussions are a great way to collect valuable feedback from your employees.

Summary and Action Items

Often the discussion of risk is applied to what happens if organizations make an investment in emergent collaboration, but what happens if organizations don't make that investment? There are very real risks associated with that. However, there are risks in investing in these tools as well. I find that the risks of not getting involved far outweigh the risks of getting involved. Although risks do exist, there is no need to panic and run away because a simple framework can be used to identify and mitigate these risks. Don't assume that just because the tools are new, employees will go nuts. Consider the following:

- Which one of the risks of not investing in emergent collaboration do you most identify with? Are there any other risks of not investing that you would include? Make sure to write down these risks or remember them as they will come up during discussions and planning.

- One of the common risks of getting involved in emergent collaboration is deciding which ones are applicable to you. Would you respond differently? Make a note of these risks and how you would respond to them. This will come in handy during conversations with people who may list these risks as objections.

- Make a list of some of the risks you feel your organization is faced with and walk through the framework.

- Make a list of the risks your employees are faced with and suggestions for how those risks can be mitigated. You may use the same framework.

Who better to learn about trust from than the trusted advisor himself, Charles H. Green. Charles is the coauthor of *The Trusted Advisor* and *The Trusted Advisor Fieldbook* and the founder of Trusted Advisor Associates.

Collaborative Software and Risk

We have talked up to this point about the risks of introducing collaborative software. But there is another aspect of risk: the business risk that is reduced by the introduction of the software itself.

Fear, Risk, and Trust

A great amount of dysfunction in a business organization comes from people's natural fears or difficulties in trusting others. Employees are human beings, and all of us bring to the workplace a common set of normal fears. We are afraid of saying the wrong thing, of not getting promoted, of not being seen as productive enough, of making a business mistake, of being misunderstood or underappreciated—the list is endless.

The way we all deal with these daily fears is for the most part to keep them to ourselves. We focus on saying the right thing, rehearsing our presentations, systematically getting approval from others, and carefully writing our memos. We tend to overfear the risk of doing a *wrong* thing and underfear the risk of *not* doing a *right* thing. All this is perfectly natural, perfectly human. The sequence goes like this:

We fear >>> we don't trust >>> we don't
take risks >>> we don't collaborate

The problem with this dynamic is a problem nearly every business organization knows: If people relate to others from fear rather than from trust, they will not collaborate. If people don't collaborate, things take longer and cost more. Innovation is stifled by lack of collaboration. Teams cannot function well if their members don't trust one another. Leaders can't lead if people are fearful and won't follow. Absent collaboration, information gets hoarded rather than shared. People develop processes, data, and rules to substitute for direct collaborative interaction.

This is where collaborative software plays a powerful role.

How Software Changes Things

People often decry online social media and other forms of electronic communication—including collaborative software—because it reduces the "personalness" of interaction. People hide behind the relative impersonality and anonymity of such media, avoiding the difficult messiness of "real" human relationships.

There is a lot of truth to that, but software is a double-edged sword. That same impersonalness is also a virtue—it lowers the risk of interacting with other people. For example, if I collaborate with others by software:

- I typically use just the written word—it doesn't involve voice dynamics, intonation, accent, or emotional content.
- It allows me some time to react; I can generally compose my thoughts before having to commit to them.
- It gives me control over just what I choose to say.
- It puts me on a level playing field emotionally—everyone else communicates in the same digital way I do.
- The "rules" are easily understood and apply to all—collaboration online feels much more meritocratic.
- There is a game quality to collaborative software for most of us—we learned such tools through some kind of online gaming—and that makes interactions feel more playlike.

People decry online communication in general for decreasing the *depth* of interpersonal interaction, but that is true only past a certain point. At early stages of interaction, collaborative software actually increases the depth of interaction by easing the difficulties of interacting with wide ranges of people we don't know well.

Risk Revisited

Collaborative software plays the role of etiquette, or custom, or school uniforms, or any set of well-defined social conventions: It eases the difficulty of interacting with others. It doesn't just make it mechanically easier to bridge the gaps of space and time; it materially eases the internal barriers of fear and risk that divide us as strongly as time zones do.

Collaboration software is easily underestimated, and not just by end users but by its proponents as well. For all the mechanical efficiencies it provides, it is also a strategic tool for organizational effectiveness. A high-trust organization has enormous competitive advantages over a low-trust organization with customers, employees, and suppliers alike. And organizational trust doesn't flow like a business process from the top down; it is a cultural set of daily norms experienced by all. Collaborative software has a role to play in creating such an environment.

---

five

Control the Center
(What Is It and
What Pieces Do You Need?)

In chess, one of the key strategies in the opening is to control the
center, but which pieces should be used to make that happen? Who
in your organization needs to be involved in the discussion and strategy
to make sure the collaboration initiative is successful?

Simply relying on the IT department to deploy and manage collaboration is not effective. Similarly, assuming that business units are going
to run with the project is also ineffective. Business unit leaders and IT
professionals both need to be involved in making emergent collaboration work.

In the survey that Chess Media Group conducted we found that
both business and IT professionals are involved in most deployments,
as is shown in Figure 5.1 (many of the responses that cited "other"
listed marketing and communications as the departments responsible
for E2.0 at their organizations, which applies to the business unit
category).

What's also interesting in this figure is that when either IT or a
business unit owns these initiatives, business units are more involved
than IT departments. The reason for this is that the barrier to entry
for business unit leaders is now very low. These technology solutions
can be simple to deploy with minimal technical knowledge and at a
very low cost. Remember how easy it was to set up that Facebook or

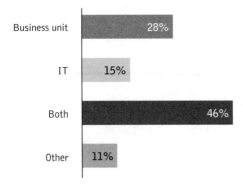

Figure 5.1 What departments are responsible for sponsoring Enterprise 2.0 efforts?

LinkedIn account? You didn't have to purchase any software, install anything, or get permission to set it up. Many of these benefits apply to the emergent collaboration space as well (even though many freemium products will eventually charge), so there is no reason a business unit leader can't deploy a collaboration solution without the help of IT.

From the organizations I have spoken to and worked with, the most effective team consists of a combination of the following:

- A senior-level executive who helps drive the initiative from the top.
- Business unit leaders who will be managing the initiative.
- IT professionals who will be managing integration and security.
- Compliance and legal professionals who will be assisting with policies and guidelines.
- A group of enthusiastic users/supporters to act as the evangelists. It's important to have several evangelists geographically and departmentally distributed throughout the organization.
- Project managers who will be the overseers of the project as a whole.
- Someone from a user experience team.
- Employees who will be day-to-day collaborators and users.
- Any other stakeholders who wish to join or participate.

Let's take a look at why these people make up an effective team.

Senior-Level Executive

Having someone from senior-level management is important for enterprise collaboration initiatives for a few reasons. First, it shows the employees that collaboration is being encouraged and supported from the top. Second, it's important to have someone who is able to make decisions at an executive level when issues are escalated or when there is lack of agreement. Third, having someone with formal power and budgetary authority increases the chances that this will be acted on. When senior-level executives are not involved, these initiatives typically turn into recommendations instead of actions.

Morten T. Hansen, author of *Collaboration*, developed the concept of T-shaped management, which is applicable here. In his book Hansen shares a story about an investment banker at a large financial institution who is up for promotion. This person is loved by his clients, is a top performer at the company, and receives great performance reviews from his managers and peers. However, the problem is that this person does not collaborate and is not a team player. Should this person be promoted to a senior-level managerial role?

Hansen states that the enemy of collaboration is modern management. Most organizations today are structured into various business units or departments, each run by a department leader who reports up to the CEO. The leaders of these units focus on achieving "their numbers" and meeting their targets. Those who exceed their targets and generate solid revenue for the company get promoted. Over time this leads to an extremely internally competitive and siloed organization; you can imagine why collaboration in such an environment does not work well.

Let's get back to the investment banker. Would you decide to promote him yet? At first it's easy to say yes, he should be promoted. But what happens if you start promoting and hiring leaders who are not collaborative? You can see how the culture of the organization and the rest of the employees are going to be affected. Collaboration in this scenario will become a problem.

Hansen's concept of T-shaped leaders means that these employees are effective not only at managing their own business units or departments but also at connecting other employees, are willing to help others, and can work and collaborate across other areas as well. I recommend reading Hansen's book for more insight on this issue.

Business Unit Leaders

These middle or senior managers can help encourage the adoption of new tools and technologies in their departments. Business unit leaders will also help guide the specific use cases that are applicable to their areas. As with senior-level management, it's crucial that business unit leaders actively participate in emergent collaboration.

IT Professionals

It's important to make sure that the professionals maintaining the infrastructure and security of the organization are involved with this initiative. They will be the ones to evaluate things such as security, integration, and maintenance and upgrades. Sometimes the IT department is actually the driving force behind enterprise collaboration, as was the case with the American Hospital Association. With the ease of deployment for many emergent collaboration solutions, the temptation to proceed without IT exists but should be quashed.

Compliance and Legal

Making sure that the way employees engage and share information complies with legal and privacy concerns is always an issue, especially in regulated organizations. I once met an executive from a pharmaceutical company who told me that employees are not even allowed to mention brand product names in their internal collaboration platforms. Making sure that the organization as a whole is not at risk of violating employee or company rights and regulations is important and is why you want to have someone from legal and compliance here. It's important to note, however, that it's not always best to agree immediately and become complacent about everything that legal throws your way; don't be afraid to push back on a few things to find a compromise. The best way to go about this is to have an open discussion on what can be done and what the possibilities are. You will find that whereas certain things might not be negotiable, in other areas one can be quite flexible.

Evangelists

This might be a large group of people or perhaps one internal champion within the organization. The evangelists are the ones who really support and drive this initiative. Evangelists help convey value to the rest of the organization, encourage adoption, help with training other employees, and act as the go-to resource for anything involving emergent collaboration. They are employees who are truly passionate about emergent collaboration and love it.

Project Managers

This person oversees much of the strategic and tactical implementation of the initiative, making sure that things are happening on time and in the right way. The project manager can be thought of as the conductor who brings everything together to make it work.

User Experience and Design

Making sure that the user experience, branding, and usability aspects meet the criteria of the organization is important. Customizations and features are usually heavily influenced by feedback from these individuals. If your employees are going to be using a central collaboration platform on a regular basis, you want to make sure that it has the company look and feel that you want to convey.

Employees

This very valuable group could consist of evangelists or other stakeholders, but I wanted to make sure to call out employees as an important part of this. At the heart of enterprise collaboration are the employees who are going to be using these tools and technologies to collaborate and communicate with one another. Therefore, employees should be involved. You don't need 10,000 of them involved, but as is mentioned later, it is important to hear feedback from employees in various business units as the use cases, business problems, success metrics, and strategies may be different. One or a few employees can act as the voices for a larger group. Simple surveys are a great way to get employee feedback.

Other Stakeholders

David Straus, the author of *How to Make Collaboration Work*, defines a stakeholder as one of the following:

1. Someone with the formal power to make a decision
2. Someone with the power to block a decision
3. Someone affected by a decision
4. Someone with relevant information or expertise

At large organizations it obviously becomes inefficient or impossible to involve every single person who wants to be involved in the planning and team process, and so in these types of situations, representatives can be selected to speak on behalf of a particular group, for example, on behalf of the employees in the marketing department or the sales department.

Team dynamics are also important here, and so putting together people you know work well together is a good idea. Gloria Burke, the director of knowledge strategy and governance at Unisys, said it best, "Cross-organization stakeholder involvement and a top-down leadership support model are essential drivers in achieving and sustaining a successful knowledge-sharing and collaboration environment; people support what they help build."

A Note on Those Who Resist

Not everyone is going to be supportive of these collaborative projects; in fact, there most likely will be some very outspoken opponents who will not want this to happen (resistance is addressed in more detail in Chapter 8). The key is not to exclude them but to involve them and let them voice their concerns, issues, and frustrations. Those who oppose something can often become the greatest evangelists. My company once conducted an assessment of a midsize organization in which we were all warned about an employee who was against anything collaborative and social. We spent some time with that employee to understand why she was so strongly against doing certain things and later discovered that the main reason was that she was unaware of how it would affect her job and had no understanding of what these platforms could do and how risks would be mitigated; basically, she was scared, and understandably so. After addressing her concerns, we found that she became quite supportive of the project. Try to identify the people you believe are not supportive and get them involved early on in the initiative. Help educate them and listen to their concerns and feedback.

Try asking them the following questions:

- What is it about this initiative that you are against?
- Do you believe employee collaboration is important?
- Do you see any areas of improvement around collaboration and communication that you think we can turn into opportunities?
- What would make you feel more comfortable with moving in the direction of collaboration?
- If you were leading this organization, what would you do to help foster collaboration?

Asking these questions will allow you to understand where an employee who shows this resistance is coming from and why. This isn't about steamrolling employees, so make sure to pay attention to feedback.

Of course, not every organization is going to have the type of collaboration team described above. In fact, I have found that no two organizations have the exact same team or the same number of people participating to make these initiatives successful.

The Next Question to Ask Is How to Get These People Involved in the Initiative

Getting employees involved doesn't need to be complicated. In fact, it starts by just asking them.

I have found that discussions about deploying these solutions are not uncommon within organizations. In fact, it's quite the opposite; they are common. The way to start is by looking at who else in the organization is having these conversations and discussions. I'd be surprised if there weren't teams at your company that haven't already deployed their own emergent collaboration technologies, such as wikis, microblogs, blogs, or other easily deployed platforms. After all, there are many free and low-cost alternatives that take a minimal amount of time to get up and running. Figure 5.2 shows that in 23 percent of all organizations the push for Enterprise 2.0 comes from the bottom up, which means that it's likely these tools are already being used in teams, groups, and departments. Keep in mind that these discussions aren't typically about emergent collaboration as a topic but instead are about business problems that employees are faced with. Emergent collaboration then becomes a potential solution to existing business problems.

You might encourage some of your colleagues to share their stories and experiences with you so that you can document them and share them with management. Surveys, as mentioned a few times in this

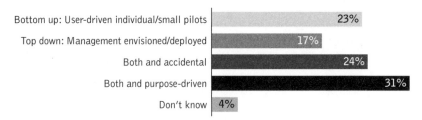

Figure 5.2   In your company, where does the push for Enterprise 2.0 come from?

book, are also effective ways to identify the collaboration problems employees are experiencing.

Many executives and employees do not like to address the elephant in the room. Because of this, many people in the organization are aware that a problem with collaboration exists but choose not to address it. This will work for only so long, and eventually it has to be addressed.

Is it more effective to have the push for Enterprise 2.0 come from the top down or from the bottom up? In the Chess Media Group survey we found that the greatest push for Enterprise 2.0 came from both the top down and the bottom up with a clear and driven purpose.

We can also see that "both and accidental" is the second largest type of push for Enterprise 2.0. This means that in 55 percent of all deployments the push came from the bottom and from the top. What does this tell us? Clearly, this is something that is being considered by most employees at an organization, and so the first step is to not be scared of having that conversation. If we include the "top down" numbers as well, senior management is involved in the push for Enterprise 2.0 in 72 percent of all deployments.

There is no template or cookie-cutter approach to getting people involved, but you should remember that based on the Chess Media Group survey, the chances of other executives and employees already having had these discussions is very high. Here are some things organizations have done to get support for these initiatives:

- Conducting employee surveys that clearly show that collaboration and/or communication is an area that employees would like to see improved.

- Developing and presenting a set of business use cases that other employees can relate to. This can be quite simple: Go out and deploy something for a small team and then show the value of what was done.

- Highlighting case studies and examples of what other companies are doing. If you can find competitors or vertically relevant companies, that's even better.

- Communicating the value of this for the employees. For example, you can go to an executive and say, "Remember how you keep mentioning that the executive team doesn't have enough insight into the ground level of our organization? Well, I think I found a way to fix this problem."

"How do we get people involved?" is a tricky question to provide a definitive answer to because it's a bit like asking, "How do I make friends?" Sure, there are some things you can do, such as not being rude and being open-minded. However, friendship happens when people click, and that is much more of a personality and personal connection factor than it is a "what can I do" factor. Although the things mentioned above can help get people involved, it is also going to depend on things such as timing, whether the people you are approaching like you and trust you, and whether you can connect and communicate with those people.

"What's in it for me?" is an important question to address for those who might potentially be involved. Unfortunately, in many companies it is rare for employees to play an integral role in something that has the potential to change the culture and the way the business operates radically. This serves as a new and exciting opportunity for employees to challenge themselves and become part of something that can change the direction of the entire company. Most of the employees at companies whom I have interviewed were excited to be a part of something new while learning new skills. Employees who are passionate about emergent collaboration and believe in connecting employees together are the best people to have on this team.

Where Does the Money Come from to Make This Happen?

One of the reasons budget becomes a factor in deciding not to invest in emergent collaboration technologies and strategies is that *budget* sometimes means "fear." In other words, the budget isn't the real reason executives don't invest in this; fear is. If your organization wants to invest in collaboration and believes in the value of connecting and engaging employees, budget should not be a problem. Penn State University cut one of its annual employee events and used that money to fund its collaboration project. Why did it do this? Because the employee event was large enough to accommodate only a small sample of the employee population; although it was an annual event, not every employee could attend. The reasoning became, why spend money every year on engaging some of our employees physically when we can engage all of them virtually? Other organizations have an emergent solution, an innovation, or a special projects budget that they pull from. Some companies rely on low-cost alternatives such as wikis or blogs. Still other organizations pool budgets from various departments such as human resources (HR), IT, and internal communications to make this a reality. I've also seen organizations shift their existing intranet budgets to emergent collaboration platform budgets. This doesn't have to be a hard and tedious process. Smart organizations will figure out a way to make this happen. I recently spoke with a team at one of the world's largest companies that told me, "How could we not invest in this?"

Can you imagine working at your company without a phone system, the Internet, or a computer? Like all these things, collaboration is not an option to build and sustain a successful organization; it should be a requirement.

I don't want to start talking numbers here because it's all relative. I know of small companies that have spent around $150,000 annually for emergent collaboration initiatives, and I know of large organizations that have spent less than that. The point is that there are options.

In developing these teams, it is also common to find that some employees are more involved than others. David Straus developed a concept called "rings of involvement" that applies to how involved relevant stakeholders are in collaboration. That concept inspired the chart shown in Figure 5.3.

In looking at how emergent collaboration platforms and strategies get implemented in an organization, it's helpful to think of several degrees of involvement, as shown in the figure.

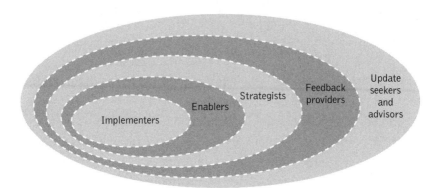

Figure 5.3 Degrees of involvement in emergent collaboration
© 2012 Chess Media Group

Implementers

This is the core team that essentially works on rolling things out. Implementers are the day-to-day employees who do everything from selecting the vendors to developing adoption strategies. The implementers are usually full-time employees devoted 100 percent to making sure the effort is successful. They can be thought of as the construction workers responsible for building the organization's emergent collaborative house.

Enablers

This is an extension of the core team but is not as involved. The extended team might work on a subset of the core project such as trying to figure who the evangelists within the organization might be or trying to predict certain risks. Ultimately, the extended team isn't a part of the big-picture strategic initiative but assists the implementers in making sure the big picture fits together. The extended team is akin to a right-hand man. The enablers effectively help make the implementers' job possible.

Strategists

The strategists work closely with the implementers and the extended team as they help develop the big picture. The strategists can be thought of as the architects who design the blueprints for the implementers and the extended team. Often there is crossover from the implementers and the extended team to the strategist role. All these categories are permeable. Strategists may not do the actual implementation.

Feedback Providers

These employees attend meetings and receive all the information they need to provide feedback and/or insight to assist in the project. Feedback providers don't actually have a hand in the roll-out or strategic decision making but contribute ideas, recommendations, and insights when and where needed. These employees are great for bouncing ideas off of.

Update Seekers and Advisors

This group of employees just wants to know what's going on with the initiative. The group can be large or small, and typically it receives updates via alerts, e-mails, newsletters, or perhaps briefings. Sometimes certain executives like to be the update seekers; they want to get enough information to know what's going on and that things are going well.

Keep in mind that we are describing nothing more than involvement. This doesn't have anything to with seniority, the size of a group, or importance. It's possible that someone senior will be part of the implementing group and an entry-level employee will be part of the update seekers group. How involved employees are can depend on all sorts of things, such as how much interest they have in the project and whether they have the time to contribute. Also, these types of involvement groups are not mutually exclusive or permanent. Employees can be a part of more than one group and can also move between groups; for example, an employee who may start getting updates and information about the project and then realize this is something he or she wants to be part of. This isn't meant to be a rigid bucket of employees; it's merely an overview of how employees are typically involved. It is something you can easily adapt and modify so that it fits your organization.

This whole group might be called the Emergent Collaboration Task Force or whatever other fun or creative name you come up with. Some companies have one core team that handles all the functions necessary, and other companies have multiple teams for separate functions. For example, you might want to have a task force as well as a governance committee or an oversight team that meets less frequently and addresses broader issues of emergent collaboration such as mandating the use of tools, changing employee incentive programs to include collaboration, permissions and policies, and other broader topical issues that help the company govern emergent collaboration. In either scenario you want to make sure to have a senior-level executive (or a few) involved.

Organizations also typically organize their teams in one of two ways. This isn't to say that one is better or more effective than the other; I believe it's situational.

Permanent Teams

Organizations with permanent enterprise collaboration teams have either hired new employees or transitioned existing employees to a new role. This is something I have typically seen in larger or more complex organizations. Permanent teams always focus on continuous ways to improve collaboration within the organization and deal with many complexities of managing robust collaboration solutions. Integrations, vendor transitions, and infrastructure changes or requirements are all handled on an ongoing basis by permanent employees. Content organization and structure also plays a crucial role here as often the larger the company is, the more content that company has and is producing. This doesn't mean that smaller companies don't have permanent teams; they often do.

When This Makes Sense

This form of organization makes sense in the following situations:

- Larger organizations in which a lot of content and information is being shared regularly

- Organizations that are just getting started with emergent collaboration initiatives and need to hire full-time employees
- Organizations that are continuously incorporating employee feedback into systems
- Dynamic organizations in which things are usually changing
- Organizations that deploy solutions that require dedicated IT staff to manage or in which vendor changes and infrastructure changes might happen

Ad Hoc Teams

These teams come together for this initiative, but the employees retain their day jobs and positions. The team meets regularly to discuss ideas and solve problems, but its members are not strictly devoted to enterprise collaboration on a full-time basis. Typically, organizations with ad hoc teams are not as large as those with permanent teams. In some large companies I have also seen one or two full-time employees remain on the team.

When This Makes Sense

This form of organization makes sense in the following situations:

- Established organizations that have already deployed these systems and are now in sustaining mode
- Organizations in which a lot of documentation and content is not created and/or shared, perhaps a small team in which everyone is in the same office
- Large companies that seek to assign distributed responsibility to a large group of employees
- Smaller companies that don't have the resources to dedicate permanent teams

Once teams are developed, it's important to maintain regular communication and meetings to discuss and address things that may arise during the course of the emergent collaboration initiative, such as brainstorming additional ways or ideas to get employees to use the platform. Large organizations with a presence in multiple countries usually have representatives from various geographies or local offices that are part of the team. There is no formula for how big or small an emergent collaboration team should be; in fact, the more evangelists and supporters you can get, the better. However, the core team will have to remain a manageable size.

Summary and Action Items

Emergent collaboration should be a joint effort between IT and business units. In fact, the research that Chess Media Group put together shows that this is the case for many organizations. Emergent collaboration teams can be composed of a diverse set of employees, and not every company will have the same kind of team involved. Your organization needs to understand what the team should be like and who should be involved. Make sure to include those who resist during the discussions; their concerns should be heard. Finally, make sure the team understands how involved the employees are going to be and how they will receive the information they need:

- Select the people you want to be part of the team; you don't need to limit this to a closed group. You may ask around and share the news of a new collaborative project to see who steps forward.
- Outline how involved each of the participants is going to be.
- Discuss whether you think this should be an ad hoc team or a permanent team.
- Address where budget can come from and come up with a few options.
- Arrange for regular meetings with the team.

Chris Hart is the vice president of IT at Random House Publishing, and during the continuing course of his company's emergent collaboration journey, Chris has learned quite a lot. He agreed to share some of his insights with us.

The value of Enterprise 2.0 tools seems so clear from a technical or business analyst position. The tools offer more real-time data, better collaboration in teams, ambient awareness of the company's independent units, and single solutions to all those internal department blog/wiki requests. But the lack of a clear ROI and the looks you get from upper management at the suggestion of adding a "social tool" to the enterprise can be a bit daunting. Additionally, a social tool at work meets with some staff derision as well: "Why do I need to Facebook for the company?" and "Don't we have enough communications already: e-mail, phone, mobile, etc.?"

So what does an Enterprise 2.0 tool set offer to a company, and who should lead the effort forward?

Who drives innovation in your company? Of course, IT has an interest in all things cool and buzzy, and so they are engaged early on in social tools. The good news is that the tools are simple to install, and moving some existing communications to microblogs and Twitter makes good technical sense and models the behavior corporate users need to display. But beyond IT, most business areas can find immediate advantage in an internal social network.

A top-down approach is rare in my experience, since E2.0 tools can be received with general derision from resistant staff. The message that senior management "wants us to tweet" may not be a clear call to effective action. It's better to build a strategy focusing on communication and collaboration and then ask for teams to coordinate those solutions. Involving senior management in your roll-out and asking them to post and set the tone of the conversations is great, but expecting people to work socially on management demand is unrealistic.

Human resources can immediately post job offers, policy changes, green initiatives, and more, creating a HR newsletter easily. HR is a great enabler, since they want to expand communications and ask for a new employee form to be delivered, a department newsletter, etc. A social networking tool may be an effective solution for HR, with many cross-functional communication features; otherwise, HR relies on e-mail and intranets and gets no direct feedback and can't judge the impact. Additionally, enabling search in your tools adds a powerful means to keep staff informed.

Sales can suddenly collaborate and share contact details. It becomes like e-mail, where IT runs the software and different business areas can use it the way they see fit. If e-mail is accelerated snail mail, social collaboration is accelerated e-mail: accelerated and expanded.

Project teams (project management offices) are often driven by technology adopters and evangelists; they are looking for tools to collaborate and report on projects. Project milestones and tasks are crucial to track but hard to communicate without spamming the enterprise. Rather than provide e-mails, Excel sheets, or solutions such as Basecamp or Salesforce, an internal social site can accomplish multiple goals with one piece of software. Project documentation, status, alerts, notification, and change management all fit nicely into social media.

Since E2.0 tools in the enterprise can lead to the evolution of business toward "social business," they can impact all areas. Social media can break out like a rash, a very positive rash of connections and engagement in all areas of the business. What do you do with people who resist, find it uncomfortable to work openly? You can leave them and circle back. Don't spend too much time convincing resisters and fighting for the value of open communications, knowledge management, and clear status views. If they don't see the value now, they will as more work is done outside of e-mail and more actions are real-time. Social media draws participants (or readers) by having energy and engagement of staff, not by being a smarter tool or being feature-rich. E2.0 tools opens the work being done to the visibility of other teams, management, and colleagues. If people are resistant to this change, over time they will engage, just as people did with e-mail.

If you can, avoid the squishy discussion of "changing the corporate culture" until later. E2.0 tools offer the on-ramp to the long-promised gift of knowledge management. If people share project status, work events, and exceptions to the rule and share real-time work issues, you start having a learning organization. The possibility to learn from others opens up staff to a broader context if all the work streams could be easily indexed in a central area, pointed to with URLs, posted to with RSS, linked, etc. The huge amount of time spent trying to find the right person or event decreases dramatically, and people can start seeing broader impacts of events within the company.

But a problem is that people don't work in the same way they socialize. Having the same consumer social tools with the same content doesn't work. The workplace is not open and free. Work has elements of individual and team competition, security, stealth projects, and poor managers, all of which should be avoided. Offering another Facebook at work doesn't sound like a value proposition, especially if you just add that and keep doing all your other work; it's just more to do. If e-mail doesn't change, no meetings get canceled, and no one gets back more value than they put in, it will fail. Generally, people use a tool only when they get more out of it than they put in. And that requires a sense of trust that others will participate. So getting started is hard. The first posts look lonely, but once the network effect kicks in and people see other people they know using the tool, it moves quickly. Activity has gravity and energy, and it pulls people in. You can add to that energy with smart choices of system automations and targeted participation.

How do we go from a reluctant internal Facebook to a rich and open knowledge management system? The move to a corporate accelerator requires thinking of your E2.0 solution as part of your systems architecture. E2.0 can be the glue point between systems and people. In the corporate framework, you want people reacting to real-time data and you want them to share and learn from their reactions. A data-driven company needs to move beyond reports and dashboards and into actionable granular system alerts that do not require interpretation and are small enough in scope to complete today. Think of your applications and systems as really smart people to follow, people who can post/tweet conditions that are based on real-time analytics, complex and deep dives into data that require multiple reports and complex interpretation. The simple statement "At the current rate of movement, three stores are out of stock of XYZ in one week, and the distribution center has no stock" can be posted and followed by any number of people: sales, manufacturing, management, warehousing, etc. That is actionable data that can be discussed, commented on, liked, shared, forwarded, and resolved within that E2.0 tool. The resolution is there for future people to review. And the resolution can be understood and coded so that next time the systems can resolve the issue further, and soon the systems post would state: "More XYZ stock has been ordered from manufacturing to a low stock/inventory position." Automating parts of the business that are repetitive and focusing on analytical exceptions can be the goal of the E2.0 system. All of that system messaging and social messaging can happen within the structure of an enterprise collaboration tool.

The real push to change team behaviors needs to come from multiple areas at once: the project managers, HR, IT, sales, and business leaders in general. If project communications are done in a collaboration tool, status and milestones are shared. Projects don't disappear into spreadsheets on shared drives, timelines aren't frozen into Gantt chart wallpaper, and redundant efforts are quickly highlighted. Getting project managers into Enterprise 2.0 tools opens projects to review and scrutiny. Projects should be seen and heard by everyone interested at all times.

If business leaders participate, especially senior management, the conversation suddenly becomes electric. If people worry about social media in the enterprise going off the corporate rails, nothing keeps it on track like management participation. Knowing that threads and conversations are being viewed by different levels of management creates a new way for staff to be noticed. Reputation management is built into most packages, so the people who have gravity, who have the most "liked" comments, become pundits for their departments. The inherent meritocracy of social networking makes people who post and participate in a meaningful fashion get noticed in the workplace or the world.

But why not use e-mail? As Bill French said, "E-mail is where knowledge goes to die." E-mail can't offer that flexible and open a solution for obvious reasons. You can search and retrieve from someone else's e-mail, you don't want to administer hundreds of mailing lists for every business issue, and you don't want interested people not to find something because it is trapped in e-mail. Forget sending more reports, because most reports require interpretation and five other reports to be meaningful. And computers are better at bumping data, defining conditions, and controlling standards than is an overworked staff. Just look at how many reports your company has. How many reports does it take to make a decision? How many people know all those interactions? What if everyone who could get value from an event, could know about it, and react to it, and it could all be captured and tracked and searched?

Search becomes a huge benefit for a social network internally. If you can include your document repositories, enterprise software systems, intranets, and social network in a search engine, you've just created "knowledge management lite." You will be able to move quickly and find what you need in people, documents, or databases; what could be better?

Remember to keep the basic 1/10/100 rule in mind for your enterprise social networking project. It is easy to be frustrated that there are hundreds of users logging in, but few posts. In general, 1 person posts, 10 people like or comment, and 100 read the post. If you keep in mind that formula, the value of the network you're creating is easier to judge. Many site managers see comments and likes as being as important as the initial posts, since that shows the engagement, which is crucial to success.

As your enterprise social environment grows, dedicated staff may be needed, the same type of staff that handles intranet communications and corporate bulletin boards. The difference is that the ease of use of these Facebook-style interfaces requires no training, and most of your younger users will easily slip into posting work status. Imagine being out of the office for a day but being able to catch up on business status, projects, problems, and the like, with the same tools you use to catch up with friends. It's the same basic stuff, just for work, not family or friends, and it can be as effective.

E2.0 gives you project status from people (which is another challenge), corporate announcements (can't live without those), exceptions management alerts (system opportunities/threats), and an index of your day's events. It's also really interesting to see all the groups your staff will create, all the closed and open team areas. It's meaningful for structure to see the real work areas emerge. Sometimes the informal groups can hint at a better logical organization of staff than the current org chart. If your groups break down the organizations silos, then maybe it's time to rethink the company structure.

So invite your systems to your E2.0 tools. Create automated alerts with standard interpretations of events/data and let staff follow them as you would other people. Enable search across systems so it's easy to find people and ideas. No department or team can own all the conversations in a company or control all the groupings. If you give everyone an account and add some clear benefits to show the way forward, such as HR and exceptions management alerts, people will converge and begin to share business information in new and exciting ways. We can't participate in the new 2.0 economy by using business 1.0 methods.

part two

THE MIDDLE GAME

six

An Overview of the Technology Landscape

There are many vendors and platforms in the emergent social software space. There are also a lot of use cases and business problems that organizations are looking to solve. Organizations need to make sure they select the right tool for the right job. The challenge is that the vendor landscape changes quickly as a result of acquisitions, new companies emerging, old ones going out of business, and so on. Instead of exploring the technology landscape from a branded vendor perspective, we are going to look at it from a category perspective. Under each category we will also explore what these types of tools are being used for, as identified by the Chess Media Group survey. Respondents were able to select more than one type of platform as well as more than one type of use for each platform.

Full-Scale Enterprise Collaboration Platforms

These are platforms that typically allow organizations to do virtually anything from developing internal blogs, to creating internal wikis, to posting group status updates, to customizing widgets, to sharing ideas. Full-scale platforms can be thought of as an entire tool set instead of something specific, such as a wrench or a hammer. These platforms are usually analogized to internal social networks and act as the "front door" for employees seeking to get work done in their organizations.

Full-scale platforms often also have a customer-facing feature that allows customers to share, collaborate, and communicate with one another as well as with employees.

More and more, these types of platforms are becoming the go-to solution of choice for organizations interested in emergent collaboration. These platforms offer organizations a host of features and functionality, and that allows them to be used in a multitude of ways; hence, they are quite flexible and robust. However, for an organization that doesn't have a clear set of business drivers, deploying something this robust (with all the features) can be a bit of a detriment (you don't need an entire tool set to hang a picture frame).

Examples of these vendors include Microsoft's SharePoint, Jive Software, Tibbr, IBM Connections, Moxie Software, and Atlassian, among many others. Keep in mind that for the purposes of this survey we asked only about internal uses of these platforms because that is the sole focus of this book.

Among 234 people who participated in the Chess Media Group survey, the top three emergent collaboration platforms being used within organizations were blogs (70 percent), full-feature collaboration platforms (60 percent), and microblogs (58 percent).

What Are Full-Feature Collaboration Tools Being Used For?

Figure 6.1 shows that the top five most common uses for these tools are employee collaboration, general communication, to ask and answer questions and get internal peer support, to improve productivity, and idea generation and innovation. This doesn't mean that this is what your organization has to use these platforms for. Don't look at this in terms of what other companies are doing; look at it in terms of what the possibilities are for your company. Aside from the top five uses for these platforms, you will notice a diverse set of other uses, such as project management, process management, and trying to shift toward a more open corporate culture. Remember that this starts with business use cases, with technology second. Following the solution mapping

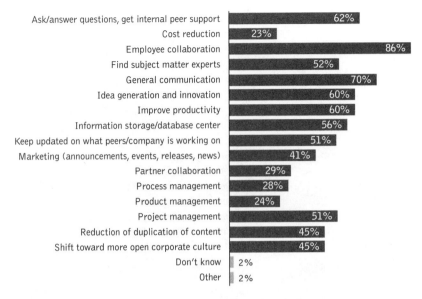

Figure 6.1   Reasons for using emergent collaboration platforms

process mentioned in Chapter 2 will allow your organization to make the best technology choice.

Mashups

This is an application that combines data from multiple internal and public sources and publishes the results to enterprise portals and application development tools. Mashups allow users to create their own way to visualize, analyze, or view data and information. Typically, data or information is taken from existing sources and developed into something new. An example of this might be a customized dashboard that visualizes data in a unique way. Vendors include JackBe and Serna Software.

According to the Chess survey, mashups are being used by only around 22 percent of organizations.

What Are Mashups Being Used For?

Figure 6.2 shows that the top reasons organizations are using mashups are improved productivity, employee collaboration, reducing duplication

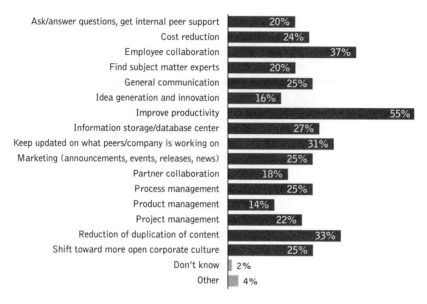

Figure 6.2 Uses for mashups

of content, keeping up to date on what peers and colleagues are working on, and as an information storage and database center. Mashups are not as prevalent as some of the other types of tools organizations are using, but they have their place.

Wikis

Wikis allow individuals in an organization to collaboratively create or edit a web page or piece of content, for example, a shared document. Wikis can also be used as information and document repositories within teams. We did not collect usage statistics on wikis, but I am finding that they are becoming less used as stand-alone applications and are more likely to be a part of a larger, more robust platform. Wikis are great information and knowledge base repositories for anything from files and presentations to proposals and marketing collateral. Example of wiki platforms are PBworks and Mediawiki (which is the free open source software that Wikipedia is built on).

Blogs

Blogs allow employees to share their thoughts and ideas via web-based pages. Blogs are a great way to showcase thought leadership or subject matter expertise either publicly or within an organization. Examples of these vendors include WordPress and TypePad. Full-scale enterprise solutions also typically have blogging functionality.

Seventy percent of the respondents said they are using blogs in their organizations.

What Are Blogs Being Used For?

As is shown in Figure 6.3, the top uses for blogs within organizations include general communication, events/news/product releases, keeping up to date on what peers and the rest of the organization are working on, employee collaboration, and asking/answering questions and getting peer support. You will find that many of the full-feature collaboration platforms already have blogging as a feature built into their offerings. As was mentioned earlier in the book, blogging internally is a great way to build weak ties within the organization.

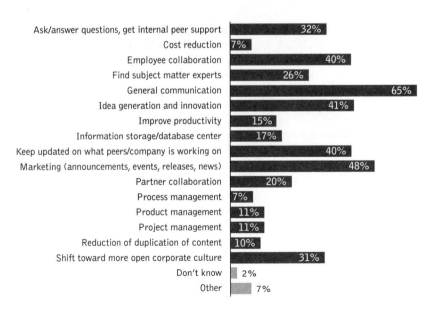

Figure 6.3 Uses for blogs

Prediction Market Platforms

These platforms allow employees to "bet" on milestones, outcomes, and decisions that the company makes. This method of collective intelligence helps organizations predict things such as product launches and performance. Vendors include Crowdcast and Inkling.

Among companies that responded to the Chess Media Group survey, only 11 percent were using prediction market platforms. This was the least used emergent collaboration platform among all the options.

What Are Prediction Markets Being Used For?

Figure 6.4 shows that the top five reasons organizations use prediction markets are idea generation and innovation, process management, to improve productivity, partner collaboration, and cost reduction. What I find interesting in this figure is that the sixth most common reason is "don't know." I interpret this as organizations deploying prediction markets either because they were sold on the software but don't understand how or why to use it or because the value is not being conveyed clearly to the employees.

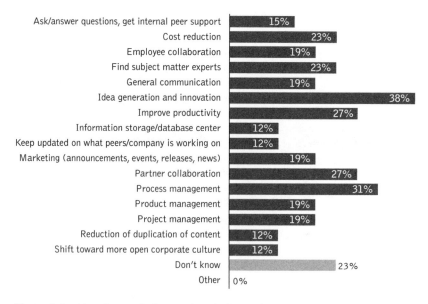

Figure 6.4 Uses for prediction market platforms

Forums

Forums are typically organized message boards and online discussion sites. Forums are web applications that manage user-generated content, usually in threaded and topically relevant conversations. Many enterprise forum solutions today also allow employees to create their own profile pages.

Forums are being used by 51 percent of organizations.

What Are Forums Being Used For?

As with some of the other categories here, forums are often a part of a larger offering in many emergent collaboration platforms. According to the Chess data and as shown in Figure 6.5, the top five reasons employees use forums are asking and answering questions and getting internal peer support, employee collaboration, general communication, idea generation and innovation, and to find subject matter experts and improve productivity (both tied for fifth).

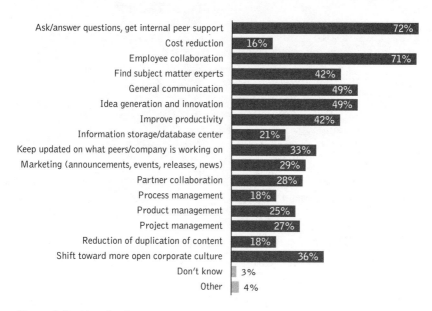

Ask/answer questions, get internal peer support	72%
Cost reduction	16%
Employee collaboration	71%
Find subject matter experts	42%
General communication	49%
Idea generation and innovation	49%
Improve productivity	42%
Information storage/database center	21%
Keep updated on what peers/company is working on	33%
Marketing (announcements, events, releases, news)	29%
Partner collaboration	28%
Process management	18%
Product management	25%
Project management	27%
Reduction of duplication of content	18%
Shift toward more open corporate culture	36%
Don't know	3%
Other	4%

Figure 6.5 Uses for forums

Ideation Platforms

These unique solutions give employees a simple way to share and recognize the ideas and contributions of their colleagues in the enterprise. Ideas are typically voted up and down by employees, and popular ideas or suggestions are implemented by the organization. Vendors include Spigit and Intuit's Bright Idea.

Ideation platforms are used by 22 percent of organizations.

What Are Ideation Platforms Being Used For?

Figure 6.6 shows that the top five reasons for using ideation platforms are idea generation and innovation, shifting toward a more open corporate culture, improved productivity, employee collaboration, and to ask and answer questions and get internal peer support.

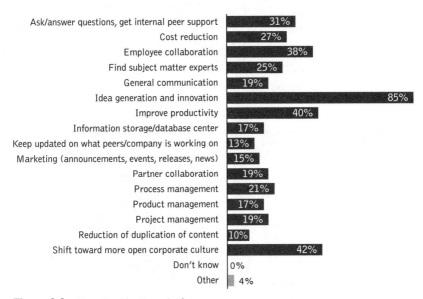

Ask/answer questions, get internal peer support	31%
Cost reduction	27%
Employee collaboration	38%
Find subject matter experts	25%
General communication	19%
Idea generation and innovation	85%
Improve productivity	40%
Information storage/database center	17%
Keep updated on what peers/company is working on	13%
Marketing (announcements, events, releases, news)	15%
Partner collaboration	19%
Process management	21%
Product management	17%
Project management	19%
Reduction of duplication of content	10%
Shift toward more open corporate culture	42%
Don't know	0%
Other	4%

Figure 6.6   Uses for ideation platforms

RSS Feeds

RSS is an acronym for Really Simple Syndication and allows users to receive the latest updates on various forms of content, such as blogs and news sources. These updates are delivered directly to the user automatically via a "reader." An example of a vendor is Attensa.

RSS feeds are being used by 34 percent of the organizations Chess surveyed.

What Are RSS Feeds Being Used For?

Figure 6.7 shows that the top five reasons employees use RSS feeds are to keep up to date on what peers and the company are working on, general communication, to ask and answer questions and get peer support, marketing, and improved productivity.

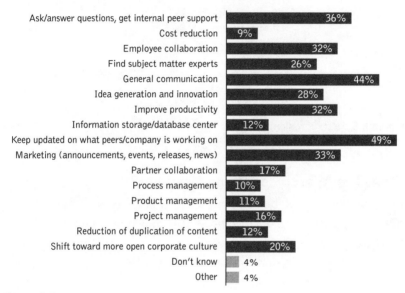

Ask/answer questions, get internal peer support	36%
Cost reduction	9%
Employee collaboration	32%
Find subject matter experts	26%
General communication	44%
Idea generation and innovation	28%
Improve productivity	32%
Information storage/database center	12%
Keep updated on what peers/company is working on	49%
Marketing (announcements, events, releases, news)	33%
Partner collaboration	17%
Process management	10%
Product management	11%
Project management	16%
Reduction of duplication of content	12%
Shift toward more open corporate culture	20%
Don't know	4%
Other	4%

Figure 6.7   Uses for RSS feeds

Microblogs

Microblogs allow employees to post short status updates or messages to their colleagues and peers. These messages can be restricted so that only a select group of people can see them. Many full-scale emergent collaboration platforms now have this functionality built into their offerings. A very simple and basic way to understand microblogs is to view them as Twitter for the enterprise. Current microblogging solutions for the enterprise also offer far more robust capabilities than just the ability to post status updates. Examples of these vendors include Salesforce's Chatter and Yammer.

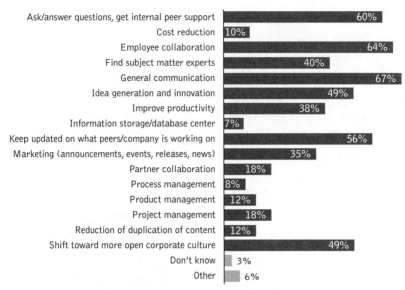

Figure 6.8 Uses for microblogs

What Are Microblogs Being Used For?

Fifty-eight percent of the companies Chess surveyed said they are using microblogs within the organization. As is shown in Figure 6.8, the top five uses are general communication, employee collaboration, to ask and answer questions and get internal peer support, to keep up to date on what peers and the company are working on, and a shift toward a more open corporate culture.

Social E-mail

The concept of social e-mail is built around using e-mail as a collaboration tool or platform to allow employees to get a holistic and contextual view of people and information that will enable social interactions. This is quite different from just seeing an e-mail message, which may or may not contain attachments. Social e-mail provides a contextual activity stream filled with updates, connections, profiles, mobile updates, and documents from multiple social platforms. An example of a social e-mail vendor is Harmon.ie. This was not a category that the Chess survey covered, but it exists, and I thank Mark Fidelman for making sure I gave it attention.

Collaborative File Sharing

These niche solutions focus specifically on making file sharing and transfer simple and effective. Often these solutions are integrated into existing emergent collaboration solutions. Many full-scale emergent collaboration solutions offer collaborative file sharing as a feature, but some companies prefer to go with niche vendors that specialize in content and file sharing and management. Examples of this include Box and Dropbox.

Video

Using video has become quite popular and useful in many organizations. The concept is the same as it is with customer-grade video applications and sites (such as YouTube), but it is used within organizations only for a business purpose.

Fifty-three percent of those surveyed stated that they use video in their organizations.

What Are Videos Being Used For?

As is shown in Figure 6.9, the top five reasons organizations use video are general communication, marketing, employee collaboration, keeping up to date on what peers and the company are working on, and idea generation and innovation.

The best way to decide what your organization should be using is to start with a solid set of use cases as described in the solution mapping process. You can see the breakdown of how various organizations are using tools behind their firewalls, but keep in mind that these uses don't necessarily apply to what your company is looking to do.

For organizations that are looking to implement emergent collaboration solutions and strategies there are a couple of key considerations that need to be made in evaluating vendors, especially for

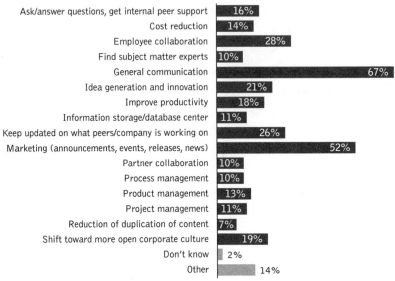

Figure 6.9 Uses for video

full-scale collaboration platforms. It's important to understand the areas on which vendors compete. If you have already begun exploring the vendor landscape, you will notice that many of the enterprise collaboration vendors have a very similar look and feel; some of them may even look identical. Regardless of the category you are looking to explore, you will find that sometimes it is difficult to distinguish the vendors from one another.

Here are the factors on which virtually all vendors compete.

Price

The basis for understanding this is simple: How much do they charge for using their platform? You will find that the two most common ways vendors will charge you are per seat (per user) and per page view. Thus, it's important to understand how many users you are thinking about including. You want to look at this in a few different time frames. Understand what it will cost now, in six months, in one year, in two years, and beyond two years. This doesn't have to be an exact science, but it will help you think in terms of cost. Perhaps for the first year you want to try piloting this concept to a small team of 100 employees. After two years you may want to roll out the platform to thousands of employees, so this is something you need to consider. Another thing you want to consider when it comes to price is the ability to add additional users or remove users without incurring any penalties or altering the cost of each seat purchased (unless, of course, the cost is lowered and not increased).

Features

What is it exactly that this platform can do for you, and what makes it different from the others? As was previously mentioned, you will find that many vendors look alike and appear to have very similar feature sets. The best way to determine the proper features is by first developing a set of use cases (see Chapter 2). Some vendors offer collaboration solutions specifically for employees, and other vendors support developing external customer communities, which is why it's important to think of this from several different timing perspectives. You may start off working with a vendor that offers only employee collaboration features and then decide you want to collaborate with employees as well and be forced to work with an additional vendor. Furthermore, there are always additional costs when you are adding customer communities and want to connect the two together.

People

You want to make sure that you're working with a vendor that not only has a great product but has people who will treat you well. I have had several clients whom I tried to refer to vendors in the past only to find that those vendors were rude or promised things that they never delivered on; this is not the type of vendor my clients will be working with. Since the emergent collaboration space is always evolving, you are most likely going to be growing and learning along with whatever vendor you go with, so making sure you are on the same page is important. Ask for previous reference customers and talk to them so that you can find out what they found easy and frustrating about working together. If the vendor typically works with enterprise clients and you are a small or midsize business, you want to make sure you are treated with the same respect and care that the enterprise-size customers get treated with.

Technology and Security

Some organizations choose on-premise solutions, some choose cloud-based solutions, and others choose a hybrid of the two. Every organization has its own measures of what it considers secure and acceptable. Whatever your choice is, you want to make sure that security is taken care of (usually by your IT folks) and that your data are safe. On the technology side you want to make sure that the platform is flexible for your needs and future plans.

In looking at the technology and security of a platform, you will no doubt run into cloud versus on-premise discussions. A brief overview of these solutions is provided later, but it's crucial to engage IT for this so that you will understand if you should have a cloud-based solution or an on-premise solution.

Customization and Integration

Most organizations want the ability to integrate other systems and customize their platform in the way they see fit. Perhaps being able to pull in legacy system documents or information and being able to edit that information within the platform are crucial. Maybe integration with a single sign-on vendor is crucial. Some vendors are flexible and others are more rigid, and so you want to make sure you have a good idea of what you want to customize and integrate.

Ease of Use and Intuitiveness

You obviously want to make sure that anyone and everyone in your organization can use the platform you select. I have seen examples in which the platform was one of the key barriers to adoption because employees had no idea what to do or how to navigate the site. I once spoke with a client who said, "We want our 60-year-old secretary who still uses a typewriter to be able to figure this out." You can also test this among your employees and collect feedback. Many vendors today have built their interfaces to look like popular social networking sites such as Facebook and Twitter to bring that level of familiarity to the enterprise. The fact that a vendor has an amazing platform doesn't mean that it is the best choice for your company. If the platform isn't easy to use and intuitive, don't bother with it.

Support and Maintenance

You want to make sure that a vendor offers an adequate support package. You will find that support and maintenance fees range quite radically, with some vendors charging upward of 20 percent of the annual license while other vendors don't charge any additional fees. Understanding when new versions of the product are released is also important, as is where those new versions and upgrade ideas are coming from. Certain vendors pride themselves on integrating customer feedback in their product development cycle, whereas others stick strictly to their own internal roadmap. Other things to look out for when it comes to support and maintenance are dedicated support lines, support hours (some are 24/7, while others are not), a customer support community, any additional fees, and what exactly the support packages cover. Some vendors provide support up to a certain point of customization and if you "over-customize" the product, those vendors don't support your modifications for future changes and versions.

Vertical Expertise

Although many disagree about whether vertical expertise is relevant for a vendor, the fact is that many organizations consider this as a factor in evaluating potential technology solutions. Some vendors tend to have more clients in a certain vertical, such as pharmaceutical or government, whereas others may be more focused on higher education and technology. Some vendors are clearly specialized for certain industries, but many platforms can be used horizontally across several verticals. I have not found vertical expertise to be that crucial a factor in vendor selection unless you need something very specific to your company.

One of the other things to look for are thought leadership and resource materials. I didn't include this in the actual scoring because it's not realistically something you would judge a vendor on, but if you find that two vendors are almost equal, then this might be something you would want to take a look at. Regular releases of educational material such as webinars, whitepapers, and speaker series are a great way for the vendor to keep educating you and sharing new ideas and insights. In an industry that's regularly changing and evolving, I like to work with vendors that continuously provide insightful and valuable resources to their customers who help them on their collaborative journey.

Now that we have the variables defined and explained, let's break them down further. In Table 6.1 you will see the variables in a grid with points assigned to them. Go through each variable and decide what your situation is on the basis of the four choices in the table. If you fall into the first column for each variable, give yourself 3 points for each one; if you fall in the second column, give yourself 2 points for each one, and so on.

Next we will look at a simple way to evaluate and compare vendors on the basis of how they score on all these variables.

A basic formula can be used to weigh vendors against one another. Keep in mind that the values and the items in the table can and should be adjusted to meet the specific needs of your organization. On pages 121 and 122 is a realistic example, but it's doubtful that it is applicable to every organization.

In this example, you can see that the variables are ranked in order of priority, where ease of use and intuitiveness is the most important variable and thus is worth the most points.

Table 6.1 Emergent Collaboration Vendor Evaluation Framework

	3 Points	2 Points	1 Points	0 Points
Ease of use and intuitiveness	Employees will find this tool easy to use and intuitive.	For the most part employees will find this tool easy to use and intuitive, but it will require a bit more training and education.	Employees will not find this easy to use and intuitive, and we run the risk of impeding adoption. Strong training and education programs are necessary.	Employees will have a hard time using this, and the success of the initiative will be compromised. Extensive training and education are going to be required.
Price	Below budget	At budget	A little over budget	Very much above budget
Features	Has every feature we want and then some.	Has all the features we need but nothing extra.	Doesn't quite have all the features we need, but we will be fine without them at this point.	Doesn't have the core features we need.
Technology and security	Offers a lot of flexibility in terms of on-premise, cloud, or hybrid cloud-based solutions. Security is very strong and meets all our requirements.	Doesn't have a wide variety of deployment options but is still secure.	Deployment options are limited, and level of security is uncertain but not a detriment.	Does not meet our security requirements.

(continued on next page)

Table 6.1 Emergent Collaboration Vendor Evaluation Framework *(continued)*

	3 Points	2 Points	1 Points	0 Points
Customization and integration	Vendor allows us to integrate all our needed systems and allows for strong customization.	For the most part we can integrate all of our desired systems and customization requirements.	Vendor allows for some customization and integration but is missing several desired or required areas.	Vendor is missing our core requirements in terms of customization and integration with other systems.
People	We have a strong fit in terms of culture, ideas, and long-term vision for growth and working together.	We disagree on a few issues in terms of how we should be doing things and what the future looks like.	We don't see eye to eye on several key issues, and we sense some tension and apprehensiveness between our teams.	We are not aligned, and there isn't a good fit culturally and in personality between our organizations.
Support and maintenance	Integrates customer feedback into the product. Offers several support options that meet our needs from a technology and pricing standpoint. We are very comfortable with their support.	Takes customer feedback into consideration. Has some support options that we can use. Their technology support and pricing options are not ideal but we can be fine with what they offer.	They pay attention to customer feedback. The support options are somewhat limited and, as a result, we are not as comfortable working with them. Either their fees or their technology support do not work for us.	They focus on their own roadmap. Support is either very limited or nonexistent. We do not feel comfortable that this vendor can support our deployment.
Vertical expertise	The vendor has strong vertical expertise in our area.	The vendor has some vertical expertise in our area.	The vendor has minimal vertical expertise in our area.	The vendor has no vertical expertise in our area.

Ease of use and intuitiveness	8
Price	7
Features	6
Technology and security	5
Customization and integration	4
People	3
Support and maintenance	2
Vertical expertise	1

Let's walk through an example of two vendors and see how they stack up against each other (see Table 6.2).

The best possible score a vendor can get in this setup is 108 points. Thus, Vendor 1 meets almost 70 percent of the overall requirements and Vendor 2 meets almost 60 percent of the overall requirements.

On the basis of this weighted formula, Vendor 2 is a better fit for the organization. You can do this with multiple vendors, and I recommend that you adjust the priorities and perhaps even the point system (or even add a new variable) and the descriptions within each variable to make this process better tailored and more relevant to your organization. For example, perhaps price is the number one concern for your

Table 6.2 Sample Vendor Scoring

	Vendor 1	Vendor 2
Ease of use and intuitiveness	8 × 3 = 24	8 × 2 = 16
Price	7 × 2 = 14	7 × 3 = 21
Features	6 × 3 = 18	6 × 0 = 0
Technology and security	5 × 1 = 5	5 × 1 = 5
Customization and integration	4 × 1 = 4	4 × 2 = 8
People	3 × 2 = 6	3 × 3 = 9
Support and maintenance	2 × 2 = 4	2 × 1 = 2
Vertical expertise	1 × 0 = 0	1 × 2 = 2
Total	75	63

organization and you weigh vertical expertise and people the same; make those adjustments and calculate as needed. The point of all this is to be as *descriptive* (not prescriptive) as possible so that organizations of all shapes, sizes, and industries can use this as a baseline.

Vendor Traps

It's important to make sure that the right vendor is selected; not doing so can become a long-term costly mistake. One of my clients at Chess Media Group hired us for several months, and one of the core responsibilities we had was to make sure that the client didn't go with the wrong vendor, something we were later told saved them well into the hundreds of thousands of dollars. There are a few common traps that organizations fall into when selecting vendors. Here are some of the traps and ways to avoid them.

The Integration Trap

Once a platform is deployed, is integrated with other systems, gains traction among employees, and has a good amount of data shared, it becomes very hard to switch to another vendor (imagine the headache of switching CRM or ERP vendors). A large organization told me that it is in the process of switching vendors and that the process has taken around 16 months (and it is still not done). This shouldn't scare you; instead, it should motivate you and encourage you to do the due diligence before selecting a solution.

How to Avoid This

Before you start the heavy integration process, try using the platform to make sure it is the best fit for your organization. Develop an integration road map and leave the heavy stuff for farther down the road. Look at this like dating: You want to get to know the person (vendor) before you start sharing all your things.

It's Free, So Let's Try It

Several vendors offer a free version of the product to try out, and that is both a blessing and a curse. The benefit of trying something for free is obvious: You have no up-front technology costs to deal with and can play around with the platform before you commit to it. The trouble with trying out free things is that your employees will get used to a platform, and this will make change difficult; in fact, you will most likely lose a percentage of your employee base every time you switch platforms. If you try a vendor, get some employees engaged, and then switch vendors, it's going to do more harm than good. This is why even though the platform may be free, it's advisable to go down the due diligence route.

Treat free vendors the same way as you would treat paid vendors. Some vendors with freemium models are quite tricky in the way they market or get you to sign up for the full version of their products. Let's say you go with a free vendor and deploy the solution for 500 of your employees. One day you see an employee post a negative comment that you want to remove, but you can't because the limited version has limited administrative functionality. Some vendors will force you to purchase a license for all 500 of your employees just to moderate the comment. In this situation organizations are stuck. They can't ignore the comment because all the employees can see it, and so they are forced to go with the licenses and emergent collaboration problems are born. I've also seen vendors with freemium models harass and spam employees at organizations to get them to sign up.

How to Avoid This

If you want to see what's out there and play around with a few technology solutions, do it with a limited group whose goal is to test various platforms. Everyone needs to be aligned on the expectations and the purpose for doing this. Make sure that you understand everything you can and cannot control with the free version of the product and get details on the costs associated with activating administrative features.

The Relationship Trap

Many organizations have technology partners that offer discount products. Often organizations will go with a particular vendor because they already have a relationship with it. This is very tempting but should at all costs be avoided. Never deploy or work with an emergent collaboration vendor because you have a relationship with it or can get its products at a discount. Although some of the large vendors may offer great products, they may also require the support of a dedicated multiperson IT team to manage the platform. Not all organizations have the resources to allocate several full-time employees to do this, and then an apparently low-cost platform becomes a very costly platform. This isn't about being nice and making friends; it is about helping your business.

How to Avoid This

If you have a partner you are considering working with, make sure to subject it to the same criteria you would apply to any other vendor. If they meet your requirements and you can get a discount on the product, you've done very well. However, if the vendor doesn't meet your requirements but offers a heavy discount, politely walk away. You want to solve business problems, not create new ones for yourself and your organization.

All in all you want to make sure you do your homework here. Get the information you need to make the best possible decision for your business.

The Data Trap

Unlike other types of enterprise software, such as CRM and ERP, emergent collaboration doesn't have common standards. This means that if you input all your data into platform X, you can't just simply pull it out and add it into platform Y. Many collaboration vendors build their solutions by using their own methods and their own standards. There is nothing an organization can do to avoid this, but it is important to be cognizant of this fact. This is why it is crucial to make sure to pick the right vendor from the start. Of course, you can always ask vendors you are interested in working with how they take information from other platforms and add it into theirs. You may get some interesting responses. Some people have built third-party apps that can help with the conversion, and your organization may have to do the same thing. I hope you will never have to do this. You should realize that these standards don't yet exist and that if you go with a vendor and decide to change later, it's going to cost you.

Build or Buy?

Organizations seeking to go down the emergent collaboration path are inevitably faced with making this decision: Is it better to license an existing emergent collaboration platform or does it make more sense to build one's own? Obviously, I cannot make the decision for you, but I can shed some light on both scenarios.

Build

This is a daunting task for many organizations. You can imagine that it is not easy to build an emergent collaboration platform from the ground up. Costs are typically going to be quite high here as a team is going to be required not just to build but also to support the project before, during, and after launch. Let's also consider the time it takes to build something and roll it out. If your organization is extremely diligent and disciplined, you may be able to get something workable live in a few months, but realistically, you are looking at a much longer time frame. Then there are the internal politics that most organizations are plagued with, including senior leaders with different visions, features that can't be prioritized because of lack of agreement, turf wars over ownership, and all the other fun things that exist within a corporation. Of course, it is possible for an organization to leverage an open-source platform and then build on it, but in that case you are going to be dealing with maintenance and support costs. If you're going to hack something to bits, you might as well build from the ground up. Most companies do not build their platforms for precisely the reasons mentioned above. There needs to be a significant strategic advantage for the organization to build an emergent collaboration platform; otherwise, it doesn't make sense.

Buy

This is the route that more organizations take because many vendors are capable of meeting most if not all of an organization's requirements for an emergent collaboration platform. The advantages of licensing a platform are many. For starters, the platform is already in existence and can be rolled out almost immediately; also, upgrades, maintenance, and new features and capabilities are taken care of by the vendor, which typically means fewer headaches for the organization deploying the platform. The costs of licensing can also be brought down significantly since there are a wide variety of vendors from which an organization can choose. In most cases this is the best and most convenient option.

Summary and Action Items

Several technology solutions are available in the emergent collaboration space. Understand which types of tools are the most relevant for your organization and why. Every vendor competes on seven variables that are going to be prioritized differently at most organizations: ease of use and intuitiveness, price, features, technology and security, customization and integration, people, and vertical expertise. The sample vendor selection framework presented in this chapter should help you narrow down your vendor choices, and the discussion of the common vendor traps will help you make sure that your emergent collaboration journey starts off strong. Complete the following steps:

- Look at the various technology platforms and what they are typically used for. Which platforms and uses are most relevant to your organization?
- Prioritize the seven variables.
- Once you have selected a few vendors, walk through the vendor selection grid and score the vendors to select the best one. Remember to consider the cloud, on-premise, and hybrid-cloud options.
- Review the vendor traps and how to avoid them. Are there any other traps you have discovered? Make sure to make a note of them and avoid them.

- Discuss the pros and cons of building versus buying an emergent collaboration platform. Which option do you think makes the most sense for your organization and why?

To learn more about emergent collaboration technology selection, I asked Karthik Chakkarapani, the former IT director of technology solutions and operations at the American Hospital Association, to share his thoughts.

Evaluating, selecting, and implementing a social enterprise platform, either a SaaS [Software as a Service] model or an on-premise model, goes beyond just the software functionality. This is just 50 percent of the equation or value proposition. Looking into the other technology aspects of the SaaS vendor is equally important.

Organizations have a lot of urgency and temptation to select and implement a social enterprise platform. Choosing the right solution that meets both business and technology requirements is very critical to the success of the project in the short term and also in the long term.

We have selected and evaluated 12 SaaS applications, including two on-premise SaaS solutions (hybrid SaaS) across various business functions over the last four years. We created a standard framework for evaluating and selecting SaaS-based products. In fact, we now have a standard SaaS legal addendum that we give to the short-listed vendors at the start of the negotiation cycle. This saves us and the vendors a lot of time. This helps us clearly set our organization's terms and conditions that the vendors will have to comply with at a minimum. Vendors also appreciate this process as it helps them see if they can meet our terms and conditions. If not, they don't have to spend their valuable time with us for weeks or months and then find out later that they cannot meet our terms and conditions. This is a win-win solution for us and the vendors. This has also helped us focus more on the product functionality and complete the procurement cycle quickly.

There is a lot of buzz in the IT industry that businesses often bypass IT when they select a SaaS product. We have fixed this gap as well. We have teamed up with the legal team. As you may know already, all contracts have to go through legal for review and approval. We leveraged this opportunity to connect with the business. Whenever legal receives a SaaS contract from business for review, they now alert us. We then connect with the business and review the SaaS vendor as a team and look into other aspects, such as security, compliance, data, identity management, single sign-on, integration, architecture flexibility, standards, support, hosting facility, service-level agreements, and so on. Business teams are very appreciative of this and are often surprised at the breadth of items we evaluate. This has resulted in great success for both IT and business by having the right SaaS solution that meets our current and future needs.

When it comes to selecting a social enterprise software product, you will need to look into additional criteria and do more due diligence because you will need to select a product you will use for a long time. This is not an e-mail, CRM, or an ERP SaaS solution, where you can easily convert and migrate all data and functionality to a new solution. The underlying data structure and standards in the CRM or ERP products are the same, and this makes conversion and migration easier. In the case of social enterprise software, there are no such standards that exist today, and I am not aware of any successful migrations either. You need to select the right product that will meet your current and future collaboration needs.

Following are the top items you will need to review and evaluate in detail to select your social enterprise software product:

1. Vendor management, product road map, and viability
2. Hosting provider and data location

3. Data access, security, segregation, and encryption
4. Regulatory compliance
5. Hosting facility security and compliance
6. Business continuity and disaster recovery
7. Identity management, security, and single sign-on
8. Standards, policies, procedures, and frameworks
9. Support and maintenance
10. Service-level agreements
11. Pricing and contract
12. Product features: people
13. Product features: process, integration, and architecture
14. Product features: infrastructure and security

The greatest lessons for us while going down this journey were the following:

1. Select the right vendor and product to meet your current and future collaboration needs. The success of enterprise collaboration at your organization is dependent on selecting the right product.
2. Do a proof of concept before signing on with the vendor and evaluate its professional services and support structure during this process.
3. Provide the legal contract terms and conditions to the vendor as early as possible.
4. Do due diligence on the vendor's integration and extension capabilities.
5. Review in detail how the vendor manages its product road map and prioritizes the features: market trends, competition, and customer input.

seven

The Adaptive Emergent Collaboration Framework

The goal of this chapter is to provide an emergent collaboration framework that organizations can use and adapt to meet their needs. This framework not only addresses collaboration within the enterprise but also includes collaboration with customers. I have found that the difference between developing a specific employee framework and developing a specific customer framework is small. Thus, although this book and this framework are meant to be used as a model for enterprise collaboration, they can also be used as a way to devise a customer collaboration strategy.

This is not the first framework that has been created; several other models and frameworks have been developed around emergent collaboration. The big problem with previous models is that they are very linear. They attempt to force organizations down a stepwise process. In my opinion, unless you are putting together IKEA furniture or baking a cake, a linear model won't do you much good. Furthermore, many of the models I have seen are quite basic and high-level and don't provide enough meat for organizations to make informed business decisions.

Every organization has a different approach to enterprise collaboration. Some organizations see these initiatives come from HR departments, and others see it come from product development or perhaps marketing. Some organizations see enterprise collaboration come from the top down, whereas others see it come from the bottom up. There are far too many variables for all organizations to go down the same path. That is why this adaptive framework was developed.

In the organizations I have interviewed, researched, and worked with, there is a common set of areas that organizations typically consider. Not all five areas may be relevant to you and your organization, but that's the beauty of an adaptive framework: It doesn't force you down a path. Furthermore, this adaptive framework shows that there is a relationship between the various elements, meaning that the way you change one may affect the others. Nothing exists in isolation.

Figure 7.1 Adoptive emergent collaboration framework
© 2011 Chess Media Group

Your organization may be great at one of the five areas, whereas another organization may be solid at three of the five. Organizations can maneuver through this framework to improve on areas where they are weak or are not as strong as they would like to be. It's adaptive because it doesn't force organizations down a single path, yet addresses the key areas for emergent collaboration. Every organization can decide which areas need to be worked on and which ones are strong.

The framework (see Figure 7.1) is designed in accordance with the business is business mindset, meaning that enterprise collaboration (or social business if you prefer to call it that) is still business. Processes, change management, leadership, and other items that are found in traditional business requirements are also found here. Let's take a look at what each of these elements means and what is contained in each one.

Goals and Objectives

Although this should be commonplace among organizations, the reality is it is often overlooked and ends up causing problems down the road, when organizations realize that they are far down a path without realizing why they are there or how they got there. Goals and objectives are typically but not always the starting point from which organizations build. Goals and objectives are broken down into a few areas.

Company

In an organization there have to be certain goals and/or objectives that executives are hoping to achieve, such as being able to communicate more effectively and collaborate across departments, across geographies, and across any other boundaries. These elements can also be phrased as business problems or opportunities the organization is looking to solve or uncover.

Department

Departmental objectives can overlap or be a subset of the company objectives. For example, perhaps the department wants to be able to communicate and collaborate more effectively within itself. Or perhaps the department wishes to improve its rate of innovation.

Employees

This one is often overlooked. It's absolutely crucial to understand the goals and objectives from an employee standpoint since employees are the ones who are going to be using the tools and deploying the strategies. It's important to convey the value to the employees and understand what the value is to begin with.

Customers

This is more relevant for customer-facing initiatives. If you are looking to engage with and collaborate with customers, it's important to define and understand why your customers should care about engaging and collaborating with you. What are their goals and objectives? What do they get out of the relationship?

Metrics

We will cover this in more detail in Chapter 12. Understanding how you want to measure success is always crucial; otherwise you have no idea what you are working toward and have no gauge for what failure or success looks like.

Organizational Culture

The culture at your company has to mesh with the strategic direction you are looking to take with enterprise collaboration. For example, if your organization is competitive and employees are incentivized to outperform one another, it's highly unlikely that deploying a collaboration platform will do much good since a culture of collaboration does not exist. One of the most important factors cited among organizations as a challenge to collaboration is culture.

Leadership

These initiatives need support from the top, and so it's important that an executive sponsor help drive this forward. Leaders at organizations need to be engaging with the rest of the employees across these platforms.

Change Management

Often, deploying a collaboration platform requires a shift in thinking in several areas, such as how employees are evaluated, how information is shared, and how people work. The entire process of shifting the organization from how it does things currently to how you want them to be done falls under change management.

Evangelists

Every organization I have interviewed and worked with has had evangelists to help propel these initiatives. Evangelists are the go-to resource for employees who want help, training, guidance, and assistance with collaborative tools and strategies. Evangelists are passionate employees who want to help others.

Openness

This is characterized by how receptive an organization is to the changes in culture and technology discussed above. Open organizations are more likely to allow collaboration and sharing of information among employees or between employees and customers in a social way. Zappos is a good example of an open company in which all employees have access to things such as sales numbers and other information usually reserved just for executives. Employees are also empowered to reach out to customers and to one another via social channels.

Mutually Beneficial Value

For this to be a win-win, there needs to be value for everyone involved. This is about understanding the value not only for the organization or the department but for the employees on an individual level.

Process

Deploying social and collaborative tools and technologies almost always means that the organization is going to have to change the way it does certain things. For example, all meeting minutes may have to be posted to a certain collaborative workplace for all the relevant employees to see. Maybe all new ideas generated by employees will have to be reviewed by someone who can evaluate their feasibility. Rest assured that processes in your organization will change.

Escalation

If an employee says something inappropriate in a company workspace, how is it going to be dealt with? What if someone inadvertently or purposely leaks confidential information? Escalation deals with how certain situations are handled and who handles them.

Automation

This is typically seen on the customer side of collaboration but is becoming more integral inside organizations. For example, if a user tweets a company to ask for the location of a store, a reply can be sent back automatically provided that the query is recognized, letting the user know of the closest store. This is done automatically, allowing these types of responses to scale. Within organizations this is typically seen around "following" and "retrieving" information, for example, subscribing to a feed that lets you know what stage of development an internal project is in or where your billing or invoicing is in the process of getting completed. Being able to control what information you see, how you see it, and when you see it is part of the automation process that some vendors are starting to incorporate into their platforms.

Information Management

With collaboration comes a lot of information. This information needs to be managed in an effective way so that employees do not get overwhelmed. Information management includes documents, conversations, reports, presentations, and anything else that can and will be shared in the organization via social and collaborative tools.

Technology

Selecting the proper technology solutions is important, and this book has discussed how to map business objectives to desired results for vendor selection. It also has explored the key variables on which vendors compete.

Tool Selection

There are a lot of new and interesting social and collaborative technologies. The challenge for organizations is to understand which ones to select to match their needs.

Integration

Tools and platforms need to communicate with one another. Simply deploying tools that sit in isolation from other systems and tools creates additional silos within organizations. It's important to make sure that various technology systems and platforms can work together or at least communicate with one another.

Training

Training and education has been instrumental for many organizations going down the enterprise collaboration road. Being able to provide resources and materials for employees is essential in ensuring success.

Adoption

This goes hand in hand with training. There is no such thing as a "build it and they will come" approach here. Adoption strategies must be considered for how organizations can get employees to use emergent collaboration solutions. I am often amazed when I hear company executives tell stories of failed deployments and wasted "efforts" when the reality is that nothing was done beyond announcing a new tool to the company.

Maintenance and Upgrades

New versions of tools and platforms are created regularly. Once you deploy a tool, how do you stay up to date with the most relevant versions? On the maintenance side, what specifically is going to be required from your team?

Governance

Governance exists to make sure that employees are all on the same page in terms of rules, policies, regulations, and the way various tools and platforms should be used.

Best Practices

This involves a recommended way of doing something to achieve the most desired result.

Guidelines

Guidelines are recommendations for the type of content that can and should be shared, how the platform should be used to gain the maximum benefit. It is important to identify things to avoid and things to be encouraged.

Policies

These are specific rules that employees must follow and addresses things such as what type of information should not be shared under any circumstances, referencing products or brands internally, proper etiquette when communicating with other employees, and so on.

Oversight Team

As was mentioned previously, this team helps drive and propel the collaboration initiative forward within an organization.

Social Service Level Agreements

Social service level agreements are clearly posted expectations for how an organization and employees and/or customers can interact with one another. This is typically seen in and more applicable to customer-facing initiatives. An example is a corporate twitter page that clearly states what types of messages are responded to or ignored, when responses will be issued, how long it takes the organization to respond, and who is managing the account.

These are the key elements that organizations need to consider. Now let's take a look at a maturity model that will help organizations evaluate where they are in these areas. The maturity model doesn't have to be followed exactly but should be used as a reference for where organizations see themselves and where they can move toward. Keep in mind that this maturity model follows the adaptive emergent collaboration framework. Therefore, in the first column of Table 7.1 we have the corresponding sphere, followed by the elements included in each sphere in the second column. The following columns show a progression from where a company gets started in that particular element to what it should progress toward. The shaded areas are more relevant for customer-facing initiatives but can be used internally as well.

On Budgets

You will also notice that "budget" is left out of this grid not because it is not important but because I wanted to focus on the strategic aspects of emergent collaboration. Budgets for these initiatives vary quite dramatically, but as I mentioned before, I strongly believe that if a company wants to make this happen, it will. This isn't to make light of budgets, because they are absolutely crucial. In looking at budgets, it's important to plan for a few things, including technology, marketing and promotion, training and education, custom integrations, and staff costs.

On this grid, I have found that organizations typically fall into one of five types of categories on emergent collaboration:

- The unaware organization
- The exploratory organization
- The defined organization
- The adoptive organization
- The adaptive organization

Why should organizations care about progressing or going down this road? As we will now discuss, when the collaborative capabilities of an organization increase, so does the business value that the organization will realize.

Table 7.1 The Maturity Model

Sphere	Elements	Stage 1	Stage 2	Stage 3	Stage 4	Stage 5	Stage 6	Stage 7
Goals and objectives	Company	Haven't started defining them	Explored	Defined	Communicated (with the rest of the company or relevant stakeholders)	Adapted		
	Department	Haven't started	Explored	Defined	Communicated	Adapted		
	Employees	Haven't started	Explored	Defined	Communicated	Adapted		
	Customers	Haven't started	Explored	Defined	Communicated	Adapted		
	Metrics	Haven't started	Explored	Defined (and benchmarked, if possible)	Communicated	Adapted		
Organizational culture	Leadership	No executive sponsorship	Potentials identified	Approached and secured	Role and involvement defined	Communicated	Adapted	
	Change management	Not addressed	In the process of developing a strategy	Strategy developed	Executed or in process of being executed	Adapted		
	Evangelists	Not identified or don't exist	Identified	Secured	Communicated	Taking action	Adapted	
	Openness (how transparent or open a company chooses to be)	Not addressed	Discussions taking place	Current and desired position identified	Plan developed	Communicated	Adapted	

		Hasn't been established	Being addressed	Defined	Communicated	Adapted	
Process	Mutually beneficial value (employees/customers/partners or other stakeholders)					Adapted	
	Escalation	No process in place	Issues and employees identified	Process developed	Implemented	Adapted	
	Automation	No automation	Processes and actions identified	Communicated	Implemented	Adapted	
	Information management	Not considered	Plan developed or in process	Communicated	Acted	Adapted	
Technology	Tool selection	Tools not selected	Potentials identified	Tool selected	Tool deployed		
	Integration	Not considered	Integration points identified	Road map developed	Communicated to vendor and team	Integration in process or completed	Adapted
	Training	None	In process of being developed	Developed	Communicated	Training started or completed	Adapted
	Adoption	Not addressed	Problems and opportunities identified	Strategy developed	Strategy in process of being implemented	Adapted	
	Maintenance and upgrades	Not addressed	Considered	Road map developed	Communicated with team and vendor	Acted on	Adapted

(continued on next page)

Table 7.1 The Maturity Model (*continued*)

Sphere	Elements	Stage 1	Stage 2	Stage 3	Stage 4	Stage 5	Stage 6	Stage 7
Governance	Best practices	Don't have any	Recognized that they need to be created	Identified who will create them	Created	Communicated	Used	Adapted/new ones developed
	Guidelines	Don't have any	Recognized that they need to be created	Identified who will create them	Created	Communicated	Used	Adapted/new ones developed
	Policies	Don't have any	Recognized that they need to be created	Identified who will create them	Created	Communicated	Used	Adapted/new ones developed
	Oversight team	Not created	Recognized that it needs to be created	Preliminary team selected	Team finalized	Meets together to implement and/or review	Adapted as organization progresses	
	Social service level agreements	Not developed	Recognized that they need to be created	Identified who will create them	Developed	Communicated	Used	Adapted/new ones developed

The Unaware Organization

Not surprisingly, unaware organizations find that they are in the stage 1 column for most of the elements but may be in stage 2 for a few. Manager resistance is going to be strongest at this stage as value and business cases have not yet been established. There is also a high degree of uncertainty and fear as the organization tries to understand how emergent collaboration applies to the way it works. Keep in mind that being unaware doesn't mean being ignorant or stupid. At some point all organizations are unaware of emergent collaboration and how it can benefit their employees and the organization as a whole. The fact that you are reading this book is a good starting point. At this stage organizations don't know what they don't know, which means the opportunity and the upside for emergent collaboration here are great. To move to the next stage, the organization should start thinking about all or most of the elements in the grid. Open discussions, education, and more in-depth research are critical for making this happen.

The Value

The value here is quite low, but the potential is the greatest.

The Exploratory Organization

At this stage organizations are spending more time researching and understanding what emergent collaboration is and how it can affect the business. In fact, organizations here may start defining what this means and what it can look like. Most of the elements here are found in the stage 2 column. Typically, organizations here start to see the possibilities of what can be done and begin to understand how emergent collaboration can solve business problems. We also start to see the formations of teams that are going to help drive this initiative within the organization. This is also where organizations will see most of their IT (and some manager) resistance. To move to the defined stage, there needs to be a very solid understanding of what emergent collaboration means to the organization and a strategic direction and vision has to start forming. Depending on the size of the organization, it can remain in this stage from one month to over three months. I've heard of some companies that have been stuck in this stage for close to a year, but that is not typical.

The Value

The organization clearly sees where collaboration can benefit the enterprise. The strategic value gap begins closing as the capabilities for emergent collaboration start to increase. Teams begin forming that will be tackling this evolution of the organization. The key value here lies in knowing that things can be improved. The organization starts to get excited, and innovative ideas for collaboration begin flowing. The organization is now educated on emergent collaboration.

The Defined Organization

Here the organization needs to have a clearly defined strategy and direction for the emergent collaboration efforts. Most of the elements here reside in the stage 3 column, and some are in the stage 4 column. At this stage, the organization is getting ready to communicate and share the direction and vision and teams and roles are clearly defined. We also see use cases developed, measures of success defined, and potential technology solutions selected. To progress to the adoptive stage, organizations have to communicate their vision and direction for emergent collaboration and start implementing everything that was outlined and put together in the defined stage. The process of defining emergent collaboration for the organization can usually be completed in one to three months.

The Value

The organization is one step closer to realizing the business value of emergent collaboration. The strategic framework to make this happen is complete, and the organization is ready to begin implementing.

The Adoptive Organization

At this stage the organization is in the process of full implementation. Everything has been explored, teams have been established, the vision has been communicated, measures of success have been established, risks have been evaluated, and the road map and strategy have been developed. Organizations here can typically implement in several of the ways that are discussed just after this section, but basically the choice is between a pilot and a full implementation. This is the stage of greatest learning for the organization as progress is evaluated and benchmarked and feedback is continuously collected. This stage can last from one to three years, depending on the size of the organization and how quickly things can get done. This is the stage at which user resistance is greatest as employees try to embrace new strategies and technologies at work. The remainder of the emergent collaboration life cycle is spent in the adaptive stage. Typically, organizations become adaptive once they have reached a steady rate of adoption and see that their emergent collaboration efforts are on solid ground. Once this happens, the organization can start to look at how to evolve and adapt.

The Value
Employees share anecdotal and data-driven information about the benefits of emergent collaboration. Information starts to be easier to find and share. Teams are more easily formed, and employees start to open up and trust one another. Company morale begins to improve as employees begin to understand their roles and the roles of their colleagues better. Senior-level leaders gain much greater insight into the way the organization operates. The organization now sees opportunities to engage and inspire employees and to retain and attract new talent by being perceived as innovative and cutting edge.

The Adaptive Organization
This adaptive stage isn't an end state; it's a continuous cycle of improvement and evolution. The adaptive organization has a very solid understanding of what works and what doesn't and is capable of making the right decisions. Organizations can easily regress into previous stages if, for example, they stop listening to and incorporating employee feedback into their efforts, which in turn can cause

employees to abandon platforms. This happened with a large and prominent management consulting firm that reached high levels of employee adoption and engagement only to see them plummet after employee feedback was no longer being integrated in the product and strategies. If employees don't feel supported and listened to, then chances are that adoption rates will never rise. The important thing here is that there are always going to be improvements, updates, changes to technologies, new best practices, new team members, new leaders, and evolved strategies. An adaptive organization is one that learns what works and what doesn't and is able to improve.

The Value

This is where the organization sees the greatest business value from emergent collaboration as problems are solved and successes are repeated. Inefficiencies begin to be eliminated. The organization is now able to adapt to new changes, behaviors, or feedback from employees. Company morale increases as employees see that they have a voice and their feedback is being implemented. All necessary components for emergent collaboration are integrated, and sharing, finding, and collaborating on information are at their peak. As new use cases emerge, the organization is quickly able to create solutions. Productivity increases, and opportunities are identified and implemented regularly and efficiently that result in cost-saving or revenue-generating opportunities.

Figure 7.2 shows the five stages of the emergent collaborative organization in the context of capabilities and business value. As the capabilities of the organization increase, so does the value of emergent collaboration. When we refer to capabilities, we're not simply referring to how advanced the technology is. Capabilities can be on the technology side or the business side. On the technology side, the organization obviously wants to make sure that the tools and platforms enable employees to do things in their flow of work; their lives should become easier as a result of these tools, not harder. On the business side, capabilities are things such as training and fostering a culture of openness and collaboration. Each stage in the maturity

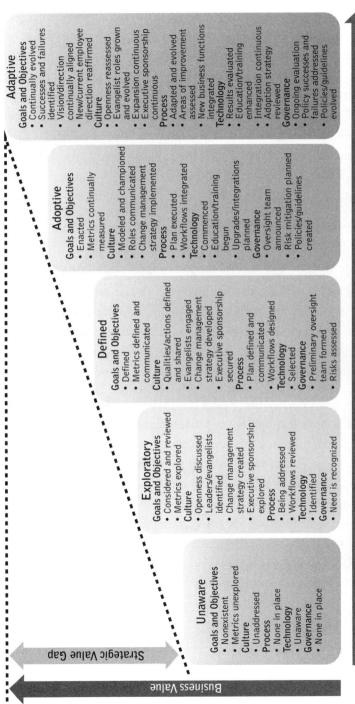

Figure 7.2 Emergent collaboration maturity model

© 2012 Chess Media Group

model shows the key differentiating factors from the adaptive emergent collaboration framework.

In developing a strategy, one of the common questions organizations are faced with is, Do we want to start off with a pilot project or should we go all-in from the beginning? Andrew McAfee dealt with this in a blog post he wrote in 2011 called "Drop the Pilot," in which he states that he believes strongly in an all-in approach. Many companies have started off with some form of pilot project: Vistaprint and CSC are two popular ones. There are a few reasons why organizations typically consider going with pilots instead of all-in deployments:

1. **Minimization of risk.** If an organization starts small and fails, the risk is minimal, as is the cost. The organization simply acknowledges that this isn't a good approach and moves on.

2. **Applied learnings.** In this situation an organization simply wants to see what happens in a small group. It's almost like a lab experiment so that the organization can learn and apply those learnings to a broader launch. The learnings can be cultural, technological, financial, process-related, or other.

Before you decide whether a pilot is something you want to consider, let's consider the various types of pilots. Pilots are typically limited in two ways: the duration of the deployment (how long will it last?) and the scope of the deployment (how broad is the deployment: across a department or across the whole company?).

Some organizations may choose to impose limits such as meeting key performance indicators in order to continue, but I have not typically seen this type of limitation on a deployment.

These four types of deployments are shown graphically in Figure 7.3 in the form of deployment quadrants.

As you can see in the figure, the type of deployment corresponds to a type of company characteristic. On the x axis we see "scope," and on the y axis we see "duration." Based on the way in which these two variables are changed, the characterization of the company changes. There are four characteristics:

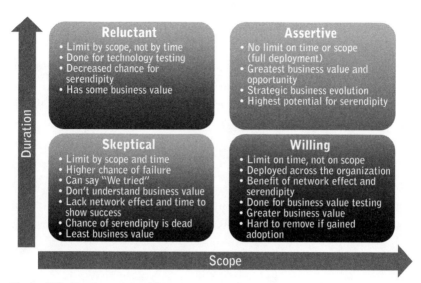

Figure 7.3 Deployment quadrants
© 2012 Chess Media Group

1. **Skeptical:** limited by duration and scope
2. **Reluctant:** limited by scope, not by duration
3. **Willing:** limited by duration, not by scope
4. **Assertive:** not limited by scope or duration

Let's take a look at each type of pilot.

Skeptical: Limited by Duration and Scope

This type of pilot is usually employed by organizations that are not entirely convinced of the value emergent collaboration can provide; in other words, they are skeptical. Sometimes these types of deployments are used so that those responsible for collaboration can say they tried to do it. For example, you might see the product development or engineering department deploy a wiki for a period of three to six months. The challenge here is that you don't have the scale that is often required for emergent collaboration to succeed; there are not enough people involved. With only a few employees using something, you are drastically decreasing the potential value that can be achieved, and the activity or use may be a bit underwhelming. Chances are that the employees in the department deploying a pilot project have already worked together or know one another.

Without having that network effect in your organization, collaboration is not as effective. Furthermore, many of the benefits that were outlined in Chapter 1 are drastically hindered, if not eliminated, for example, cross-department communication or being able to find subject matter experts.

Finally, putting a time limit on emergent collaboration is not the best approach, as collaboration is not bound by time. Collaboration does not have a shelf life.

Reluctant: Limited by Scope, Not by Duration

The challenge in this scenario, as was mentioned above, is that you are limiting the potential value of deploying an emergent collaboration tool because you lose the network and the serendipity effect. You have eliminated time as a barrier, but the scope is still a barrier. This type of scenario is typically seen among companies that are looking to test various technology solutions in a controlled environment, limiting the amount of people involved. Because the scope of this type of deployment is limited, a considerable amount of business value is lost and many of the benefits addressed in Chapter 1 will not be realized.

Willing: Limited by Time, Not by Scope

The challenge with this type of pilot is gaining adoption for a particular tool and then removing that tool after a certain period. If the organization deploys a tool only to find that nobody is using it well, adoption is the problem that needs to be addressed, and that can't happen if the entire effort is completely abandoned. Organizations need to focus on identifying and fixing the problems, not on scrapping entire emergent collaboration projects; that does nothing.

With this type of pilot, I mostly have seen organizations that focus on business value testing and use case development as opposed to the technology testing done by reluctant organizations. In this scenario many of the benefits addressed in Chapter 1 can be realized as the entire organization is exposed to emergent collaboration.

Assertive: Unlimited Amount of Time Deployed Across the Enterprise

In my opinion, this scenario really isn't considered a pilot. If something is deployed without restrictions, it's most likely not being tested; it's being deployed. Some organizations will deploy something, pay for it, and hope it works out eventually (and will keep paying for it because they have the money to do so). Other organizations make the decision that "this is how we are going to work from now on" and provide the necessary support to help ensure success. Assertive organizations see the greatest value from their collaborative efforts and a maximum serendipity effect.

Ultimately, the decision for going with a pilot or with an all-in approach is yours. I have seen successes with various approaches. However, if you are in the early stages and are trying to prove a business case, gathering enterprisewide support is clearly not going to be possible (unless this initiative is coming directly from the executive team). In these situations the pilot is the best approach, and I advocate being a "willing" organization when possible. Some organizations believe that emergent collaboration is not a trial-and-error project but is simply the direction in which they need to head. These organizations typically have fewer budgetary constraints and greater support from the leadership, which means that an enterprisewide approach is suitable.

Keep in mind that just because you start off with a pilot, that doesn't mean you are committed; you can just as easily switch approaches as you can evolve into a full deployment. These are just starting points.

That Special Something

Have you ever walked into a store or a company office and gotten a particular vibe or feeling? How about from a person, perhaps a first date or a new acquaintance? This is something I never hear anyone talk about, yet it is present in every company today. Regardless of how meticulous or granular I can be in terms of providing an emergent collaboration strategy blueprint, one thing I will never be able to capture in this book is that special something that makes companies unique. It's analogous to giving two people the exact same recipe to make something and finding that one of the dishes tastes better. Sometimes we joke around and say, "It tastes better because it was made with love," but it's this unique something that makes one dish taste better than another that can be found in organizations. You can't quite put your finger on it and it's not tangible, but it's there.

You can call this whatever you want, but what I'm referring to is the chemistry or the vibe of the organization. This is something that no strategy can account for; instead, what I can do is help make you aware of this and point out the fact that it exists. In considering all the elements in this book, try to remember that this special something does exist and acknowledge it. The fact that I write something here doesn't mean you should do it or follow a particular framework exactly. This needs to fit with the vibe of your company, which is why I want to be as descriptive as possible (and less prescriptive).

Summary and Action Items

A common set of areas that need to be considered by organizations interested in investing in emergent collaboration exists in the form of the adaptive emergent collaboration framework. Evolving and moving through this framework presents us with five categories of organizations: unaware, exploratory, defined, adoptive, and adaptive. As organizations progress through these stages and evolve their capabilities, the strategic value gap diminishes. Deploying emergent collaboration within an organization can be done in one of four ways presented in terms of four company characteristics: skeptical, reluctant, willing, and assertive. Take the following steps:

- Review all the variables in the adaptive emergent collaboration framework so that you understand them.

- With your team, walk through the adaptive emergent collaboration framework grid to understand where you are in terms of maturity. What has been done and what hasn't?

- Look at the five categories of companies and be able to place your company in a category.

- With your team, review what your organization needs to do to evolve to the next category of organization; set some timelines and key actions around this.

- Determine the best type of approach for your deployment based on the variables of scope and duration. What characteristic best matches your company?

- Discuss what that special something means in your organization. What does it feel like?

Carl Frappaolo is one of the leading practitioners when it comes to emergent collaboration strategy. Carl was formerly a principal at Information Architected, a consulting company where he worked with companies such as Google, Baxter, GlaxoSmithKline, and Alcoa, among many others. Today Carl is working at FSG (social impact consultants), where he is the director of knowledge management. Since Carl has such a broad and in-depth experience in emergent collaboration, I asked him to share his experiences and insights with you.

One of the primary benefits of Enterprise 2.0 and social computing is the adaptive and organic nature of the software and thus the business models it can support. Although this can be extended to include grassroots organization approaches to system design and deployment, it is prudent and much more time-effective to establish a strategy for Enterprise 2.0 in the organization. (Indeed, even if you do not undertake an initial assessment, prudent management and maximum return on investment come from monitoring the system.) In each case what is monitored or should be appreciated is that the system must function holistically but is composed of people (i.e., organizational culture), process, strategy (which includes broad goals and objectives not just for E2.0 but for the organization), and technology.

Each is important, but what is most important is *alignment.* One should not get too far ahead of the other or it will cause frustration. Equally important, the most poorly defined and understood element will create the weakest link in your strategy. Social computing in the business setting is an entire ecosystem. The primary role of the manager of an E2.0 "solution" is to ensure that people predisposed to sharing and seeking know-how and input from others are supported by business processes that facilitate the capture and reuse of knowledge as a normal course of doing business in a way that moves business and personal goals forward while minimizing any risk to the organization (e.g., protects against accidental misappropriation of knowledge).

Although each component of this ecosystem is important, in my experience, culture is the single greatest potential asset or detriment. A culture conducive to collaboration will compensate to some degree for awkward processes and inadequate technology. In contrast, a culture not conducive to collaboration will ignore, or in the worst case sabotage, even the most sophisticated technology and process approaches to open transparent sharing.

For that same reason, the technology component is the least important. Typically, technology should be positioned as a catalyst that propels processes and user habits. It can certainly take a healthy culture and motivate it to new levels of sharing and can be used to alter processes to make them more adept at knowledge capture. But rarely will even the "best" technology deployments make up for or change culture and process. I once worked with a quasi-governmental agency in the Washington, D.C., area. They could not understand why their rather substantial investments in E2.0 technology had had no real impact. Senior management was vocal about its desire to become a more sharing organization and "put their money where their mouth was" by supporting the IT budget. But what I found when assessing the situation was that the underlying processes and culture were linear, siloed. The actions and habits of management (promoting individual knowledge, not team-based success, managing in well-defined and delineated departments that were encouraged to "protect" their know-how as this was related to departmental budgets) clouded the words and dollars of management. Similarly, several months ago I was called into a company in the Boston area that was impassioned by the market promises of social collaboration inside the firewall. Using a popular product, they had a collaborative online community up and running in 15 days. But that success quickly turned to failure when the user community abandoned it as quickly as they took it up. The site lacked a clear objective, had a poorly defined audience ("everyone"), and mostly consisted of random content. It was a technology success, but a business failure.

In contrast, in many other cases in which I orchestrated the strategy of organizations across verticals, including finance and healthcare, I have seen E2.0 environments flourishing despite any formidable presence of technology. The introduction of aligned technologies into these situations was readily accepted and greatly increased the rate and nature of collaboration.

Lastly, it is very important to recognize that although in some cases the Web 2.0 world has demonstrated viral adoptions, this is not necessarily the case inside the firewall. Why? In the case of E2.0, the community is confined (it is not the world at large but a community of coworkers who are not necessarily driven to collaboration for purely social reasons, as is the case with tools such as Facebook). This situation imposes a culture that includes motivation and goals not just for E2.0 itself but for what the community wants to achieve. The goal is probably not to see how many "friends" you can acquire or even to get involved in communities of interest per se. The goals are aligned to business objectives. In fact, the more you can demonstrate that, the easier it is to demonstrate the ROI. A well-orchestrated strategy will identify what the critical success factors (business goals and objectives) are and tie each action and outcome of the

E2.0 system to one or more of those critical success factors. I continue to be amazed at the number of Enterprise 2.0 initiatives I encounter that fail initially for this very reason. Indeed, my last client, a major financial institution in New York, had put in place an E2.0 team and program over a year ago. Despite the good intentions of business and technical staff, the program never came to fruition. It took me less than a day to realize the root of this failure. There was no consensus on what the purpose of the initiative was, the direction in which it would take them, its primary benefactors, and the goals it would achieve beyond "make us more collaborative, smarter, and more aware."

Thus, building a strategy that defines the specific components but, more important, the impact each component has on the others can be the single most important step to ensuring success with E2.0. This competency should be positioned as an integral part of the system, because the nature of an organization's profile as defined by "the model" probably will change. An ability to assess and react to it on a periodic basis ensures that the system remains current and relevant.

How often do you need to realign your strategy? It's hard to say, at least from a fixed timeline perspective. Keep an eye and ear focused on the components of the model and be sensitive to their level of change. Whenever you feel your community changes (significant new hires/acquisitions/turnover), your processes change (formal and informal), your governance changes, or your business goals and objectives change, these are serious red flags, indications to reassess your situation and realign your E2.0 strategy. This includes technology. The introduction of any technology, especially social technology, probably will exert change on an organization. Approaches to work (processes) may change given unprecedented ways to communicate and collaborate. Culture may change, one hopes for better, as the technology makes transparency and speed of sharing increase. Rules and processes related to governance may also have to be altered to adapt to new potential ways of sharing and collaborating.

Monitoring and executing via this model is an ongoing task and one that is not simple. You must remain vigilant and make the time and effort to assess each component. This requires ongoing collaboration with human resources, executive management, risk and compliance officers, and IT. Periodically you must perform exploration, including defining usage models to identify the needs of individual users.

Make no mistake about it; building such a strategy takes time and concerted effort, but without doing so, you seriously increase the chances that your deployment will miss the mark or grow stale and irrelevant.

The benefit of taking this approach to building an E2.0 strategy for your organization is simple. It identifies the exact needs of the organization, the physical and cultural challenges/requirements of the organization, the value of collaboration and content sharing within the organization, the types and availability of knowledge throughout the organization, and the benefits associated with knowledge sharing within the organization. It provides a benchmark against which progress can be measured so that you are not building your solution in the dark. Finally, it provides the insight necessary to approach development effectively and in a timely manner.

---

eight

Resistance
Is Futile

Y ou remember the Borg, those creepy characters from the *Star
Trek* series, right? They had a saying: "Resistance is futile." I hope
they don't mind that I borrowed their catchphrase for the title of this
chapter.

Resistance can come in all shapes and sizes, from someone refusing to
fund a project, to an employee not wanting to use a tool, to someone in
IT not being willing to implement a solution. The important thing here
to realize is that resistance does exist but there are ways to overcome it.

When organizations see resistance to enterprise collaboration initiatives, it usually manifests itself in one of three ways: manager resistance,
IT resistance, and/or user resistance (see Figure 8.1). Based on the
Chess Media Group research, we found that 30 percent of organizations
report not having resistance, whereas 21 percent see manager resistance,
20 percent see user resistance, and 17 percent see IT resistance (the
remaining responses were classified under "I don't know"). When 30
percent of organizations claim that they are not having any resistance, I
find this number to be quite high, especially since all the organizations
I have spoken with have told me that they have faced resistance of some
sort. Resistance should be expected, and there is nothing wrong with
that; resistance always happens when change is present.

Let's take a look at each type of resistance.

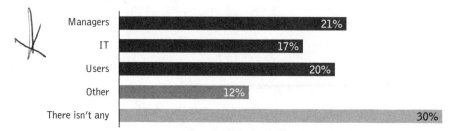

Figure 8.1 Types of resistance to enterprise collaboration

Manager Resistance

The top four reasons organizations experience manager resistance are as follows:

- It's not a priority (32 percent).
- There is uncertainty about tangible ROI (26 percent).
- There is uncertainty about the overall value and how it will meet business objectives (26 percent).
- The company culture is not supportive (22 percent).

User Resistance

The top three reasons organizations experience user resistance are as follows:

- Users don't want to learn a new technology (33 percent).
- Users say they don't have time (32 percent).
- Users are already overwhelmed by existing technology platforms (24 percent).

IT Resistance

The top four reasons organizations experience resistance from IT are as follows:

- It's not a priority (24 percent).

- There are security issues or threats (20 percent).
- There is no manpower (18 percent).
- There is no budget (18 percent).

Now that we know what the most common types of resistance are from managers, employees, and IT professionals, what can executives and decision makers do to overcome resistance at their organizations? Let's take an in-depth look at each type of resistance and what can be done about it.

Manager Resistance

Not a Priority

I have found that often this response happens not because it's not a priority but because there is a lack of education about the benefits that can be achieved and because of a high degree of fear. In these situations a few things can be done. First, I recommend drumming up support from employees and colleagues throughout the organization. Surveys, focus groups, and one-on-one meetings with employees can be an effective way to show managers that this should be a priority. Second, sitting down and speaking with several managers one on one to understand their fears, concerns, and perceived benefits is also effective. Chess Media Group conducted several multiday interviews in which we sat down and spoke one on one with almost all the VPs and key stakeholders as well as several employees during a client project (often it's best if a third party does this because people are more comfortable sharing personal information when they know they won't be judged or reprimanded for it). Third, I recommend education and training on what exactly all this means to the organization. Several hours devoted to introducing the concept, what other organizations are doing, case studies, and potential benefits and risks and then brainstorming some potential next steps can be very effective. Simply approaching someone and saying, "We want to invest in emergent collaborative software" doesn't mean much to many people, and so "It's not a priority" is a very easy answer to give. But by focusing on solving very real and tangible existing problems with new tools and strategies, the chances of support are much greater. Showing practical use cases for collaboration is also effective. Focus on existing problems with the organization that can be solved with these new tools and strategies.

Uncertainty about Tangible ROI

This is a very common form of resistance, and it's quite understandable. Why would an executive want to invest in something without understanding the financial impact it will have on the organization? Then again, there are many investments organizations make without clearly understanding the financial return: Billboards, print ads, printers for the office, phone systems, and television commercials are all difficult to show a return on, but that shouldn't be an excuse. I'm not going to lie and say that I have an ROI formula or a simple way to calculate exactly what the ROI of collaboration is. In fact, there is only one formula for ROI, which is (gain from investment − cost of investment)/cost of investment. Instead, I can point to research conducted by McKinsey, which surveyed around 1,600 people. McKinsey found that 77 percent of respondents saw increasing speed of access to knowledge, 60 percent saw a reduction in communication costs, 52 percent saw increasing speed of access to internal experts, 44 percent saw a decrease in travel costs, 40 percent saw a reduction in operational costs, 29 percent saw a reduction in time to market for products and/or services, 28 percent saw an increasing number of successful innovations for new products and services, and 18 percent saw increasing revenue. There are several pieces of data on the web that all point to the business value of collaboration. Collaboration is part of the fuel that makes a company run. There is a very clear and real business value of enterprise collaboration that we explore in greater detail in Chapter 12.

Uncertainty About Overall Value and How It Will Meet Business Objectives

This type of response typically means that an organization is considering deploying a tool first and then will find a problem for the tool to solve.

I have found that when organizations use the approach of mapping a business problem to a desired result, it becomes quite clear what the overall value is and how it will meet business objectives. Always start with a business problem; don't worry about technology yet. That's like having the dessert before the appetizer. I guarantee that virtually every organization in the world can benefit from effective enterprise collaboration.

The Company Culture Is Not Supportive

We keep hearing about the culture of a company and the impact that it can have on collaboration, but what exactly does that mean? Culture is one of those things that is a bit hard to define, but a good way to look at it is like the personality of the organization, the behaviors of the employees, and the shared understandings and assumptions of how people work, behave, and communicate. Therefore, if an organization is very competitive, fragmented, and noncommunicative, it will be much harder to adopt a set of collaboration tools and strategies. Many companies have run into this obstacle because they assume that tools alone can help change the culture of a company; this is false. If the company culture does not support collaboration, then you already know what needs to be done before reading the next sentence: you have to change the company culture. An entire book can be written on that topic alone, but culture is typically instilled by leaders of an organization and so they have the power to change it. This can involve things such as incorporating a new set of public values that encourage collaboration, rewarding employees for collaborating with each other and helping each other, leading by example, and removing cubicles that segment employees. Nonsupportive collaborative cultures at organizations can destroy efforts to build a collaborative organization; therefore, they must be addressed.

User Resistance

Users Don't Want to Learn a New Technology

The key here is to convey that this is not about technology but about improving the way employees work, collaborate, and communicate. If you simply tell employees about a new platform that the company is rolling out, of course many will be reluctant to join. Employees have a certain way they work, and this process and method shouldn't be disrupted; instead, it should be enhanced. Social and collaborative technologies are not meant to act as additional things to do or to be the ugly duckling of the enterprise. These tools are integrated into an existing way of work, which means that if an employee has a four-step process for doing something, that process will either stay the same or be shortened as a result of these deployments. User resistance is a factor only when you threaten to change how things get done and convey that employees are going to have to do more work instead of less. Also keep in mind that collaboration has a certain amount of self-interest to the individuals collaborating. This means that employees need to understand what's in it for them, not just what's in it for the company.

Users Say They Don't Have Time

Education can play a crucial role in showing employees that using these tools isn't going to take more time but will help them save time by making their jobs easier. Understand where your users are spending their time and show them how using the new tools will cause them to spend less time doing the tasks they are doing now. For example, if employees say they already spend a lot of time searching for information or people to work with, let them know that those tasks will be shortened.

Users Are Already Overwhelmed by Existing Technology Platforms

It's completely understandable that employees are overwhelmed by the many social and collaborative tools and platforms that exist today. I have found that in the most successful instances these enterprise collaboration tools don't serve as additional tools; they serve as the central resource for employees within an enterprise. Think of it as the operating system for the enterprise in which everything they need can be done or located from within a central hub. This isn't a technology add-on; it's a platform that will become a part of an employee's day-to-day job. From this platform employees will be able to access anything they need. Of course this isn't always the case; often these social tools are used as replacements for corporate intranets. But in every case I have seen thus far, these tools have replaced something or have been used as aggregators of other tools. Also keep in mind that when these new tools are implemented, features should be rolled out in phases to avoid overwhelming employees, something covered in greater detail in Chapter 10.

IT Resistance

It's Not a Priority

As with the manager response mentioned above, fear and lack of education are a factor in why this isn't a priority. However, it's true there are situations in which an organization is focused on other projects and needs to wait until they are completed before investing in something else. I would recommend asking the IT folks why this isn't a priority. I have also found that bringing business and IT professionals together to discuss priorities often makes for interesting and enlightening discussions. If employees and executives decide that effective collaboration and communication is a priority, IT usually follows. You don't want to separate IT from the decision-making process as their approval and input are integral. Bring them into the conversation and try to understand their perspective. Sometimes IT leads the collaboration initiative and team members in this department may not all agree on things such as security or feasibility. Education is also a crucial component not just for the employees on the business side but also for those on the IT side. There have been several instances where CIOs or VPs in the IT department have had to force the use of these collaborative tools because their own teams were not familiar with them and thus didn't understand what they were really resisting.

There Are Security Issues or Threats

This is a common concern, but if some of the world's largest and most heavily regulated companies are able to make this work, security is an issue that can be overcome. In all my research and case studies I have not found a single example of a security threat that has done a company serious harm. Security is and will always be a concern, but that doesn't mean enterprise collaboration platforms are less secure than any other system. Part of selecting a vendor entails reviewing security; don't go with vendors about which you are skeptical. Pabst Brewing Company is one of the largest breweries in the United States with about 300 employees, and they had to overcome this very problem. Ben Haines, the CIO of Pabst, had to take a top-down approach with IT and basically force the transition to using more social and collaborative tools. At the beginning, Ben's IT team didn't really understand the security behind these news tools (whereas Ben already had prior experience with this), but after implementation all of IT saw how secure these new tools were. When I spoke to Ben, he told me that many IT professionals don't always have "security" as their focus; they concentrate on architecture, integration, support, and a host of other issues. However, vendors such as Box (which is what Pabst is using; it moved from SharePoint to Box) have a whole team devoted to making sure their product is secure, so it's more efficient to go with them. Keep in mind that Pabst is not a company with thousands of employees; they have just a few hundred, and 80 percent of their workforce works remotely thanks to the use of collaborative tools.

There Is No Manpower

This is a very legitimate concern. However, many business units have the ability to deploy these tools and platforms without the involvement of IT. Of course, it is always preferable to have the IT department involved here, but chances are that your business units are already deploying customer-grade collaboration tools that are not as secure as enterprise-grade tools and platforms. As far as manpower goes, it should be stressed that this is not an IT project; it is a company project that will necessitate a team of which IT will have to be a part. However, this isn't something that IT is going to be slaving over (or at least, it shouldn't). Smaller organizations can go with cloud-based vendors, which require little if any IT involvement. Many of the collaboration vendors today can act as allies and partners who already consider complex issues such as security and integration. This is why it's important to make sure your company goes with the proper vendor (something discussed in detail in Chapter 6).

There Is No Budget

Budget is always a concern from an IT and a managerial perspective. However, I have found that organizations are usually able to find the budget for these programs, especially when the platforms replace legacy intranet systems that the organization pays for. Furthermore, there are several free and/or low-cost options for collaborating, such as blogs and wikis. Océ (see Chapter 3) was able to save around 350 euros annually by shifting its budget from a legacy intranet system to social and collaborative tools. Penn State Outreach (see Chapter 3) canceled one of its annual employee events and used that money to fund its collaboration project. The annual event allowed only 500 of the 1,500 employees to attend, so it wasn't very effective at engaging employees. Now all the employees are able to connect with one another in a way that was never before possible. Companies don't need to go automatically with the best and most expensive enterprise collaboration solution. There are plenty of lower-cost, if not free, options available. Transferring budgets from legacy deployments is also something I have seen done many times with great effectiveness, typically when an organization realizes that it needs to update its intranet. Organizations can get creative when it comes to budgets, especially when it comes to deploying cloud-based solutions, which can save the company money on hardware and server costs. This money saved alone can often pay for the use of the new tools and then some.

The E-mail Culture

It's an interesting phenomenon when you think about it. We are so reliant on e-mail in our professional and even in our personal lives that it has become part of our culture. I think some of us enjoy getting e-mail because it usually means that someone needs our help, which makes us feel valuable or important. However, many of us hate e-mail when we get bombarded with spam, when angry bosses "yell" at us, or when we need to search through old messages to find information. But did you ever think about why we use e-mail to begin with?

Is e-mail a great collaboration platform? No.

Does e-mail make it easy for us to find information? Not really.

Is e-mail secure? Definitely not.

Does it make us more productive or make our jobs easier? Nope.

Why do people use e-mail to begin with? I believe the only reason e-mail is used is that everyone else uses it. E-mail used to be necessary for business, and so it became ubiquitous, but things have changed and e-mail is now no longer the most effective tool for communication and collaboration.

Luis Suarez works at IBM and is someone I have come to know over the last few years. IBM is one of the largest companies in the world, so you can imagine that the amount of information and e-mail flowing through the walls there is massive. But not for everyone. Luis has been able to reduce his e-mail by around 90 percent through the use of emergent collaboration solutions. In fact, he doesn't check e-mail that often, and when he does, there aren't many messages in his inbox. I'm not saying that Luis has everything figured out when it comes to e-mail, but his ability to decrease his reliance on it is quite an impressive feat.

I don't think e-mail is going to die, but I think organizations need to realize that there are better, more effective alternatives. This isn't a technology problem, it's a behavior-changing problem, but Luis's example shows that even someone working at one of the world's largest companies can make this change happen.

Summary and Action Items

Organizations are typically faced with three types of resistance: manager, user/employee, and IT resistance. Often there is an underlying theme that points to the real reason for resistance. E-mail is still a vastly popular form of collaboration and communication even though it is lacking in its ability to do either thing effectively. E-mail is in fact used because it is the lowest common denominator among individuals and companies. Everyone has e-mail, and so everyone uses e-mail not because there is nothing better but because everyone already uses e-mail. Take the following steps:

- Understand which groups you see the greatest resistance from and why; this can be done via an internal survey or one-on-one interviews.
- Develop responses to address the common forms of resistance that you will hear; try to find the root of the problem.
- Discuss how e-mail affects collaboration and communication in your organization. Do you have an e-mail culture? If so, why do you think that is and is it something you want to change?
- Do employees at your organization feel that e-mail is not a great collaboration and/or communication tool?

Let's hear from Ria Breuer, the global intranet manager for Océ, a document management outsourcing company and provider of printing equipment to companies around the world. Océ has over 20,000 employees, and Ria has learned quite a few things about employee resistance to emergent collaboration.

Employee Resistance

There are many reasons why employees are not using the social and collaborative tools available to them. Most are related to generational differences. Some will not use them because of misconceptions or unfamiliarity with the tools (mainly baby boomers and Gen X members), whereas others claim that the use of these tools is not related to their daily work. Some of the baby boomers are still of the opinion that knowledge is power and are therefore reluctant to share that knowledge.

All these issues can be resolved by educating employees. Teach them when to use which tool for which task and how to use each tool most efficiently (incorporate collaboration training in human resource development programs, organize workshops/webinars, join online conversations, create tutorials, and offer advice). Identify workflows where social media can add value and communicate best practices. And, very important, identify and award (recognize) leaders, preferably by adding that information to their personnel files.

You will also have to accept the fact that not everyone is willing (or able) to share knowledge actively. As in a business meeting, there will be some who lead the discussion and others who are only listening. That does not mean that they don't get value from the discussion.

Management Resistance

Management support is crucial for a successful companywide adoption of collaboration tools. If you cannot get top management to participate and support the initiative, concentrate on getting support from middle management.

The generational differences also apply to the management group, and therefore they also need to be informed and educated. However, management also needs to be shown the value (return on investment) of these tools for the company not only in terms of money and time saved but also in terms of "return on ignorance." Think of the consequences of recruiting and keeping new employees who use these tools in their private lives and expect to use them at work too and the active participation of employees in external online conversations and missed opportunities of connecting with (potential) customers. It's always better to start from the inside out.

Management can drive adoption of collaboration tools by actively participating in conversations and by blogging. For example, organize live chat sessions about hot items and guide management during those sessions.

IT Resistance

Until today, IT was in charge of selecting and rolling out tools for business users. However, times have changed and IT support is no longer required to roll out social and collaborative tools. IT sees its role diminished; that is the source of its resistance, usually expressed by raising security issues.

To overcome this resistance, it is advisable to involve them from the start. They can help select the right tools based on business requirements, and they can help in fine-tuning tools (think of ADS [Active Directory Service]-based access, search, adding functions or changing functions, statistic tools, and contract negotiations). The security issues are real but can be overcome by defining appropriate security measures, controls, and use policies and making sure all employees know how to apply them.

nine

Let's Roll

Once the vendor is selected, the next step is to go live with the emergent collaboration solution. Depending on the vendor and the requirements you have stipulated, this can take anywhere from a few hours to a few months.

Chances are that the technology solution you go with will have several features and capabilities. It's tempting to launch these platforms as is with everything enabled and let your employees have at it. However, I have found that this is not always the best approach for two reasons.

Employees Get Overwhelmed

As was mentioned earlier, many of these platforms and tools have a whole list of features and capabilities that can be used by employees. A common problem is that starting with too many things at once causes employees not to use anything at all. Think about how you would feel if all of a sudden your company implemented an emergent collaboration solution that allowed you to create wikis, join groups, share information, submit ideas, and do a host of other things. Where would you get started, and how would you manage the use of all those things? I'm not saying that you shouldn't deploy the tools, but I would use a phased approach to keep employees from getting overwhelmed.

A Steep Learning Curve Is Created

It always takes time and effort to learn something new, and emergent collaboration platforms are no exception. Employees need to learn how to use the new tools gradually or they may not learn how to use them at all. The more you pile on from the start, the harder it's going to be for employees to adopt the new tools, and eventually you are going to see a separation between employees who are quick to learn new tools (perhaps they are already familiar with them) and those who aren't. I don't recommend creating this kind of tension in the workplace, so my recommendation is to start with something easier to use and roll out additional features over time.

Start off with simple features that provide a clear and unique value to employees. For example, microblogging, rich profiles, and wikis might be a good starting point. Later, personal blogs, prediction markets, and forums can be added. An example of a feature roll-out plan as well as the value of the various features is discussed in more detail in Chapter 10. The key here is to make sure to account for the comfort levels and use of these features before adding to the mix. If you find that your employees are quick to adopt and understand how to use these tools and features, you can begin to roll out additional features sooner. However, if you see the employees are struggling to understand why or how they should be using something, adding more is not going to help. How long of a roll-out you have is up to you and should depend on what you are seeing with your employees. You might have everything rolled out in a few months or a year (or longer).

Marketing and support are also crucial for initial success, so you want to let your employees know about the new initiative before it goes live. I've seen organizations start internal marketing and communications efforts anywhere between a few weeks and five to six months in advance of the launch. The timeline is something you are going to have to gauge for yourself, depending on how receptive your organization is to marketing, how large the company is, and whether this is an initiative that employees are excited about. For example, if your company is large and the employees are already bombarded by internal marketing communications messages, you might want to give yourself a longer timeline to launch, say, four months. If your organization is smaller (a few hundred employees) and the employees are receptive to innovations and improvements, you can give yourself a bit less time, perhaps a month or so. To be safe, give yourself around 90 days to market and drum up excitement about the launch. I'm sure your marketing team is capable of reaching your organization, but make sure it has the resources and staff to make this happen.

Keep in mind that this isn't just a marketing project; it is an organization-wide project. Here are a few ideas I have seen companies implement along with a few of my own:

Marketing strat

- Announce a "secret project" that the company is working on slowly, dropping clues about what the project is over the course of a few months.

- Showcase regular video interviews of employees who talk about the challenges they are faced with at work when it comes to collaboration. Have the employees talk about the challenges and what a solution would mean for them (you don't need to tell them that the organization is looking to deploy something yet, but you can).

- Issue very clear senior directives stating that during a certain time period employees will be able to find only certain information on the new platform.

- Implement employee surveys, focus groups, and discussions that highlight the importance of improved collaboration.

- Show comedy videos that depict the frustrations employees have with the current ways of doing things.

- Send messages and announcements directly from senior-level executives talking about their support for and excitement about the emergent collaboration project.

- Distribute physical flyers and little gifts to employees to help generate buzz around the new launch.

Penn State Outreach planned its roll-out almost two months before the launch and used its creative potential to make it successful. Posters and banners were hung throughout offices saying things such as "Who was on *Romper Room* at age five?" (referring, of course, to an employee). Penn State also asked that everyone not schedule anything on the day of the launch: no meetings, no conferences, nothing. This was the day to try out the new platform and experiment with it. Fifteen hundred welcome packages were put together for all the employees, and a video was created with someone from the executive team supporting the initiative and was then distributed. Finally, a video tour of the platform was put together to help employees navigate the features.

One of my favorite creative examples of an emergent collaboration roll-out came from Yum! Brands, the company behind the brands Taco Bell, KFC, Pizza Hut, Long John Silver's, A&W Restaurants, and Wing-Street (around 38,000 restaurants in total with almost 400,000 employees). Yum! named and branded its platform iCHING. Yum! embarked on a heavy marketing campaign that included everything from iCHING T-shirts, notepads, mouse pads, and welcome starter kits (which looked like the box for an iPhone) to bathroom and elevator marketing.

Who would have thought that the rest room would be a great place to promote and market an emergent collaboration platform? When employees entered the rest rooms at Yum!, they were greeted with a little mirror decal that included fake profile information along with a message for everyone to "now go create your real profile" (see Figure 9.1).

Since the iCHING logo and branding shows two people connecting, Yum! decided to leverage the elevators to help promote that concept. Every time employees get in an elevator at Yum!, they are reminded of the iCHING platform (as is shown in Figure 9.2, the decal is shown on the inside and the outside).

Yum! is a massive company with a lot of resources at its disposal, but if you think about what it did with the elevators and bathrooms, the company simply found the most common places that employees access. The point here is that creativity should not be left out of the marketing equation.

The most effective way to start the marketing process is by assigning key activities or tasks that need to get done each week and the person or people responsible for completing those tasks. For example, the

Figure 9.1 The roll-out at Yum!

Figure 9.2 Leveraging the elevators at Yum!

first week of the roll-out plan might entail sending out an initial teaser e-mail and designing the creative for the flyers you will hand out to the employees. Week 6 might include sharing employee interviews that address why collaboration is important to those being interviewed. Again, this is where your team needs to get creative. Remember that you have to communicate with your employees. I spoke with an executive from one of the world's largest hotel chains in Las Vegas who told me that his company deployed a platform but that nobody knew about it and thus nobody used it.

The branding and design components should not be overlooked. Think of the time and effort that go into designing and branding a new customer-facing product; the same time and effort is going to be needed for your emergent collaboration initiative: everything from colors and logos to messaging and the customization of the collaboration platform to include those colors and logos. Start this process early as you are going to have to do several revisions and have discussions with various departments about what works and what doesn't.

Everyone who is part of the emergent collaboration team also needs to be an evangelist: someone who encourages and supports the use of the new technologies and strategies within the enterprise. When the platform is rolled out, you want the employees to feel excited about it, not annoyed that they are going to have to use a new platform. This is where the human aspect of communication and connecting with your employees is crucial. Employees not only need to hear about and understand the benefits of emergent collaboration, they need to *feel* that the organization and the senior leaders care about making it work.

Rolling out an emergent collaboration platform is not that different from announcing a new product, a feature, or a special event your company is putting on. The main difference is that you are doing all of this internally.

Summary and Action Items

In rolling out the platform, the most effective approach is to release the various features in phases. Start with the easiest features that offer a clear value to employees, such as rich profiles and microblogging. The more advanced features can be rolled out later. Rolling out the platform takes the effort of the entire organization led by the emergent collaboration team. Everyone needs to act as an evangelist to get things going. Thinking out of the box is also highly effective, and the use of creative and unique ways to engage employees to let them know about the initiative is highly encouraged:

- Develop a marketing road map with key milestones and responsibilities that have to be done each week.

- Brainstorm creative ways to engage and excite employees. Make sure support from the senior leadership team is clearly shown and conveyed.

To help us better understand what goes into the launch, marketing, and communication strategy of a collaboration platform, the chief information officer of the Children's Hospital in Boston, Naomi Fried, Ph.D., has shared her insights.

_____

As chief innovation officer at Children's Hospital Boston, I lead a department with a unique mission: to accelerate innovation by providing resources and support to empower innovators in developing and testing their novel ideas, to collaborate on strategic clinical and business model innovation opportunities, and to initiate innovative cross-disciplinary projects to address unmet clinical needs.

Fortunately, Children's already has a culture that embraces innovation. Last year our employees filed for over 200 patents, and we've had two Nobel Prize winners on the faculty. To enhance this culture, we launched an internal social networking site in February 2011. Our site is named SPARC, which stands for the Social Platform for Accelerating Resources and Connections.

The purpose of SPARC is to promote communication, interaction, and sharing of ideas between clinicians, healthcare providers, support staff, and researchers within Children's and with outside academic institutions. On SPARC, innovators form communities that allow them to "meet," problem solve, and exchange information, ideas, advice, and opinions. Innovators can pose questions, share tips and links, and virtually "chat" with one another. Moderators help stimulate discussions by posting interesting links, asking questions, and finding "guest experts" at Children's to participate as needed.

The overall goals of the community are as follows:

- Facilitate efforts to move laboratory advances, devices, and clinical innovations closer to clinical trials and practice
- Foster innovation by providing an easy, spontaneous mechanism of interaction in the Children's community
- Facilitate brainstorming about new ideas, procedures, and equipment
- Provide an environment in which innovators can get feedback on a concept's merit and relevance
- Increase awareness of others' projects and activities that may advance one's own
- Identify resources and equipment that could help advance an innovative idea
- Identify users with a particular skill set needed for a project
- Connect innovators with supportive internal organizations such as the Children's Innovation Acceleration Program and Technology Development and Innovation Office

Communications Plan

It is necessary to create a marketing and communications plan before rolling out a community. For us, the most important part of the communication plan was defining "what's in it for me?" (WIIFM) for the users. Although we have an innovative culture, we knew our employees needed a reason to visit another website throughout their busy day. Physicians, nurses, researchers, and administrators have very different motivations for visiting the site. We cannot assume that users will come to the site just to be social; there has to be a clear business objective for employees to make the time.

We created a comprehensive list of the WIIFM for each user. Below are some points that were consistent across all user populations:

1. Reduce e-mail and in-person meetings.
2. Increase transparency and influence by showing off your skills to colleagues.
3. Improve mobility because SPARC can be accessed off the virtual private network and on mobile devices.

[handwritten: What's in it for me]

We had to pause a few times and remind ourselves that the goal of the site is not to change how employees work; it is to enhance their efforts and accelerate their ability to connect to resources and colleagues.

We knew we wanted to avoid the common pitfall of having a big launch too early in the community's maturity. Although it's a logical promotional step, we avoided issuing press releases, hosting kickoff events, and sending mass e-mails. We knew we could drive traffic to the site, but it would make a bad first impression if people saw very little activity on their first visit. What's in it for them if it looks like a community of one? For this reason, we opted for a slow, viral launch.

The Community Manager's Role

We learned very quickly how important the community manager is to the success of the community. The community managers must have a crystal-clear understanding of the community's business objective. They must have the ability to balance many distinct functions. A community manager needs to be a *teacher*—a good teacher. Thinking about the site like a new car, the community manager needs to be able to teach users how to drive the car, not just show them all the parts.

The community managers need to be the community's *help desk*. If anything goes wrong on the site, they are the first ones users reach out to. The community managers need to build time into their schedule to be responsive to any requests for help. They must also have enough technical understanding to articulate the bug clearly to their vendor or support partner. This is especially important in first rolling out the community.

The community managers also play the role of *custodian* by cleaning up the forums, removing old user profiles, and watching for inappropriate activity. They must also feel comfortable with conflict because there are times when they will have to enter into uncomfortable situations or steer a conversation in a more professional direction. An organization needs to make sure the community managers know the appropriate boundaries for community members because they set the majority of the expectations.

A community manager needs to be an excellent *writer* and *promoter*. They have to have the confidence to put themselves and their words out there. However, they have to know when to be an *observer*. If the community manager is the first person to comment on all posts and always tops the most active member list, users can feel discouraged or intimidated about sharing their content.

As if we haven't asked enough of this person, he or she also needs to be an excellent *project manager* and *liaison* to the technology vendor.

ten

Adoption
(Not Babies)

Once an organization selects and deploys an emergent collaboration solution, the next step is to get employees to use the new
tool or tools. Every organization has its own ways of getting employees
to adopt new tools and solutions; in fact, I haven't seen many similar
approaches to increasing adoption. Strategies for adoption are not as
effective when they are simply white labeled or copied because many
variables differ from one organization to another. Before we begin
exploring adoption, let's take a look at where companies are currently
in the grand scheme of things (Figure 10.1).

By examining these data we can see that most companies are still
at the very early stages of getting these tools and strategies adopted by
their organizations. In fact, 27 percent of companies don't even have
a 10 percent adoption rate yet and 45 percent of those who responded
are seeing anywhere from 10 to 25 percent of their employees actively
engaged. These low numbers show that there is still a lot of work to be
done to get emergent collaboration in full swing.

Figure 10.2 shows that the business development and sales teams
are the most actively engaged in these tools, followed closely by marketing and communications and then operations and IT.

Figure 10.3 shows a comparison of organization size and the most
actively engaged departments. If you look closely, you will notice

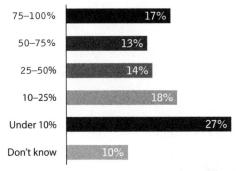

75–100%	17%
50–75%	13%
25–50%	14%
10–25%	18%
Under 10%	27%
Don't know	10%

Figure 10.1 What percent of the target employee base is actively engaged in E2.0?

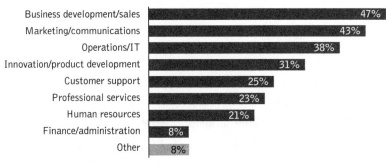

Business development/sales	47%
Marketing/communications	43%
Operations/IT	38%
Innovation/product development	31%
Customer support	25%
Professional services	23%
Human resources	21%
Finance/administration	8%
Other	8%

Figure 10.2 Which departments are most actively engaged in E2.0 efforts?

an interesting trend. Smaller organizations see their business development and sales team most actively engaged, midsize organizations see a shift in focus toward marketing and communications, midsize to large organizations focus on operations and IT, and large enterprises focus on innovation and product development. On a spectrum we can see something like this:

- Smaller organizations focus on growing the business through business development and sales.
- Midsize organizations focus on marketing and communications to create awareness and visibility.
- Midsize to large organizations focus on operations and IT to sustain and support their infrastructure and growth.
- Large enterprises focus on innovation and product development to stay competitive and innovative.

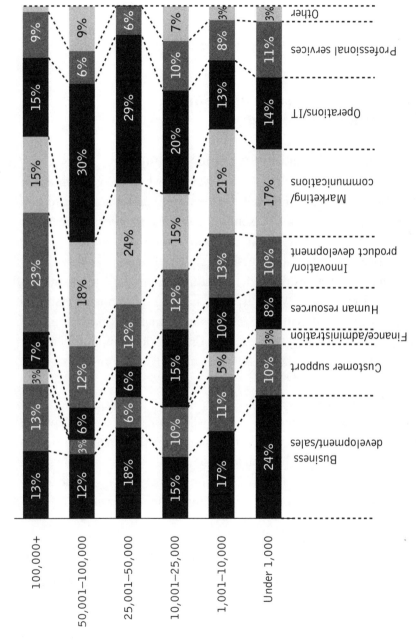

Figure 10.3 Which departments are most actively engaged in Enterprise 2.0 efforts (breakdown by organization size)?

Regardless of where your organization is on this spectrum, there are some common elements among organizations that deploy emergent collaboration solutions in their organizations.

What the Successful and Smart Companies Are Doing

Developing a Taxonomy for Information

Procter & Gamble learned the hard way that when you give employees complete freedom to information, there is going to be a lack of standardization and a lack of taxonomy around how information is presented and shared. To solve this problem, taxonomies can be developed or guidelines can be established to help employees make sure that an "information soup" isn't created. A simple example is the naming of files or group spaces. What types of naming conventions should be used? Does every department get its own internal workspace along with subgroups? This doesn't have to be a difficult decision, but there does need to be consistency to preserve the integrity of information.

Conveying Value

I have touched on this topic throughout the book, but it's worth repeating here. Employees will not use something unless there is a clear and real benefit to them. Part of being able to convey value is understanding what the business problems and use cases are, so make sure you understand them. Don't focus on features or technology; focus on value.

Investing in Education and Training

Virtually every organization I have worked with or researched has had some sort of training and education program for emergent collaboration. As with anything new, employees will have questions and will need to get answers to those questions. You can gauge how in-depth an education and training program you need to develop, but the point is that it has to exist. Most companies deploy a combination of group training and some one-on-one training sessions as well as best practices

and other online resources. Training for the new emergent collaboration platform should be part of the onboarding process for every
employee who joins the organization. I realize that many vendors
claim that their platforms are so intuitive that training and education is
not necessary, but keep in mind that there are two sides to this: business
and technology. On the business side, employees need to understand
how collaboration can benefit them and why it matters. They need
to understand the strategic and business implications of collaboration.
On the technology side, employees need to understand how to use
the tools and platforms. Just because the technology may be intuitive
doesn't mean training shouldn't be a part of the plan.

Reaching the Exemplars

Find who the employees are whom everyone looks up to and admires.
Employees often emulate the behavior of exemplars, so if you can
get them on board, you will have a good chance of speeding up and
increasing adoption. Exemplars don't have to be executives at an organization; they can be absolutely anyone.

Removing Barriers, Not Building Them

It's tempting to develop pages of rules, policies, and guidelines for
employees to follow. However, organizations need to learn how to get
out of the way of their employees. Whenever possible, try to limit rules
and governance and let the employees dictate how these tools should
be used. There is nothing wrong with encouraging employees and providing recommendations, but try to avoid strict policing of usage unless
it is absolutely necessary.

Integrating into the Flow of Work

One of the most common things I have observed in organizations
deploying emergent collaboration technologies is the importance of
integrating new tools into the existing flow of work. This means that
if employees have a five-step process to get something done, the new
tool should have just as many steps (and ideally less). Emergent collaboration shouldn't prevent employees from getting their jobs done;

it should be a more effective way of allowing them to get their jobs done. For example, if employees traditionally have to log in to multiple systems to access information, try to limit the number of logins by integrating them via a single sign-on with a new emergent collaboration platform. Thus, employees will still be able to access the information they need but with fewer steps.

Enlisting Evangelists

As was stated earlier in this book, evangelists are valuable in helping with the adoption of new tools and strategies. Think of evangelists as the special forces for your emergent collaboration efforts.

Emphasizing Senior Leadership Support

Showing that senior-level leaders are involved with emergent collaboration is always effective. In Chapter 16, Andrew McAfee identifies lack of senior-level support as one of the key predictors of failure. Successful organizations make sure that senior-level leaders are *visibly* involved. Unisys is a great example of a company that led collaboration from the top. Senior leaders were among the first to complete their profiles, start blogging, and post status updates of client meetings. This helped to create trust and transparency among employees. Within one year, Unisys went from 5,000 active employees to over 15,000 active employees, representing more than 80 percent of the target population.

Putting Information on the Platform

Organizations communicate frequently with their employees through newsletters and other forms of communication. Instead, place the relevant information on the emergent collaboration platform so that employees will have to access it to get the information they need. This will allow employees to get familiar with the platform while seeing the value and benefit of using the new solution.

Integrating Employee Feedback

Not integrating employee feedback is a sure route to failure. It is crucial to listen to employee feedback, ideas, and insights and to integrate them into the product and the processes of emergent collaboration. The last thing you want to do is not listen to your employees.

Developing an Information Skeleton

Often, before tools are deployed to the general employee base, the team members will begin to populate the emergent collaboration platform with some content, perhaps the most recent training information, upcoming news and events, or any other relevant documents or information. Sometimes groups are precreated for various teams and/or departments as well. Doing this will help employees get up to speed more quickly as some of the information has already been uploaded and created for them. When deploying its wiki, Vistaprint created an information structure (like a table of contents) but left the content within that structure blank for employees to fill out and populate as they saw appropriate. This is like having chapter titles in a book but without the chapter content. It's not advisable to launch an emergent collaboration platform with absolutely nothing populated or created on the platform. When possible, try to make things as easy as possible for the employees.

Creating the "Front Door"

New tools make sense only if employees don't have to consistently access multiple platforms to get their jobs done. Even if your company uses multiple tools, there needs to be a way for the information to be accessed, shared, edited, and curated from a central area. This is where researching the integration capabilities of vendors becomes important. The easier you can make it for your employees, the better (for example, using single-sign-on functionality).

Highlighting Successes

I have seen this done very effectively in several organizations. Some have made use of employee video testimonials and featurettes, which were distributed to the organization. You want to make sure that employees know of and can relate to successes that other employees are having using these new tools. Feature it in your employee newsletter and bring it up at your meetings and conferences.

Making Sure the Technology Is Intuitive

This will help make sure employees can use whatever tools the organization deploys. If the new technology has to come with a training manual, chances are that the platform is not going to be very intuitive. This is why so many emergent collaboration vendors are building their platforms with user interfaces that are similar to those in popular consumer social media platforms; people are already familiar with them.

Conveying the Strategy and a Clear Mission

If employees don't understand what the strategy or the vision of emergent collaboration is, why should they bother using it? Employees need to be able to align on something, and if they don't know what that something is, it becomes very hard to align. This shared vision is a critical component for the success of any emergent collaboration initiative.

Incentivizing Employees and Forcing Adoption

There are two parts to this that need to be discussed. The first is the concept or idea of incentivizing or rewarding employees for using emergent collaboration solutions. The second involves mandating that employees use the new tools the company deploys.

Incentives

Should employees be rewarded or enticed to use emergent collaboration technologies (for example, financially or with some other compensation)? This is a question that many people ask. Unfortunately, there isn't a clear-cut answer. One of the biggest problems I see with these types of incentives for using new tools is that this implies that tools are not valuable in and of themselves and so in addition to being provided with new tools, employees get some kind of reward. Furthermore, this creates a certain expectation in the mind of the employee. For example, if you reward me for doing something on the platform, I'm going to expect that reward and over time I'm going to want the reward to grow in value. This of course is not scalable or realistic at most companies. We also need to consider that different employees perceive incentives differently, and so what may be valuable to one employee may not be valuable to another. Perhaps these types of incentives will work as a short-term approach, but then you have the challenge of slowly removing the incentives, which might cause drops in adoption. You want employees to use tools because they are valuable, not because there is a reward for doing so.

The greatest incentive you can provide to your employees is to make their jobs and lives easier. Show them that the value of these new tools is so great that they will feel that they have to use them.

Most employees want recognition in the eyes of their peers, coworkers, and managers. One effective way to do this is by developing leader boards where employees are publicly recognized for their contributions. I've also seen employees mentioned in newsletters for their collaborative efforts. Applying gaming concepts or "gamification" may also be something you wish to experiment with. Examples include badges or "status" for employees who are active on the emergent collaboration tools. Again, the goal is to be able to make this scale and capture the attention of the employees consistently.

Instead of trying to hang a carrot in front of employees, focus on giving them valuable tools and technologies that will make their lives easier.

Organizations also have another option: changing the way they evaluate employees by incorporating their activity of collaborating and knowledge sharing into their reviews. The employee review process is typically quite static at many companies, but this may be the time for a change. Incorporating collaboration as a part of the employee review process is a great way to foster and encourage collaboration.

Forcing Adoption

Is it possible to force employees to use new tools and technologies? In the few examples I have heard of this happening, there were very mixed results. My recommendation is never to force anything because that inevitably ends up causing a lot of tension and friction in the workplace. Most of the companies I work with and have researched take the exact opposite approach of not forcing but encouraging. One of the things I have noticed over time is that employees begin to force one another to use these tools and technologies to access information. For example, during a group meeting notes are placed on a wiki, and for other employees to access these notes, they have to access the wiki.

A Note on Community Managers

Community managers have become a core part of engaging with customers on social channels, and this role has made its way into the enterprise. Many vendors also offer community management as a part of their professional services package to increase adoption of their platforms. The tricky thing here is that *community manager* can mean a lot of different things and can encompass a wide spectrum of responsibilities. Sometimes this role overlaps with that of the evangelist or champion. It doesn't matter what you call this role; the important thing is that the role needs to exist. The role of a community manager isn't about just trying to engage with employees and start discussions, because discussions and engagement just for the sake of it aren't that valuable. You can think of the community manager almost as an advisor or a close friend, someone you go to with questions, ideas, and requests for advice or when you want to learn something new.

The community manager is there to make your life easier. Some of the key responsibilities of a community manager include:

- Training and educating employees on how to use new tools
- Encouraging employees and providing recommendations for how tools can be used more effectively
- Monitoring internal platforms to extract learnings and ideas by observing employees' use and behavior
- Developing and sharing resources and best practices
- Project managing

It's tempting to want to focus all the engagements, discussions, and ideas on work topics: How can we sell more products? Does anyone know how we can cut costs? What's going on with our competitors? These are the types of discussions you would expect to see in a workplace. But how would you feel if you saw discussion groups around things such as a weekly runners group or chess enthusiasts? Perhaps there is a group for employees who like to sail or an amateur photography circle. Should these types of things be banned or frowned upon in the enterprise? After all, why should employees be starting discussion groups on playing chess or racquetball?

This is the wrong approach. Remember that employees are humans and allowing people to connect with one another to share ideas, passions, and interests is a big part of making employees feel fulfilled and happy at work; this also helps build trust. It's crucial for employees to get to know one another, make friends, and learn to trust one another. This means that if your employees want to create a runners group or a sailing group, by all means let them create it and be active in it. Organizations should never take the human aspects out of work. Employees are not worker bees or drones; they want to feel as though they have a network and can make a connection with those they work with, so don't restrict discussions or activity to work-related content. Remember that inspiration and ideas don't always happen when one is thinking about work.

One thing that is not typically looked at is adoption from a technology or feature perspective. In other words, many organizations want to know how features affect adoption. This framework can help guide you down that road (Figure 10.4).

Let's walk through each stage in detail.

Stage 1

Implement basic and intuitive features that can help solve problems right out of the gate. Rich profiles and microblogs are a great starting point, along with the ability to share files and search for information. Enabling single sign-on functionality is also crucial to implement early on as it can be a huge factor in ramping up early adoption and solves a very clear and immediate need in most organizations. Depending on the size of your organization, you may be in this stage for one to six months. Instead of basing this on a timeline, look at employee use and feedback as an indicator for when to advance.

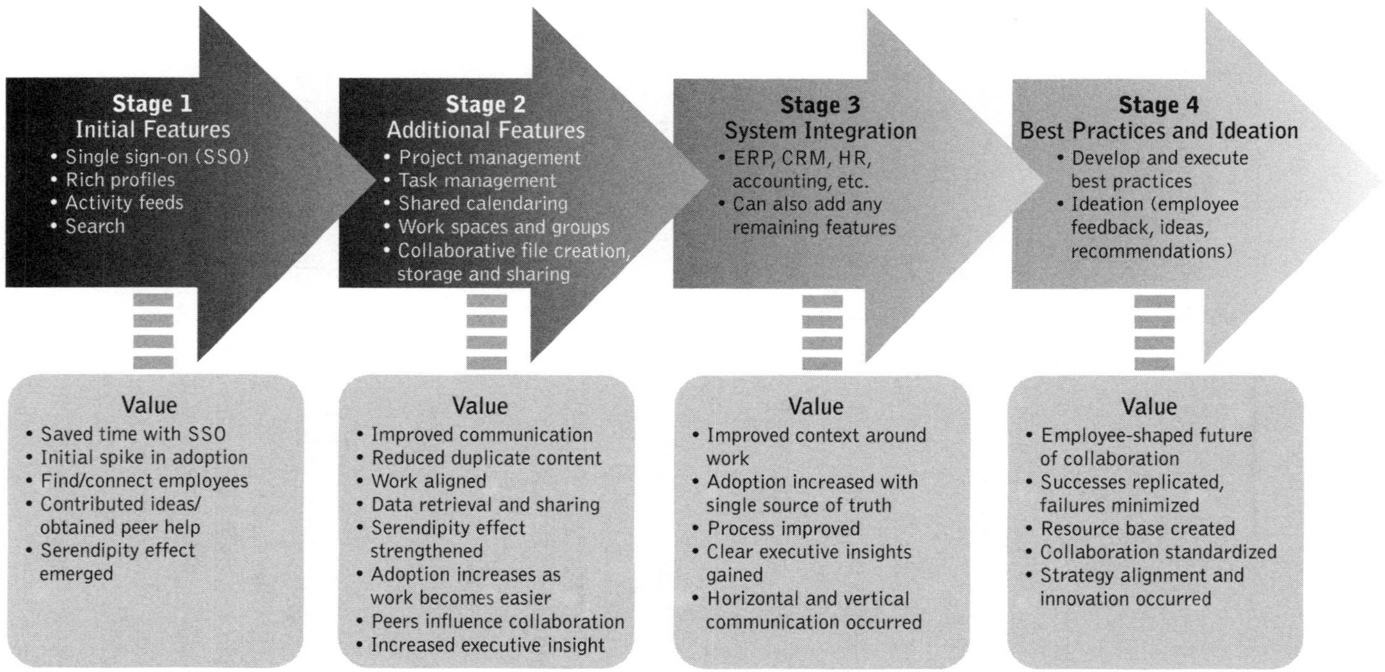

Stage 1
Initial Features
- Single sign-on (SSO)
- Rich profiles
- Activity feeds
- Search

Value
- Saved time with SSO
- Initial spike in adoption
- Find/connect employees
- Contributed ideas/ obtained peer help
- Serendipity effect emerged

Stage 2
Additional Features
- Project management
- Task management
- Shared calendaring
- Work spaces and groups
- Collaborative file creation, storage and sharing

Value
- Improved communication
- Reduced duplicate content
- Work aligned
- Data retrieval and sharing
- Serendipity effect strengthened
- Adoption increases as work becomes easier
- Peers influence collaboration
- Increased executive insight

Stage 3
System Integration
- ERP, CRM, HR, accounting, etc.
- Can also add any remaining features

Value
- Improved context around work
- Adoption increased with single source of truth
- Process improved
- Clear executive insights gained
- Horizontal and vertical communication occurred

Stage 4
Best Practices and Ideation
- Develop and execute best practices
- Ideation (employee feedback, ideas, recommendations)

Value
- Employee-shaped future of collaboration
- Successes replicated, failures minimized
- Resource base created
- Collaboration standardized
- Strategy alignment and innovation occurred

Figure 10.4 Framework for feature adoption

© 2012 Chess Media Group

Value

Employees will start being able to find and connect with their colleagues at work through the use of rich profiles. They will also be able to share ideas and content and ask and answer questions via the microblogging functionality. Instead of relying on e-mail as the content repository, employees will be able to share files with one another easily. They will no longer have to sign on to multiple platforms to access information; they will only need to log into one system that can authenticate them across all other systems. Executives will start to gain insight into how employees work and how the organization as a whole functions. The organization also will start to see the serendipity effect emerge.

Stage 2

Once employees become more comfortable with and accustomed to the initial set of features, you can begin to turn on additional capabilities. Project and task management features should be added as well as group and workspace creation capabilities, shared calendaring, and collaborative file creation, storage, and sharing. These features will help employees add more context to the way they work while providing them with the additional tools they need to solve business problems. Organizations are typically in this stage for around three months.

Value

Employees will be able to manage more of their day-to-day work lives on the emergent collaboration platform. Tasks can be created and assigned, and special project groups or department groups can be created to keep everyone on the same page. It also becomes much easier for employees to retrieve and share information with one another. Adoption will increase as employees will need to access the collaboration platform to get the information required to get their jobs done. Employees will also start to see a reduction in duplicate content as well as improved communication. A "single source of truth" for projects and information begins to be formed here. At this stage colleagues also typically begin to influence one another to collaborate. Finally, executives gain greater insight into their organizations.

Stage 3

Once the set of features and capabilities is rolled out, integration can begin with other legacy and back-end systems such as customer relationship management (CRM), enterprise resource planning (ERP), billing and invoicing, and ticketing systems. All required and relevant integrations are rolled out here as well as any remaining features the organization wishes to roll out. Organizations typically are in this phase for 6 to 18 months or more.

Value

The emergent collaboration platform now becomes the front door for the enterprise, and everything employees need to get their jobs done is found in one place. Adoption increases even further as employees no longer need to access other applications or sites and can instead utilize one platform to get everything done. Process improvement is very noticeable here. Context around collaboration becomes prevalent, and communication becomes increasingly horizontal rather than vertical. Executives now have a very solid understanding of what is happening in their organizations at the ground level.

Stage 4

The final stage involves employee ideation and innovation and the creation of best practices. Here we see employees being able to contribute their ideas and feedback to help shape the future of collaboration in the enterprise. New ideas, use cases, and opportunities are identified and pursued. Best practices are developed regularly to address issues or recommendations for how employees can best leverage the emergent collaboration solution. This isn't to say that best practices and ideation can't and won't take shape in earlier stages, but this is when it really starts to become formalized and distributed. Some organizations put a heavy emphasis on developing best practices and including employee ideation concurrently with earlier stages, which of course is another option. Organizations typically remain in this stage once the other three are completed, but they can regress, for example, if a deployed platform is being replaced for another one or if the organization feels that new features were rolled out too quickly.

Value

Through the use of best practices successes can be replicated and failures can be minimized. Employees are now able to share and access a resource base to help educate, train, and guide new and existing employees to make the most of emergent collaboration. Employees are able to contribute their own ideas and provide feedback to help shape the future of collaboration and work at the organization. Emergent collaboration becomes the standard for how work gets done. I also don't want to suggest that this is the only phase where employee feedback should be considered; that should be ongoing through all the phases of deployment.

Keep in mind that this is one framework you can use but that it can be adapted. For example, instead of having two feature stages, your organization might have three. This needs to be mapped to what works best for your organization.

Finally, getting and sustaining desired adoption levels does take time. Nobody likes to hear that things take time, but that's the reality, especially in large organizations. Successful emergent collaboration initiatives aren't looked at as projects or campaigns; they are looked at as an evolution of doing business. Smart organizations understand that this is how things need to be done in the future. Can you imagine your organization not deploying these tools in the next three to five years?

Summary and Action Items

Many companies are still at the early stages of their emergent collaboration initiatives. Companies that are actively involved see the greatest engagement coming from the business development/sales departments, the marketing/communications departments, and the operations/IT departments. Different-size companies see department engagement vary, and an interesting trend emerges that shows how companies focus their efforts on different business drivers, depending on company size. Smart organizations do several things that separate them from the rest. These include everything from education and training, to reaching out to the exemplars, to obtaining senior leadership support. The features of a platform can be strategically rolled out to maximize adoption levels at organizations:

- Conduct an employee survey to see what percentage of employees is actively engaged.

- Explore which departments are the most actively engaged and why.

- Look at where your company falls on the organization size spectrum. Do you see the same trends at your company that were presented in this chapter?

- Review the list of things other organizations are doing. Which ones is your organization doing? Are you having success with these initiatives?

- Are you incentivizing or forcing your employees to use these tools, and what role do community managers play in the success of the project?

- Walk through the feature adoption framework. Which features is your organization rolling out and when? What benefits do you see from each phase of the roll-out?

To help us learn some valuable lessons about emergent collaboration adoption, I asked two members of the Elizabeth Glaser Pediatric AIDS Foundation to contribute to this chapter: Keith Fleming, IT manager, and Sara Teitelman, senior technical editor. The foundation currently has over 1,500 employees in 17 countries.

Different groups in our organization have adopted the platform at different rates. Since we are a geographically dispersed organization (more than 80 percent of our staff is based outside the United States, mostly in various African countries), the challenge was to encourage rapid adoption among those with an immediate business need or a high level of enthusiasm (i.e., champions) while acknowledging that there would be slower, more gradual uptake among the majority of staff, especially those outside the United States. We did this by staging our efforts, first training content managers in the United States within each department and assisting them with build-out of their team areas prior to launch and then hosting virtual orientation sessions after the launch with each country office. We also provided training to U.S.-based country liaison officers by using a training of trainers model so that they in turn could train in-country content managers during their country visits. With all these efforts, we are depending to some extent on word-of-mouth promotion by early adopters as well as senior management and respected opinion leaders, and this has turned out to be an important factor. Departments with managers who show great enthusiasm for the platform have typically been much quicker to adopt it.

Among our U.S. staff, we have seen that those departments with business needs that the platform could easily address, such as financial planning, accounting, and human resources, quickly embrace the platform and start using it almost immediately as a go-to resource and central repository for all content related to their work. Slower rates of adoption have been seen among medical and scientific teams, as those groups are generally a bit wary of new technology and are still trying to decide on the best use for the platform in their daily work. Since the work they engage in is highly collaborative and content-rich, we feel it will be greatly enhanced by such a platform, but spaces must be built out that are both safe and functional havens for the exchange of ideas, the asking of complex questions, and the formulation of strategies and approaches. We are still working with these teams to determine the best mix of functionalities for these collaborative spaces and expect this to be a highly iterative process as we try out different mixes of features for different groups. The key going forward will be to get these teams to define specific business needs that we can help them address, which in turn is hoped to drive further adoption among these groups.

For non-U.S. staff, the challenge is promoting a culture of openness and sharing. Office culture tends to be very hierarchical in our African offices, and so we have engaged managers in those countries to encourage their staffs to contribute to and form their own discussion forums and blogs. We believe that once a few respected staff members lead the way, more will follow. Again the focus is on empowering decision leaders to be agents of change in this regard. Many people on these staffs do not typically sit in front of a computer all day, so making it fast and convenient for them to log on and quickly access the information they need is a priority. This includes a roll-out of the platform on mobile devices so that they can access the system on the go.

The four most crucial things that we would recommend other organizations pay attention to are the following.

Senior Staff Buy-In

Senior staff buy-in has proved to be an essential part of adoption at EGPAF. Many of our work processes were based on entrenched impractical models of sharing information—e-mail file attachments, network drive file folder structures. Directed by the CEO, senior leadership encouraged the staff members to think more creatively about how they conduct their daily work and to use the intranet as the main collaborative tool.

The core intranet team engaged the senior leadership team early in the development process and presented the business case for adoption of the new platform. In response, the CEO saw the intranet as being in line with the organization's strategic objectives, directed senior leadership to make adoption a priority, and requested quarterly quantitative feedback on the adoption process.

Intranet Content Managers

We recommend forming an intranet content managers group early in the site development process. This group should include a representative from each department who will serve as the owner of the departmental content and intranet champion. At EGPAF, this group participated in vendor presentation meetings and was involved in the final vendor selection process. This served to build a sense of ownership that built excitement that team members took back to their departments.

Accessibility and Performance

The staff should be able to access the site easily, and the site should consistently perform at a high level. If your site is difficult to access (confusing URL, too many clicks, awkward security) or performance is slow, the staff will quickly disengage. With more than 80 percent of our staff located in Africa and not networked with U.S.-based staff, this posed a challenge. Accessibility was made easy by adding the site URL to the autoauthenticated local intranet zone in U.S. offices and setting the intranet home page as the default home page for all users. To improve performance, we host our site in London, England, which significantly reduces the number of "hops" for Africa staff, and we installed network optimizers at the London hosting location and in all our African offices. Staff members outside the U.S.-based offices log in by using Windows Authentication.

Ease of Use of the System

Choose a system platform that is user-friendly and easy to administer. This was the largest lesson learned from our previous intranet platform roll-out. At EGPAF, our intranet content development is decentralized. As such, it's essential to the upkeep of the site that the system be intuitive and easy to navigate. Despite numerous training sessions, several sections of our previous intranet went without updates for months because the content owners struggled with using the system. It is obvious, based on the volume of content and activity on the new site, that content managers are embracing the system and finding it easy to use.

Overall, successful adoption will be driven by us meeting people where they are in terms of their personal comfort level and work style so that we can reduce barriers to use and convince them that this is something that benefits them and will lead to greater efficiencies rather than being an additional task or step that is being added to their workload.

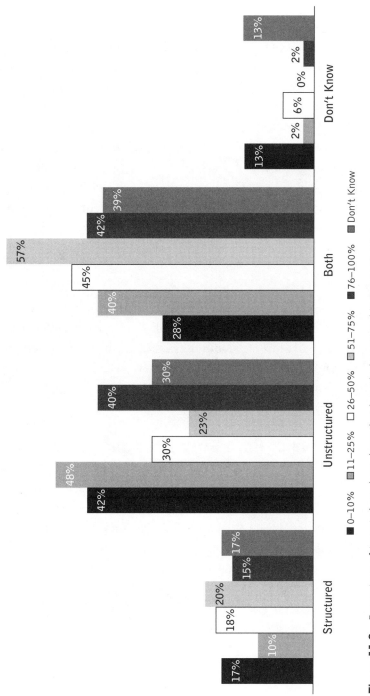

Figure 11.2 Percentage of targeted employee base that is actively engaged in Enterprise 2.0

Legend: ■ 0–10% ■ 11–25% ☐ 26–50% ☐ 51–75% ■ 76–100% ■ Don't Know

Structured
- 0–10%: 17%
- 11–25%: 10%
- 26–50%: 18%
- 51–75%: 20%
- 76–100%: 15%
- Don't Know: 17%

Unstructured
- 0–10%: 42%
- 11–25%: 48%
- 26–50%: 30%
- 51–75%: 23%
- 76–100%: 40%
- Don't Know: 30%

Both
- 0–10%: 28%
- 11–25%: 40%
- 26–50%: 45%
- 51–75%: 57%
- 76–100%: 42%
- Don't Know: 39%

Don't Know
- 0–10%: 13%
- 11–25%: 2%
- 26–50%: 6%
- 51–75%: 0%
- 76–100%: 2%
- Don't Know: 13%

Structured

This type of governance model is strict and rigid, with specific rules and regulations in place for what employees can and cannot do. You might see this type of model at regulated organizations such as banks or pharmaceutical companies. The main challenge with this approach is the concept of regulating, policing, and enforcing collaboration. The reason collaboration as a concept is successful is that employees have the freedom to share ideas and work. When you start to enforce specific rules for what employees can say and how they can collaborate, you are effectively kicking out one of the legs of the stool. The desire of managers wanting to control every aspect of emergent collaboration is understandable, but it's a battle that will surely be lost.

Unstructured

This model is quite flexible as it mainly involves self-organization and policing within the emergent collaboration solutions. Best practices and guidelines are leveraged, but the organization as a whole does not strictly enforce how employees should behave, what they should share, or what they can and cannot say.

Combination of Both Structured and Unstructured

Not surprisingly, this model makes use of some specific rules and regulations but also gives employees the freedom they need to make collaboration work. As was mentioned above, this is the most common approach utilized by organizations today as indicated by the Chess Media Group report.

There is no secret to putting together policies and guidelines; however, it is most effective to sit down with the emergent collaboration team to discuss what policies and guidelines should look like. Here are some questions to get you started:

- Should employees always have to identify themselves internally (for example, if they comment on an internal blog)?

- What happens if an employee acts inappropriately on an emergent collaboration platform?
- What features should be accessible to whom?
- Is it okay for employees to share any type of internal information they come across?
- Are there specific laws or rules that must be followed that are outside the control of the organization?
- Do employees know that they are supported if they notice and report a violation of some sort?
- How is the employees' personal information handled on collaboration platforms?
- If an employee contributes an idea that is implemented, is he or she rewarded? Who gets credit for the idea?
- When different types of issues arise, who should be contacted? An example would be a legal issue versus a rude comment or the leaking of private information.
- What are the core values and/or behaviors that you want employees to show?
- Is it important for employees to be themselves and let their personalities come through in the ways in which they interact?

Chances are that your organization already has a set of business conduct guidelines that employees are expected to follow. Creating emergent collaboration guidelines can fit in nicely with them. These guidelines don't need to be epic sagas; in fact, you can fit them neatly into around one to three pages. If you're starting to go beyond that, then perhaps you are trying to be too controlling; don't be scared to pull back a little bit. Remember that you have to trust your employees if you want them to trust you.

Best Practices (or Policies)

These are very valuable pieces of content that you should share with the employees to help them get the most out of the emergent collaboration initiative. Best practices are typically created on a regular basis whenever a best practice arises that needs to be shared. For example, a best practice might be "Instead of e-mailing a group of people information about a project and creating a long e-mail thread, why not create a shared wiki or private workspace where you and your team collaborate and share ideas?" Then show employees how to make this happen with either posted video walk-throughs or documents with screen shots. Another common best practice can be "Instead of sending out mass e-mails trying to find a particular team member, try utilizing the rich profile directory to find the person you are looking for. You can search by tags, location, first/last name, or job title or function. This helps save time and simplifies your work." This can be accompanied by clear instructions on how to do it.

You can create a "home" on your emergent collaboration platform where all these best practices and guidelines can live, and you can organize them in any way you wish. What's great about utilizing emergent collaboration to distribute the guidelines is that employees can comment, update, or contribute additional ideas or best practices of their own, transforming this into an evolving and active repository of best practices for the organization.

The best way to get started on creating best practices is by observing where you can see the largest areas of improvement or by noticing where large groups of employees are having trouble. It's exciting and rewarding to create something that you know will benefit the rest of the organization.

Keep in mind that governance at your organization will continue to change and evolve, so you don't need to figure everything out on day one. Start by building a foundation and tackling the questions that you know and need the answers to at the beginning. The rest will continue to build as you learn and understand more about how collaboration works within and impacts your organization.

Summary and Action Items

There are three ways to approach governance within organizations: structured, unstructured, and a combination of both. A combination of the structured and unstructured approaches yields the highest level of engagement. Best practices are essential for making sure that new and existing employees are trained and educated on the best ways to leverage emergent collaboration platforms. Policies and guidelines are more formal recommendations and suggestions for how employees can leverage these emergent platforms and are also crucial to have. Consider taking these steps:

- Explore what governance means to your organization.
- What type of governance model is your organization choosing to go with and why?
- Identify topical areas where immediate best practices can be created and shared.
- What policies and guidelines do you want employees to adhere to or follow?

To learn more about governance in organizations, I asked Abha Kumar, principal, Vanguard, and Eric Ziegler, senior manager, Vanguard, to share their insights and learnings. They have thought through and developed a comprehensive governance framework that many companies can learn from. Vanguard is an investment management company, and so it is in a heavily regulated industry.

Vanguard, headquartered in Valley Forge, Pennsylvania, is the largest fund company based in the United States. Financial services organizations are highly regulated, and Vanguard is very security-conscious, describing security as a top commitment to its clients. Although these two factors can present challenges to Enterprise 2.0 (E2.0) initiatives, Vanguard has been successful at implementing the E2.0 agenda while simultaneously honoring its security and regulatory commitments to its clients. A key component of this success has been the alignment of the E2.0 program to the business, ensuring the success of the program.

At Vanguard the E2.0 program is far-reaching. To help focus its efforts, the program has been divided into three pillars: mobility, enriching communication, and collaboration. The goal of the mobility pillar is to provide parity of access to Vanguard systems from any device, from anywhere, at any time, while maintaining a highly secure environment. The second pillar, enriching communication, enables the Crew (what employees at Vanguard are referred to) to communicate with one another in real time by using rich audio and video capabilities that diminish distance barriers. Enriching communication also includes self-provisioning tools that allow the Crew to create multimedia communication and training materials. The third pillar, collaboration, creates an environment where the Crew can easily collaborate in real time and offline. Collaboration reduces the hurdles of distance and allows the Crew to search easily for answers to questions, collaborate with an expert, and be productive and engaged. Although each pillar provides unique capabilities, the pillars overlap, creating opportunities for integration. By integrating the capabilities, Vanguard is attempting to provide a cohesive solution for Crew engagement across the pillars that are intuitive and easy to use by the Crew.

Governance

E2.0 governance at Vanguard is multifaceted and flexible. It spans the enterprise, with direction, control, implementation, and feedback coming from a cross section of senior executives at Vanguard who represent the entire organization. The E2.0 program has instituted a distributed implementation model, allowing groups to implement relevant parts of the E2.0 agenda at the local level. The local groups can make many decisions surrounding implementation and direction to meet their specific needs while following the enterprisewide governance directives.

Enterprisewide Governance

Figure 11.3 represents the E2.0 governance structure at the enterprise level. At the center of the E2.0 governance model is

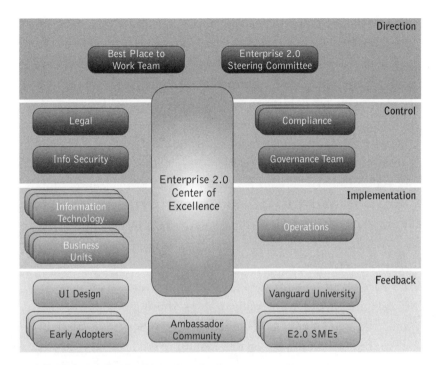

Figure 11.3 Vanguard governance framework

the E2.0 Center of Excellence. This consists of members from business and IT and is responsible for implementing solutions that meet the strategic goals of the entire enterprise.

Direction

The E2.0 Center of Excellence receives direction from two sources: the E2.0 business sponsor, the Best Place to Work Team, which is part of the office of culture and diversity in the human resources division, and the Enterprise 2.0 steering committee represented by senior executives from each of the company's divisions.

Control

In the diagram, control organizations at Vanguard (i.e., security, legal, and compliance) provide direction to the E2.0 Center of

Excellence by defining the guidelines and rules that must be followed as defined by regulatory agencies and Vanguard's security program. The E2.0 Center of Excellence team receives input from the legal, information security, and compliance departments on guidelines for implementing a wide variety of E2.0 technologies. At Vanguard there are several IT governance teams that provide direction and guidance to development teams throughout the organization. These teams provide guidance and direction to development teams on how to develop new code, bring in new products, operationally implement technology, and integrate applications into other enterprise applications.

Implementation

As part of the enterprisewide governance, the E2.0 Center of Excellence works with many groups throughout the organization to implement E2.0 technologies at Vanguard. It starts by ensuring that there is sound direction from the business sponsor and solicits input from a variety of business units. This is accomplished by gathering requirements, understanding how the Crew do their jobs (business processes), and making recommendations on technologies that could improve their existing business processes. In this way the E2.0 team plays a consultancy role as much as it operates as an implementation team for some projects.

When the E2.0 Center of Excellence team implements a new technology, it partners with systems integration (SI) teams throughout the enterprise to integrate it into the existing business processes. The team coordinates with both SI and business to ensure a smooth transition from the original business process to a new business process. Part of the transition includes ensuring that the teams using the E2.0 technologies adhere to the enterprisewide governance directives.

As an example, the E2.0 Center of Excellence works closely with teams that use the E2.0 collaboration platform. For every collaboration site created, a local implementation team for the site is defined. Owners and officer sponsors are identified for each site. If the site contains regulated data, a licensed officer is also identified. The owner and the sponsoring officer are responsible for ensuring that (1) the content of their site adheres to its security classification, (2) regulatory-based content is placed in the correct sites, and (3) the content of the site follows the field of use and complies with Vanguard's defined policies.

Feedback

The E2.0 Center of Excellence receives feedback from a variety of sources. These groups continuously help the team understand the needs of the enterprise through usability testing and gathering feedback from training courses. The E2.0 Center of Excellence identifies early adopters, allowing them to beta test and participate in pilots of new technology. The goal is to ensure user acceptance, gather early feedback, and make improvements before the technology is rolled out to the entire enterprise. Frequently adopters become ambassadors who promote the new technologies. The ambassadors gather feedback and provide input into future enhancements and business process improvements enabled by E2.0 tools. The E2.0 SMEs (subject matter experts) are Crew members who obtain a deep understanding of the technology and provide feedback based on their interactions with Crew members who are just learning the new technologies.

Summary

Combining enterprisewide governance with locally distributed implementations affords Vanguard the ability to scale E2.0 beyond a small implementation to the entire enterprise. Direction, control, implementation, and feedback are centrally managed by the E2.0 Center of Excellence, and the local implementation teams have the autonomy to make decisions. The governance structure enables Vanguard to adhere to strict regulations and security policies while maintaining flexibility.

part three

THE END GAME

twelve

Measures
of Success

I want to make it clear that there is no ROI formula for collaboration or for deploying emergent collaboration platforms. There also isn't a set of simple steps you can follow that will lead you to some sort of ROI number. It's ironic, but none of the companies I have worked with or researched have been able to predict the ROI or the value that their emergent collaboration deployments would bring. Yet every one of those companies has stated that it has seen enough value to justify the investment (this is not to say that this is true for every company).

Emergent collaboration solutions are simply pieces of technology that enable employees to do something. The ROI or value doesn't come from the actual platform or the technology but from the use of that platform by the employees. Investing in these solutions is not like investing in a stock that will go up or down regardless of what you do. Emergent collaboration ROI or value comes from activity, not from purchase.

When you step back to think about this ROI or value, it's really coming from collaboration. These emergent technologies are just new ways to do something we have been doing for many, many years.

The value of deploying an emergent collaboration platform and strategy can be seen in two ways: anecdotal (or soft benefits) and financial (hard benefits). Let's start the discussion by looking at both types of value.

Soft Benefits

The soft benefits of emergent collaboration can vary quite a bit from company to company. These are some of the soft benefits I have seen.

Company Morale Improvement

Employees who are a part of an organization that is doing something innovative and different (deploying emergent collaboration solutions) usually get excited and invigorated about their work and their company. Many employees at the companies I have been working with and researching have grown tired of and irritated with stale technologies and inefficient ways of working. In addition to being able to solve business problems, emergent collaboration technologies tend to pump up the workforce, especially when the value of the tools and strategies is communicated as an employee benefit.

Speed of Access to Information and to People

Virtually every company I have worked with and researched to date has reported that its employees are able to access information and find subject matter experts faster than they could before these tools were deployed. Most companies don't have a quantifiable number in terms of how much time was saved or how this translated into an actual dollar amount; that is why this is listed as a soft and not a hard benefit.

Improved Communication and Collaboration

Virtually every company has reported that its ability to communicate and collaborate has improved. Employees who have never met and even those who have met are more actively sharing ideas and insights and departments are sharing information with one another.

Insight into the Organization (Alignment)

Several executives have told me that as a result of deploying emergent collaboration technologies, they now have much greater insights into what is happening at their organizations and how it's happening. The same is true for midlevel managers and entry-level employees who are trying to get a greater sense of clarity about how what they do affects others and what the company is working on. The company as a whole is able to stay on the same page.

Agility of the Organization

Agility in this case is synonymous with adaptability and ability to change. As a whole the organization is able to do things such as identify new opportunities and risks more quickly (and act on them), prioritize projects and budget allocation, and stay on top of the competition. In short, these tools allow organizations to respond to changes effectively and efficiently.

Learning Among Employees

As employees gain insight into how their colleagues and other departments are working and getting things done, they learn new things and processes. This can range from how to stay productive, to how to develop a strategy for a new product, to where to access or find something. Constantly being able to learn new things is a key motivator for many employees to stay at their companies.

Innovation

Employees are able to identify new opportunities or come up with new and unique ideas to solve problems that the organization is faced with. Intuit is a great example of a company that uses collaboration to come up with new product ideas for its customers. When employees can connect with each other and collaborate, it helps spur creativity and innovation.

Improve Quality of Life

I'm not just talking about the life of employees at the workplace, I'm talking about their overall well being. Collaboration in the workplace means that employees feel a greater sense of purpose and fulfillment with the work they are doing and they feel more inspired to go to work each day. Since it becomes easier for employees to do their jobs and to access information, they can now have more time to spend with their families and therefore reduce the amount of stress they bring home with them from work each day.

Positive Company Perception

Organizations that deploy these tools and strategies are often perceived as being innovative, which reflects positively on them in the opinion of their clients, partners, prospects, and employees, along with the general media. Competitors feel threatened, and the overall perception of the company is more positive and innovative.

I'm sure you can identify several other soft benefits of emergent collaboration in your organization as this is by no means an exhaustive list. Let's take a look at some of the hard benefits.

Hard Benefits

Let's start by looking at the value of collaboration through several pieces of research that have been conducted over the last few years. Frost & Sullivan released two reports that address this issue. The first report was conducted in 2006 and included the responses from 946 decision makers in enterprises in Europe, Asia, and the United States. Figure 12.1 sums up the findings.

Frost & Sullivan compared the impact of collaboration (collaboration index) with both strategy orientation and market turbulence. These three factors were then measured against the variables seen on the x axis. In every single area collaboration has the greatest business impact. However, what I think speaks volumes is the section titled "Overall Performance." According to this research, collaboration has a 36 percent impact on overall business performance.

The second report, which was released in 2009, compares business performance among basic, intermediate, and advanced collaborators.

Figure 12.2 shows that the more advanced an organization is when it comes to collaboration, the greater is the business impact of that collaboration on various business units. I want to point out that neither of these tools was specific to emergent collaboration platforms.

McKinsey, one of the top management consulting companies in the world, also released a study on the impact of using emergent tools in organizations called "How social technologies are extending the organization." This comparison was done to show the impact of these

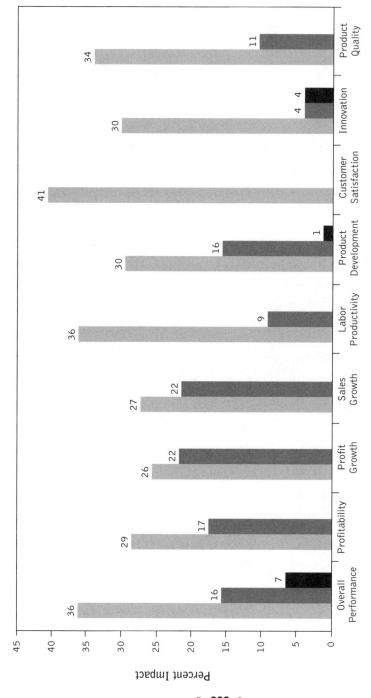

Figure 12.1 The relative impact of collaboration on business performance

Source: Brian Cotton, "Meetings Around the World: The Impact of Collaboration on Business Performance," Frost & Sullivan, June 2006.

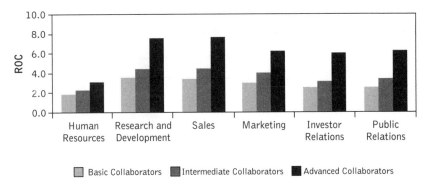

Basic Collaborators | Intermediate Collaborators | Advanced Collaborators

Figure 12.2 Deployment of collaboration and business-critical processes

Source: Brian Cotton, "Meetings Around the World II: Charting the Course of Advanced Collaboration," Frost & Sullivan, October 2009.

tools on customers, employees, and partners. Figure 12.3 shows the responses from the participants. The section that is most relevant to us are "Internal Purposes."

We can see that there has been a strong business impact in all three areas, but let's take a look at the first column. Notice that both hard and soft benefits are seen here.

Percent of respondents reporting at least one measurable benefit at their companies

Top three measurable benefits of technology adoption, by use

Internal Purposes[1]		Customer Purposes[2]		Partners, suppliers, and external-expert purposes[3]	
Increasing speed to access knowledge	74 77 69	Increasing effectiveness of marketing	69 63 54	Increasing speed to access knowledge	65 57 53
Reducing communication costs	58 60 56	Increasing customer satisfaction	47 50 44	Reducing communication costs	61 53 50
Increasing speed to access internal experts	51 52 44	Reducing marketing costs	43 45 39	Increasing speed to access external experts	50 40 43

[1] In 2011, n = 1,949; in 2010, n = 1,598; in 2009, n = 1,008.
[2] In 2011, n = 2,227; in 2010, n = 1,708; in 2009, n = 956.
[3] In 2011, n = 1,142; in 2010, n = 1,008; in 2009, n = 686.

■ 2011
■ 2010
■ 2009

Figure 12.3 Benefits remain consistent over time

Source: Exhibit from "How social technologies are extending the organization," *McKinsey Quarterly*, www.mckinseyquarterly.com, November 2011. Copyright (c) McKinsey & Company. All rights reserved. Reprinted by permission.

In 2011 Deloitte released a report titled "Social Software for Business Performance" in which it showcased two companies that deployed emergent collaboration tools and the impact it had on their business. The first example is from Alcoa, which is one of the world's leading producers of aluminum and has around 60,000 employees globally. Alcoa deployed wikis to its IT group, which consisted of 305 employees, through Traction Software. The impact can be seen in Figure 12.4.

Here we can clearly see that the number of monthly compliance hours was significantly reduced after the wikis were deployed at Alcoa.

The second example is just as telling. OSIsoft is a global company with over 500 employees that develops enterprise architecture software. OSIsoft deployed wikis via a platform called Socialtext and as a result (see Figure 12.5) saw a 22 percent decrease in issue resolution time (improvement in call center productivity). Chapter 3 of this book contains several other case studies of companies that have deployed emergent collaboration technologies and strategies and the results they have gotten.

Clearly, a financial ROI does exist and companies are reporting that they are experiencing it. However, I want to stress again that the ROI does not come from the technology but from the use of the technology and that activity that happens across the platforms. Simply deploying a wiki will do absolutely nothing.

I think that when it comes to ROI, we are asking the wrong questions. My favorite question to ask organizations interested in emergent collaboration is, Is solving a business problem or achieving an objective as good as being able to show a financial ROI? Think about that for a moment before you answer. For example, let's say you wanted to improve communication at your organization, wanted to get more insight into what is happening at the ground level of your organization, or sought to improve company morale. If you were able to achieve any of these things but couldn't show a financial ROI at the end, would it be worthwhile? What if you are looking to improve your rate of innovation or make it easier for employees to get their jobs done. Would achieving those things be good enough?

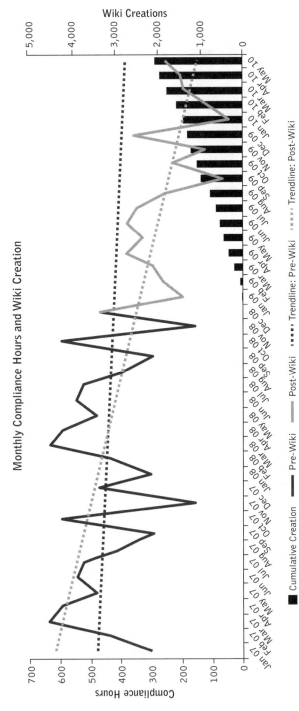

Figure 12.4 Benefits of emergent collaboration at Alcoa

Source: Deloitte LLP, "Social Software for Business Peformance," 2011

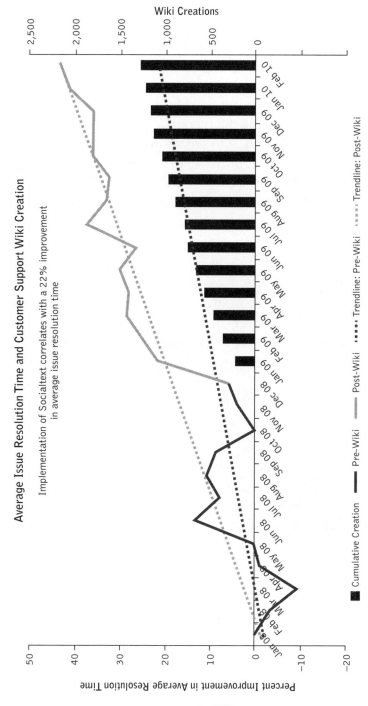

Figure 12.5 Benefits of emergent collaboration at OSIsoft

Source: Deloitte LLP, "Social Software for Business Peformance," 2011

According to the majority of the people the Chess Media Group surveyed, the answer is a resounding yes. In fact, 73 percent of the respondents said that solving a business problem or achieving an objective is as good as being able to show a financial ROI. Only 9 percent said that this wasn't good enough (Figure 12.6).

It amazed us to see that 73 percent of the respondents believed that solving a business problem or achieving an objective is as good as being able to show a financial ROI. After we saw these results, we decided to break things down further by looking at how this compares with seniority at the organization (see Figure 12.7).

This figure reveals a couple of interesting things. The first thing to notice is that C-level executive employees are the group that most frequently answered yes to the question "Is solving a business problem or achieving an objective as good as being able to show a financial ROI?" The second thing to notice is that midlevel business employees were the largest group that said no. Senior-level business managers were by far the largest group to answer "don't know." Looking at these three findings together paints a bit of a "spectrum" picture going from "no"

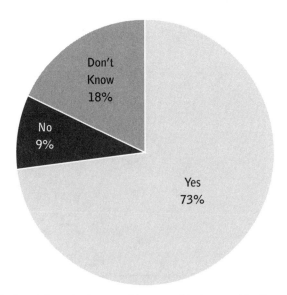

Figure 12.6 Is solving a business problem or achieving an objective as good as being able to show a financial ROI?

Figure 12.7 Is solving a business problem or achieving an objective as good as being able to show a financial ROI? (Breakdown by role within the organizaton)

to "don't know" to "yes." The farther down the organization we go in seniority (for business-level employees), the more likely the response is to be "no." Clearly, we see a bit of a misalignment here, which could be the result of poor communication. If a C-level executive believes that solving a business problem or achieving an objective is as good as being able to show a financial ROI, that needs to be conveyed and communicated to less-senior employees.

When I saw the results, the first thing that came to my mind was, "Wait a minute. If such high numbers of people say that solving a business problem or achieving an objective is as good as showing a financial ROI, why is this whole ROI debate even happening and why are organizations using lack of ROI as a reason not to invest?"

The answer to that question is that organizations are often not able to show that they are achieving an objective or solving a business problem. Basically, what is going on is that many organizations are deploying the tools without understanding why they are deploying them. This lack of understanding makes it virtually impossible to tie the emergent collaboration technology and strategy to a financial ROI, a business objective, or the ability to solve a problem.

Take a look at Figure 12.8 for a shocking and telling picture of what is happening.

Only one of four organizations is defining any performance indicators that can be used to measure success or progress of any kind. The majority of companies did not define any type of performance

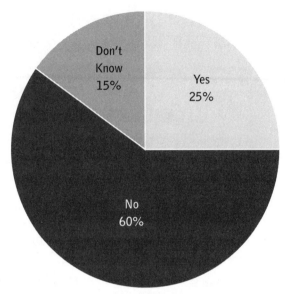

Figure 12.8   Did you define performance indicators before you began your E2.0 initiatives?

indicators, meaning they are embarking on an emergent collaboration journey without a compass. There has to be a way to measure or gauge success or progress. Whether it is anecdotal or data driven is up to you (in fact, a combination of both is probably most effective); the point is that it needs to exist.

As a follow-up to this question we asked respondents who answered yes to the question about defining performance indicators how close they were to achieving their performance indicators. The results, as shown in Figure 12.9, were just as shocking.

Forty-eight percent of the people who responded to this question stated that they don't know how close they are to achieving their performance indicators. Thus, we have double trouble. Few organizations are defining performance indicators, and those which are defining them appear not to be doing a good job of following up and checking on how they are doing. Basically, they define the indicators and then let them sit. I don't think I need to say that this is far from an effective way to gauge or measure success or progress. In fact, there

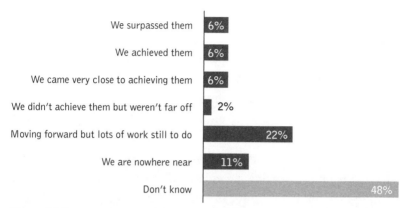

Figure 12.9 Generally speaking, how close are you to achieving your performance indicators?

is no way that organizations in this situation can understand what impact emergent collaboration is having on their organizations, let alone the value it brings.

Setting up these performance indicators doesn't have to be difficult or complex. Here are a few basic examples of both hard and soft metrics that organizations use:

- Improvement in communication measured by quarterly surveys
- Onboarding time for new employees
- Executive insight into the organization
- Activity on the platforms (comments, ideas shared, groups created, etc.)
- Decrease in e-mail use
- Improvement in rate of innovation
- Improvement in company morale
- Improvement in ease of finding people and information
- Decreased travel costs

These are just a few examples of things organizations can use as a starting point. Some organizations also include groups created, ideas shared, comments contributed, and other engagement metrics that show employee use.

The point isn't to tell you what you should be measuring or looking at, but to tell you that you should be looking at the things that are relevant to you, whatever those things may be.

Where does this leave us with the question about the ROI of emergent collaboration? When I have to address this, my answer is quite simple: "It's part of the sauce." Emergent collaboration (in fact, any type of collaboration) is one of several ingredients that come together to make something happen. For example, let's say I was working on developing a marketing plan for product X. As a part of the marketing plan development I used a wiki for my team to collaborate, a project workspace for it to share thoughts and ideas, and the rich profiles of employees to find the right subject matter experts to collaborate on this project. We research the competition, segment our customers, choose all the relevant channels for the team, and do everything else we need to do to develop a successful marketing plan (which anyone who has developed a marketing plan knows is quite a lot of work).

Would the marketing plan not have come together without the use of the emergent collaboration platform? Doubtful. The ability to collaborate with my team is a part of the sauce that allowed us to complete the marketing plan, so how do you extract the value or the ROI from one ingredient? Some people try to match inputs to outcomes, which is fair enough, but even that can require its own set of resources while not providing the full picture of how emergent collaboration is affecting the organization.

Georgette Parsons is the CIO of MEC, an outdoor sporting goods and gear co-op retailer based in Vancouver. MEC has over 1,500 employees and deployed an emergent collaboration platform known as ThoughtFamer. In discussing the business impact Parsons stated:

> I'd like to think it has generated increased productivity, reduced waste, possibly improved user service. I think it has. The question is, how to tangibly measure that—and by the way, as a medium-size business, is it really worth our time trying to measure it?

The previous examples and the case studies in this book have clearly shown that organizations have seen cost reduction and revenue generation opportunities. Ben Haines, the CIO of Pabst Brewing Company, saw a reduction in spending on servers and hardware (if you recall from Chapter 8, they switched from SharePoint to Box). Perhaps more important is the fact that the IT team at Pabst has been able to spend less time on support and more time focusing on projects and innovation ideas to add value to Pabst. We have also explored some of the soft benefits of emergent collaboration. However, all these things fail to paint an accurate picture of the overall impact of these tools and strategies. When employees collaborate by using these emergent tools, that activity permeates everything and anything the company does.

In the book *Strategy Maps: Converting Intangible Assets into Tangible Outcomes*, Bob Kaplan and David Norton note:

> None of these intangible assets has value that can be measured separately or independently. The value of these intangible assets derives from their ability to help the organization implement its strategy. . . . Intangible assets such as knowledge and technology seldom have a direct impact on financial outcomes such as increased revenues, lowered costs, and higher profits. Improvements in intangible assets affect financial outcomes through chains of cause-and-effect relationships.

I completely agree with that sentiment. Trying to get to an ROI number is in my opinion a fruitless and time-consuming task with more questions and rabbit holes than solutions and answers. The ROI formula can be written as follows:

$$\frac{\text{Gain from investment} - \text{cost of investment}}{\text{cost of investment}}$$

Typically, this formula is used in situations in which there is an end date such as selling a stock, selling a piece of property, or concluding a sales campaign. Emergent collaboration has no end date: It is not sold, and it does not expire. I want to reiterate that I'm not suggesting that organizations abandon trying to understand the value or impact of emergent collaboration on the enterprise. I'm suggesting the opposite, that organizations not limit themselves by focusing on ROI, which many organizations will never be able to prove. In fact, ask yourself and your team this question: If you knew for a fact that your organization would never see a single penny made or saved as a result of emergent collaboration but you knew you were solving problems and enabling and empowering your employees, would you still make the investment? Most of the time when I ask this question, I get back a resounding yes.

What are some of the metrics that companies are using? They include:

- Ideas generated/submitted
- Comments
- Number of employees actively using the platform
- Money saved (for example, on hardware, software, travel costs, and so on)
- Revenue generated (for example, with new ideas that employees come up with that are implemented and result in more money made)
- Time saved by using these new tools
- Employee satisfaction
- Groups created
- Decrease in e-mail
- Improved productivity

The list can go on and on. There are many metrics an organization can use, but the important metrics to measure are the ones that tie back to the objectives the organization has defined. I'm personally not a fan of focusing on "busy metrics" because they don't really say much; they simply look at activity. Some organizations typically define an "engaged" employee as someone who participated in these various platforms, which is a backward way of looking at this. Employees may use these new tools because they have to, not because they want to.

Instead, I prefer to look at it as it's the engaged employee who uses the tools and not the tools that make the employee engaged. Tools have been and will always be just that, tools.

Gallup, for example, asks 12 questions when seeking to understand engagement:

- Do I know what is expected of me at work?
- Do I have the materials and equipment I need to do my work right?
- At work, do I have the opportunity to do what I do best every day?
- In the last seven days, have I received recognition or praise for doing good work?
- Does my supervisor or someone at work seem to care about me as a person?
- Is there someone at work who encourages my development?
- At work, do my opinions seem to count?
- Does the mission and purpose of my company make me feel that my job is important?
- Are my coworkers committed to doing quality work?
- Do I have a best friend at work?
- In the last six months, has someone at work talked to me about my progress?
- This past year, have I had opportunities at work to learn and grow?

Having said all this, if I had to pick just one metric to measure, what would it be? I've given this a lot of thought and debated about focusing on engagement, productivity, time saved, and a host of other metrics. However, I don't think any of these are really as important as company morale or "engagement" (as in how connected or fulfilled employees feel about their jobs and the work they do), or how happy the employees are. Regardless of how you spin emergent collaboration solutions and how great you make them sound, if employees don't feel fulfilled and inspired at work, why should they bother collaborating, sharing, and engaging? In fact, why should they even bother doing any work at all? This doesn't mean that you shouldn't look at other metrics;

in fact, you can measure pretty much anything. However, I believe that engaged, happy, and inspired employees will be the ones who come up with great ideas and the ones who share and collaborate with one another most effectively.

At the end of the day, spending all your time focusing on metrics and trying to predict value is like learning to swim by watching YouTube videos. Sure, the videos will help you a bit and show you what the perfect stroke looks like, but until you actually get in the water, you won't be able to swim. In other words, if you want to see the business value, get involved.

Summary and Action Items

There is no such thing as an ROI formula for emergent collaboration. We are simply talking about pieces of technology; the business value of those technologies comes from use, not from deployment. There are both soft and hard benefits to deploying emergent collaboration technologies and strategies. Several research reports have noted the significant business value that organizations realize as a result of emergent collaboration, yet organizations are not able to predict what this return is going to look like.

Organizations fall into the value paradox situation, meaning that they want to understand the business value of collaboration but don't set up metrics or data points (either anecdotal or numerical) to track and measure progress. Companies that assign metrics don't follow up on them regularly to measure progress. Thus, organizations want to see the business value, yet aren't doing what is necessary to see it. Most people believe that solving a business problem is as good as being able to show a financial ROI. Here are things an organization can do to measure the benefits:

- Go through the list of soft benefits. Which ones are you hoping to see and achieve and what metrics or data points are you going to use to achieve them? How often and how are you going to measure these?

- Do the same thing for the hard benefits.
- Get clarity and alignment on the question of solving a business problem or achieving a financial ROI. What is it that you are trying to do?
- Define and regularly benchmark the metrics you identify.

To learn more about measures of success, let's hear from Joe Johnson, a former global solutions provider and solutions designer for one of the largest companies on the planet, UPS.

An emergent collaboration solution was in progress when I "accidentally" found the value in sharing individual content across the enterprise. I wanted to implement a real-time event notification system at a large customer's request. The idea was shot down because the needed skills were not available and the cost was projected to be too high. Because the project management systems were being merged, I searched for and found an employee who had developed a working example of the technology. The major objection was removed, and the solution moved into production without delay or great cost. There is no fancy measure of the ROI here, but the customer was happy and a small cross-division team cranked out the application at a very low cost.

Platforms that make it simple for several experts to solve a problem in real time from anywhere in the world can pay for themselves the first time they are used. It is not just the travel time and expense saved. Nothing can replace the ability to have several experts on the scene collaborating to solve a problem in a matter of minutes or to have a recording of a problem available for analysis by people who may have been sleeping in a different time zone when the problem occurred. That type of collaboration is measured in problems solved and satisfied, if not amazed, customers. Soon after we had these tools, we began to use them for projects that would have been much too costly to consider without them.

Not everybody adapts to the use of collaboration solutions. That is not a problem. In my opinion, it is a fact of life. My point is that small groups of highly motivated employees who adopt collaboration solutions can provide more than enough return to cover the investment.

Deploying and helping manage emergent collaboration at UPS taught me several things when it comes to ROI:

- Measure ROI in terms of problems solved using collaboration tools. Upper management rewards those who solve problems.
- Collaboration is a game changer. When employees experience a positive collaboration experience, they feel they can accomplish more and they do.
- Individuals benefit from collaboration and feel more a part of the larger organization. In a global company the potential for unexpected benefits is very high.

An understanding of emergent collaboration greatly helps the ROI discussions with executives. When they hear that business problems get solved, they are quick to get onboard regardless of the financial numbers that are shown.

---

thirteen

Sustaining

Over the last few years several enterprise collaboration initiatives have been touted as being successful. However, a few years later those successes were being called failures. Why? Because adoption rates of deployed enterprise collaboration tools have begun to plummet. A few months ago I had a conversation with an executive who told me that his company's adoption rates have traditionally been over 80 percent but that now adoption is somewhere in the range of 20 percent. The executive had no idea why this was happening.

I believe that sustaining these initiatives is the hardest part. Once organizations make the investment and see adoption rates climb over a few years, how do they keep the momentum going for 2 more years, 5 more years, or 10 more years? How can this be sustained when there are organizational changes, new employees leaving and old employees joining, and other changes?

There are a few key things that every executive and decision maker should consider in regard to the longevity of enterprise collaboration initiatives.

Playfulness

This is a concept I first heard about from Euan Semple, and it makes a lot of sense. If using emergent tools and technologies is dry, not stimulating, and not fun for employees, why would they bother using it? There has to be a certain amount of enjoyment and playfulness baked into these solutions. We have seen this already with various technology solutions awarding badges or points for active participation. Those who are most active and collaborative are usually featured on some sort of a leader board and are recognized among the employees. Playfulness can also be subtle with simple features that allow employees to "like" something or vote something up or down. Most platforms today have "gamification" concepts built in. However, this looks at playfulness from the standpoint of the technology.

Playfulness also needs to be embedded in the culture. For example, there is nothing wrong with employees sharing occasional interesting links or fun videos with their coworkers. This gives employees the freedom to communicate and share with one another. If employees are allowed to post only business-related content, things can become stale rather quickly. Human beings inherently want to connect with one another, and that isn't always done via a status report or a strategy document. Give your employees the freedom they need to maintain playfulness. I'm sure if you examine the e-mails that employees send one another, you will find plenty of jokes, videos, bantering, and other non-work-related content.

Incorporating Feedback Regularly

Employees usually have regular feedback that they can provide in regard to what they would like to see in the platform or what the next updates and upgrades should be. Incorporating user feedback into the design and applications of whatever solution you select is paramount. The challenge here is to maintain the expectations of the employees. For example, a large consulting organization was implementing employee feedback every few weeks. Over time this slowed down, and eventually the voice of the employee was no longer being listened to. Employees stopped using the platform, and adoption rates plummeted after reaching a high of over 75 percent. Not only do organizations want to incorporate feedback regularly, they also want to manage employee expectations and be consistent. Remember that these tools and strategies are put in place for the employees, so let them have a say in how the platform looks, what it does, and how it's done.

Conveying Individual as Well as Corporate Value

If I were your boss and came over to you and said, "Hey, we are going to start using a collaboration platform that will help the company make more money; you should use it. And by the way, I'm going to need those TPS reports done by the end of the day (*Office Space*, anyone?)," you probably would be indifferent. However, what if I came to you and said, "We want to really help make the lives of our employees easier. One of the things we heard from employees is that it takes too long to find information. This new platform we are going to deploy will help solve problems such as that and many others. I'd really appreciate it if you could test it out and let me know what you think"? All of a sudden the focus is on the employee and how it can benefit him or her. I would recommend focusing the conversation and positioning on the value to the employees, not on features or corporate value, as the primary reason for use.

Training and Educating New and Existing Employees

I remember a conversation I had with an executive at a large event management company who told me that the annual turnover rate was 100 to 200 percent. Yes, you read that correctly. This is perhaps an extreme case, but the question still arises, What do you do? Training and education need to be a staple of the employee onboarding diet. New employees need to be trained and shown how to use the new tools and technologies the organization is deploying; this should become a part of their day-to-day work. Existing employees need to be encouraged and educated continuously on the value of these collaboration solutions and how and why to use them. I have seen organizations get very creative with this, using everything from road shows to all regional offices, to declaring a mandate that all communication must now be done via a new platform, to developing scavenger hunts in the collaboration tools to help employees get accustomed to using them. The point is that these education and training programs for new and existing employees need to exist and need to be formalized.

Evangelists Within the Organization

The best way to think of evangelists is as employees who are passionate about people and the use of social and collaborative tools. Typically, these employees are already active on social sites such as Twitter and Facebook, and they are probably already helping some of their colleagues by answering questions about these social sites. Evangelists love helping others understand how to use these tools and are usually the go-to employees for questions.

I have yet to find an organization that does not have a group of evangelists or champions to educate and encourage people. Evangelists are not always the people you would expect them to be. In fact, an evangelist can be anyone who is passionate about using emergent collaborative tools in an organization. It's not hard to find evangelists; a good way to start is by looking at who in the organization is active on social networks. Did someone try to start a company Facebook or Twitter account? One of the clients I worked with had someone from the video department become the company's greatest evangelist. Don't limit this role to someone in the marketing, communications, or PR department, as the role of an evangelist has nothing to do with an employee's job title.

Continuous Executive Support

In the interview I conducted with Andrew McAfee (see Chapter 16), he stated that one of the key predictors of success for these initiatives is the support of the executive team. He meant that if the executives are not actively using these tools and supporting them, the chances of failure are high. This doesn't mean temporary support. Being involved for a few months to help with adoption and dropping off the grid is not going to do much good. This needs to be a long-term commitment from the executive team.

This Should Be Part of the Way Employees Work

One of the crucial things organizations need to remember is that these tools and platforms have to become part of the way employees work. Simply deploying something as an addition to what employees are already doing is ineffective. New platforms should replace something that already exists and/or integrate with other systems. If employees have a process that takes four steps, whatever you deploy should take four steps or less. The key here is to make this a standard for how employees can get their jobs done without impeding what they currently do. It should make their jobs and their lives easier. If it does not, you're in trouble.

Continuous Evolution and Iteration

It's important to stay relevant and current. You can expect that whatever tools or platforms you deploy today are going to evolve and change in the future. It's important that your organization evolve its practices and technology stack to keep pace with other companies and the changing world. This doesn't mean that your company should follow technology, but it does mean that you should continuously be looking to improve based on the business requirements and the needs of your organization. Iteration and evolution is a continuous, never-ending process. When you stop evolving, you die.

Establish a Team of Practice

This can be a person, a team, or a department, but you want to make sure that within your organization someone is keeping a pulse on what is happening within the organization and in the world of collaboration. Employees will always have questions, new challenges will always arise, and things will keep changing; there needs to be someone (or more likely a team) within your company that keeps collaboration initiatives moving in the right direction.

Summary and Action Items

Sustaining emergent collaboration can be as hard as, if not harder than, gaining the initial adoption. To sustain adoption there are many things organizations can do, such as making sure emergent collaboration platforms fit into the way employees naturally work, developing training and education programs for new and existing employees, and consistently integrating employee feedback and ideas into the platform. Organizations that set employee expectations and then mismanage them will not do well. In other words, if you tell your employees you are going to integrate their feedback and ideas into emergent collaboration regularly and then stop doing that, your adoption rates will sink. Here are a few suggestions:

- Go through the list of ideas to help sustain adoption. Which of these ideas are you planning to utilize?
- Do you have other ideas that are not listed here?
- Commit to these ideas and develop regular checks with yourself and your team to make sure you are following up with your commitments.

Euan Semple spent the last 6 years of his 25-year career at BBC, where he was the director of knowledge management solutions. During his time with the BBC, Euan learned some very valuable lessons that he agreed to share with the readers of this book.

Sustaining 2.0

Getting social platforms accepted and working in corporate environments is hard enough, but how do you keep them going once you have them? How do you make it more likely that they will survive and flourish rather than wither and die? One of the things

I was most proud of about the social spaces we developed inside the BBC was that they survived our departure despite the fact that when we left, no one took particular ownership of them. The following are suggestions based on what I believe we got right:

1. Make your spaces unashamedly social. That is the glue that will hold them together and give them longevity. There is nothing wrong or new in being sociable at work, and it is the ability to establish relationships that enables us all to get things done. The better your environment allows people to do this, the longer it will last. If it has strong social ties between the participants and a frequent and robust exchange between them, you will have a sustainable solution that should outlast you.

2. Rather than putting all your eggs in one basket and buying a whole social platform from a single vendor, buy a lot of small but perfectly formed tools and start building them into an ecology. Don't overdo the structure either; make it easy for people to link from one tool to the other but don't overengineer the connections. What you think is a sensible structure may be bewildering to the users. Allow them to work out what relates to what and why. Once you have a clearer idea of the topography of your spaces, you can start to signpost them better and reinforce the bits that are working.

3. Use your blog to talk about managing the environment in which it sits. Blog about the challenges and the successes. Blog about the things you are not sure about and blog about the things you are grappling with. Use your forums to ask questions about the use you are putting the tool to and ask if this is what people want, what they want to change, and how they think you should run the tool. Keep pushing debates about the tools back into the tools themselves. Use the tools to develop and record your processes, policies, and guidelines.

4. Make it an ideal that as many issues as possible are dealt by the users in the tool itself. Involve as many people as possible in running the online environment. You should aim to have as many sectors as possible of your business using it anyway, but make sure the more formal governance of it reflects this variety. The more of a sense of shared ownership you can cultivate, the more smoothly things will run. Have a way of dealing with issues and a clear way of escalating problems if necessary.

5. Be patient. Be patient when people don't join your system fast enough. Be patient when people don't learn as quickly as you expect. Be patient when people get things wrong. Be patient with yourself when you make mistakes.

6. *Culture* is a slippery word that gets used in all sorts of ways, but you should be trying to cultivate a robust and appropriate culture in your online spaces. Establish norms of behavior and shared values. Encourage tolerance and a willingness to work together to create supportive environments. Foster relationships and bonds that shape the culture and help sustain it.

7. Be prepared to be edgy. Allow people to talk about things they can't talk about elsewhere. This will make your online space attractive. Why would people bother to use it if all it did was mirror the conversations they can already have elsewhere? You probably want to stop short of courting gossip and scandal, but sailing as close to the wind as you can is a good thing. Lead the way yourself. Be prepared to name as many elephants in as many rooms as possible and wake things up a bit.

If you get these things right, your online environment should be largely self-sustaining. You should have less and less to do with running it as time goes by, and it should be capable of adapting itself to changing circumstances.

fourteen

Putting It
All Together

We have covered many aspects of emergent collaboration, and this chapter is devoted to putting it all together. You can use it as a baseline guide for making your own emergent collaboration journey and modify it as you see fit for your organization.

I've been adamant thus far about conveying a descriptive and not prescriptive approach and will emphasize that again here. I don't expect you to go back to your organization and develop a 200-page strategic document based on the contents of this book; in fact, I encourage you *not* to do that. Instead, I would like you to use the book as a guide for your collaborative journey. Utilize everything you can in this chapter and in the book, adapt it, change it, and make it your own. After all, what works for your company may not work for another company. I'm giving you the Play-Doh, and you should mold it into something you would like to see.

Let's pretend you are working at an organization that is at the very basic stages of emergent collaboration. How can you walk through the content in this book and come out with a successful plan of attack? Table 14.1 will help guide you through answering that question. The first column lists a step you need to take, the second column provides more context and clarity about what that step entails, and the third column tells you which chapter contains information about that step.

Table 14.1 Strategic Plan for Emergent Collaboration

Step	Explanation	Where to Go
Do research	Review information about what emergent collaboration is and why it is important	Chapters 1 and 2
Review case studies	Look at what other organizations are doing; there are plenty of examples	Chapter 3
Develop team	Put together the key members of the emergent collaboration team and their degrees of involvement	Chapter 5
Review benefits	Review the unique benefits of emergent collaboration and identify which ones are relevant to you	Chapter 2
Understand business drivers	Explore why emergent collaboration is an area of interest for your organization	Chapter 2
Evaluate risks	Walk through the risk assessment framework to prioritize and mitigate the risks	Chapter 4
Develop use cases	Walk through the solution mapping process for your use cases	Chapter 2
Assign performance indicators	Determine how you are going to measure success and/or progress; this can be quantitative or qualitative or both	Chapters 10 and 12
Determine relevant vendor category	Determine what type of emergent collaboration solution makes the most sense for your organization and why	Chapter 6
Prioritize vendors' competitive variables and assign scoring	With your team walk through the variables on which vendors compete and prioritize the variables and assign weights to them	Chapter 6
Walk through vendor scoring	Once you have a list of vendors, walk through the scoring and compare the results to decide on a vendor	Chapter 6
Formulate adaptive business framework and maturity model	Make sure you have addressed and discussed the items in the framework; walk through the maturity model to evaluate where your strengths and weaknesses are	Chapter 7
Develop feature roll-out plan	Develop a timeline for when and how you want to roll out various features of the technology	Chapter 8

Determine type of rollout (pilot? if so, what kind? full deployment?)	Decide what type of approach makes the most sense for your company and why; explore the various options and determine the best course of action	Chapter 7
Determine governance	Decide what types of rules, regulations, guidelines, and best practices are going to be encouraged and enforced	Chapter 11
Roll out the platform	Implement the solution	Chapter 9
Review adoption strategies	Examine what other organizations have done and determine what techniques make the most sense for your organization	Chapter 10
Look for resistance	Understand where resistance is coming from and why it is happening; the earlier you can identify it, the better	Chapter 8
Evaluate progress	Analyze what has been done so far; determine whether you are where you want to be	Chapter 12
Sustaining and adapting	Determine what can be done to continue sustaining this initiative at the organization and what changes or adaptations need to take place for continued success; decide what is working and what isn't; explore what the future of collaboration can look like for your company; what's next?	Chapters 7, 13, and 15

A Note on Failure

This has been mentioned before, but it's worth repeating that emergent collaboration is not a short-term initiative. It's a long-term strategic direction for the company, which means that it will take time and that there will be obstacles. However, obstacles are not failures. My favorite example of this came when I saw Chip Heath, the coauthor of *Made to Stick and Switch*, speak at a conference in New York a few years ago. The analogy Chip used was babies learning to walk. When babies first learn to walk, they stumble, but we don't look at them and say, "Well, it looks like walking isn't for you." Instead we encourage them to get back up and try again. The same is true for emergent collaboration. Organizations will stumble along the way, but that doesn't mean they have failed. Obstacles are to be expected; the important thing is to learn from those obstacles and keep moving toward your goals.

Where Organizations Typically Run into Obstacles or Fail (aka Things You Want to Avoid)

No Budget to Sustain Emergent Collaboration

You don't need to spend millions of dollars to make this work, but you need to be realistic about funding an emergent collaboration initiative. Keep in mind that this is ideally a new strategic direction for your organization, and so you're going to get out of it what you put in. If you purchase a technology solution but don't allocate budget to training, marketing, community management, and an emergent collaboration team, chances are that this isn't going to give you the business value you want to see. I don't mean to scare you by saying that everything is going to require a massive budget; it's simply my way of recommending that you think about the various items that will require budget beyond just the technology costs to make this work. I also don't mean to suggest that just because you have a lot of money to spend, you're going to succeed. Sure, budget is important, but the execution and proper implementation of tools and strategy are the crucial factors for success.

Lack of Senior Leadership Support

Andrew McAfee believes that lack of senior leadership support is the single greatest factor that makes or breaks the success of emergent collaboration for an organization. If leaders are not involved, why should employees be?

Poorly Managed Employee Expectations

If emergent collaboration is positioned as something that will solve all the problems in an organization and make everything better, that is what employees are going to expect, and when that doesn't happen, you are going to have a lot of angry employees. Emergent collaboration is supposed to make the lives of employees easier, but it's not a panacea for all the organization's problems. Another thing to note here is employee feedback. Emergent collaboration solutions evolve and adapt, and it's important to integrate employee feedback regularly and continuously.

Owned Entirely by IT or a Business Unit

Emergent collaboration is not an IT or a business unit initiative; it's a collaboration in which both units and departments work together to solve a problem. Business units are needed to help define the specific use cases and encourage employee adoption, and IT is needed to evaluate security, integration, and technology and to help roll this out. The only way this can succeed is for both to work together.

Stringent Regulations

If I told you to pick any color as long as it was black, you'd probably look at me like I was crazy. The same thing is true for emergent collaboration. You can't tell employees you want to create a culture of collaboration and then turn around and say, "We want you to collaborate and connect with one another, but you have to do it the way we say you should." That defeats the entire purpose. Sure, there are mandatory policies or rules that some companies need to put in place, but organizations have to learn to get out of the way. Try to minimize the amount of rules and restrictions you put on employees.

Wrong Platform or Tool Selection

This was addressed in Chapter 6, but it's important to pick the right vendor for your business. This doesn't mean going with the cheapest vendor or the one with which you already have a relationship. Make sure the vendor you go with can solve the business problems you need solved and ranks highest on the variables discussed in Chapter 6.

Lack of Planning and Strategy Development

Strategy should always come before technology. Not having a strategic plan is the quickest way to get this initiative killed. You want to make sure you clearly understand what it is you are trying to achieve, why you want to achieve it, and how you are going to get it done. When you pick a technology platform, you don't have the answers to any of these questions, and that makes it hard to see the business value in emergent collaboration.

Focus on ROI, Not on Business Value

If you are simply looking to see a dollar return on an emergent collaboration investment, don't waste your time. This was discussed at length in Chapter 12. Most organizations fall into this business value paradox: They expect to see an ROI or business value, yet don't assign metrics (and follow up on those metrics) to gauge success. Typically, the primary reason organizations invest in emergent collaboration is not financial; it's to connect their employees together to solve a business problem or achieve a goal.

The Person Responsible Leaves

This is one of the important factors in creating emergent collaboration teams. If everything falls on the shoulders of one person and that person leaves the company, you're in a lot of trouble. These initiatives should never fall solely on one individual; it's unfair to that person and dangerous for you.

Summary and Action Items

The purpose of this chapter is to bring together all the information covered in the book.

Table 14.1 can be used as a strategic blueprint or road map as you take the emergent collaboration journey. However, during this journey there are a few common obstacles or pitfalls that organizations have to overcome to succeed:

- Go through the strategic plan for emergent collaboration.
- Will you adapt this plan or use it as is? If you adapt it, what changes are you going to make?
- What do you believe are the obstacles your organization is going to face? Try to anticipate them and plan for them.

The U.S. Department of State has been involved with collaboration initiatives for several years and they have learned quite a lot during that time. I asked Richard Boly, Director of eDiplomacy at the U.S. Department of State, to share some of his insights and learnings about strategy.

Nothing begets success like failure. It took three big ones to ignite the spark that led to the State Department's Office of eDiplomacy. The first came to light following the 1998 bombings of American embassies in East Africa, when a blue-ribbon commission found that State needed to do much, much better at sharing knowledge and communicating with other foreign affairs agencies. The second was 9/11, which underscored that knowledge sharing had become a critical, governmentwide necessity for national security. The third was an expensive flop at addressing the first two; State's proposed online foreign affairs collaboration zone received no buy-in from other agencies or from State's users, who found the system too clunky. So State set up eDiplomacy in 2002 to do three things: give State's end users a voice in IT decision making; improve communication and collaboration within State and with foreign affairs partner agencies; and design and implement a better way to share knowledge and information. More recently, we have added a fourth role— techcraft for diplomats—to catalyze collaboration among the worlds of technology, diplomacy, and development.

Through the support and advocacy of new technology like blogs, wikis, professional networking, global TechCamps, Tech@ State conferences, and virtual student einterns, eDiplomacy promotes an organizational culture for innovation that allows State diplomats to lead the foreign policy process at home and abroad.

Innovation is hard. Making it work in an organizational context is difficult because there is a need to build out technical infrastructure, and also to change how work is done. Perhaps the most important key to unlocking the capacity for techno-organizational innovation in a large organization is to embrace bureaucratic entrepreneurship. While the concept may sound absurd, it is not. The capacity for entrepreneurial behavior in a large organization is essential, so that it can adapt to the external forces. Even risk-averse organizations need to innovate.

Accepting that entrepreneurial behavior is the path to techno-organizational innovation, you can drown in the fountain of knowledge without clear focus or direction. It's good to have a filter for teasing out what is important from what is not—a strategy. Strategy is vital to decision, communication, measurement, and the allocation of resources. It also persuades your skeptics and comforts your bosses that you know what you're doing. In fact, without strategy the technology is useless and collaboration efforts will likely fail.

Once a strategy is developed (and strategies can change, they are neither immutable nor fixed), the change agents need to be brought together. Create an office. Let the innovators have a place to hang their hats, take time to think about how to improve processes, learn new tricks, and engage in collaborative tinkering with others. It's also important to make sure those change agents have the mandate and mindset to get out of the office and engage the rest of the organization. The office has to evangelize.

There are several things that need to be considered when developing a strategy. Leadership must create an enabling environment. I moved from an office to a cubicle, both to stay more closely connected with our team and to reinforce our office's flat organizational structure. Allow team members to set their own ceilings.

Accept failure and protect your team from demotivating external naysayers. While we often feel innovation is in some way quick, a great deal of trial and error goes into it. Many ideas that at first glance appear promising may not be. That's okay. Little failures allow the organization to avoid making large bad bets. The key is to be patient and understand that the path to innovation takes time. It took the State Department four years to notice significant progress and build up the processes surrounding its most valuable innovative knowledge-sharing programs.

Don't buy into technology as a panacea. On the technical side, complexity kills. Technologies need to be simple, intuitive, and cheap for the user. Don't buy into technologies that come with an onerous administrative burden. Also, let your users innovate. They'll pleasantly surprise you. Plus, they do the work. Finally, don't wait; get started and get down to work. That's probably the most important thing to do. Launch, learn, and iterate. All these things combined help make for a successful collaboration strategy.

So to summarize, when developing a strategy consider the following:

- Culture of collaboration is crucial
- Encourage internal entrepreneurism
- Give the innovators a place to congregate and innovate
- Evangelism from all levels is key
- Leadership must create an enabling environment
- Accept failure but protect your team from negativity
- Little failures help keep the organization from making large bad bets
- Be patient as this does take time
- Technology is not a panacea
- Complexity kills
- Launch, learn, and iterate

fifteen

What's Next?

It's hard to imagine that just a few years ago many of the platforms and technologies we use in our personal and professional lives did not exist. What was the world like before Wikipedia, Twitter, Facebook, and blogs? A lot can happen in a few years, as we have seen.

In fact, a few years ago there were debates over whether these tools belonged in enterprises and whether they would succeed. Today it seems as though those debates have been quashed by the many examples, case studies, and stories of small, medium-size, and enterprise-size companies deploying these new tools and strategies across their organizations. Although we are seeing a positive momentum toward building collaborative organizations, there is still a lot of work to be done. Many organizations are still at the early stages of their emergent collaboration journeys, and some have not yet gotten involved.

In looking ahead, it's hard to imagine organizations around the world not using these tools to improve collaboration in the workplace, not just among employees, but with customers and partners as well.

As mentioned earlier, I was born in a digital world and don't remember what it was like to do business without the Internet and social and collaborative tools. I can only imagine what my children are going to say about the world into which they are born.

Smart Platforms and Collaboration

In the future it's hard not to see the integral (and perhaps scary) role that computers and artificial intelligence are going to play. Imagine sharing and creating content and having everything filtered through a "smart" platform that recommends where the information should go, categorizes it and places it in the proper place, and automatically lets the relevant people know about it. Instead of having to upload something onto a platform and create a group, what if you could just drag and drop it into a folder and the rest was taken care of for you? Or better yet, what if the platform knew contextually what you were working on and created folders and groups automatically? The platform analyzes your network and your connections, analyzes the content of the document, and already "knows" what you need to do with it and who should receive that information. In fact, computers might understand our intentions and the possibilities of information and data better than we can and as a result will be able to make recommendations that we are incapable of seeing or putting together.

In a chess game humans can think several moves in advance, but computers can play out entire game scenarios through virtually limitless calculations. What if this was applied to business scenarios? It's a bit scary to think that one day computers will be capable of understanding and making better decisions than humans, but that doesn't mean it can't become a reality. I always joke that future collaboration platforms are going to have Siri-like functionality, but for the entire enterprise. (Siri is the voice-controlled virtual assistant that Apple recently added to its new line of iPhones.) I believe that voice-controlled collaboration platforms will be a key part of how we collaborate in the future.

Perhaps that's a bit farther out than the "near" future, but it seems probable that we will one day live in a world where many of our actions in the workplace are analyzed by computers to check if we are making the right decisions. This would be a very sophisticated and in-depth type of behavioral analytics.

Future of Management

It's also clear that management models are going to have to change. Employees should not feel miserable and unfulfilled at work. They should understand where they fit in the big picture of an organization and how they contribute to the organization but also how the organization contributes to them. I don't know when it happened or how, but somewhere along the road to profits we began ignoring the people who help generate those profits. We began treating people as expendable accessories and expecting the most from them. People come home tired and exhausted after work, often not looking forward to the next day when they will have to wake up early and come home late. Instead, people should feel energized and happy about the work they are doing. People should like their jobs and the people they work with, and I'm hopeful that we will get there and that emergent collaboration is a step in that direction.

The whole mentality of managing by fear or by command and control is done for. We are going to see new collaborative leaders take the helms of their companies. Technology always changes, but in order for organizations to sustain and grow, their management models are also going to have to change.

Gamification

Perhaps in the not so distant future we will see the heavy gamification of the enterprise, in which gaming concepts are deployed to make work more enjoyable. We might see real-time analysis and analytics of employee performance and activity that can gauge what tasks employees should do next to keep up their morale and energy levels. We already see this to some degree at companies such as TELUS, which leverages gaming concepts and badges for new employees during their onboarding. Employees are taken through a 90-day scavenger hunt in which they have to complete certain tasks to show their fluency with the emergent collaboration platforms.

Vendors

One of the things we are definitely going to see is a continued evolution of collaboration platforms. Today many products look the same and do similar things, but over the last year or two a few vendors have emerged that have started to challenge conventional emergent collaboration platforms. I think we can expect to see many more changes, experiments, adaptations, and evolutions of existing platforms in the coming years along with the development of new ones.

We've seen an interesting trend over the past few years where vendors started out in their niche areas, focusing on specific areas such as microblogging, wikis, document management, ideation, and so forth. Today vendors are converging to offer a full suite of products and services to meet the collaboration needs of organizations. The point solutions, I think, will be acquired and absorbed into larger organizations that have collaboration suites. Right now there's a great opportunity for an enterprise collaboration ecosystem, something like the iTunes store, but for collaboration, where companies can buy and integrate modules and applications that are relevant to them. The analogy I like to use is LEGOs. Today when a company buys a collaboration platform, it has to buy a specific LEGO set that allows it to construct something. In the future these LEGO pieces are going to connect with each other based on collaboration standards, so new designs, shapes, and platforms can be built. This will be the collaboration ecosystem.

Collaborative Operating Systems

We will see a fully functioning operating system built with the concepts of collaboration in mind. I have already seen some vendors moving in this direction. This will be something far more advanced than the icons we click on our computers. What if the future operating system was in and of itself a collaborative platform with all the applications and features we needed built into it? This wouldn't be something you would need to log on to or access; it would simply be a part of everything you did: one central hub to access anything and everyone you need to get your job done.

Mobility and E-mail

There are many people out there who constantly decry the death of e-mail, but let's step back and think about that for a second. Today, there are really only two things that are unique to all individuals: their e-mail addresses and their phone numbers. This is very important when we think about collaboration. Today, phone numbers and e-mail addresses are the two lowest common denominators for individuals when it comes to collaboration and communication. I'm not confident we will see the end of e-mail, though. It may instead be repurposed to act as an alert notification system that alerts us of people trying to communicate with us on other platforms. With the rise of collaborative platforms, though, it's hard to see the purpose of e-mail not changing.

Surely mobility will also play an integral role for the future of our enterprises as our phones become smarter and more capable of taking on the functions of computers today. Most emergent collaboration vendors also offer intuitive mobile applications and interfaces so that employees can take emergent collaboration with them anywhere they go. We also have to consider the role of telecommuting, or working from home, which is a trend I believe will continue to rise as employees are often no longer needed at an office; as long as they can access the people and the information they need to get their jobs done, physical location is going to become less of a factor for job roles. Boundaries for organizations will be severely diminished or eliminated.

The Cloud

I struggle with seeing how organizations at some point will not move to fully cloud-based collaboration (and other) solutions. It will still take a few years, but eventually we will get to a point where on-premise deployments and physical devices that run collaboration applications will not be used. Everything will be run and operated online. It's cheaper, easier, and more effective.

Relationships

Collaboration centers on the relationships we have with people or the potential relationships we can build with people. Right now there isn't an effective way to match our relationships to the work we do. For example, let's say I'm tweeting with someone at a large organization who is also in the process of working on a deal with someone else at my company. Right now there is no way to make that connection, so relational collaboration databases are going to be an interesting area that we will see explored in the future. The future collaboration platform will be able to match the people we are connected to with the work we do, or the people that we *should* be connected to with the work that we do.

One thing is for sure, we are still near the early stages of emergent collaboration and it is becoming a strategic imperative for companies of all sizes. As this continues, we will see more attention paid to how collaboration impacts the lives of employees, not just while they are at work but also when they are at home.

To help us understand what the future of emergent collaboration and business will look like, I can think of no better person than J. P. Rangaswami, who is the chief scientist at Salesforce.

The defining characteristic of the world economy has grown beyond its agricultural roots and forged past the industrial age into one dominated by services. Knowledge workers are now the norm; knowledge work is lumpy, with unpredictable peaks and troughs.

Throughout the industrial age, manufacturers had end-to-end control of the processes of production and consumption: any color you liked as long as it was black. When it comes to services, this control has evaporated; as a result, processes are no longer as repeatable and standardized as they used to be, exception handling has become the norm, and nonlinearity is common as we move from process to pattern.

This evolution of "lumpy" work, coupled with the increasing nonlinearity of processes, comes at a time when there's a new generation at work, a generation that knows nothing about life before the web, a generation weaned on smart mobile devices, a generation resident in social networks.

As a result of all this, work as we know it will change beyond all recognition over the next five years. By 2017, the following things are likely to happen.

We won't have any desktops. There won't be any desks to put them on; workplaces will resemble a hybrid of coffee shops and airport lounges.

We won't have any laptops. We will have smart mobile devices. Not just the tablets and phones we see today but devices we haven't even dreamed of will be in use.

We won't have any keyboards. We'll use our voices as the primary way to create information, communicate, search, and instruct; touch will be a close second, more for navigation than for anything else.

We won't have any paper. Using printers and paper will be perceived as akin to smoking at work: irresponsible and damaging to the environment.

We won't have any software. Instead, we will consume services from the cloud, sometimes via HTML5 apps, sometimes via browser–operating system mutants, and sometimes via apps native to specific devices.

Businesses, as Boston professor N. Venkatraman stated a decade ago, will morph from being hierarchies of customers and products into networks of relationships and capabilities. As a result, we will learn more about how to value relationships and capabilities. Skill, expertise, and knowledge will continue to be important, but increasingly, the focus will shift to the wisdom that comes from tempering skill and expertise and knowledge with learning and experience.

As the social network paradigm evolves into its next iteration, work will begin to resemble a hybrid between a video game and a virtual world. Firms will have sandboxes where new employees will discover how the company works, the "mechanics" and "controls" that they need to know to navigate the organization. They will choose their own teammates "bottom up" as they unearth affinities and complementarities as peers. They will select their own tasks: the missions and quests that appeal most to their values, abilities, and aspirations.

E-mail, by then 40 years old, will go the way of desks and PCs. All communications will be publish-subscribe, with power in the hands of the recipient, not the sender. Presence will become more important, a prerequisite for short synchronous communications; longer communications will usually be asynchronous as people shift place and time.

Teamwork will become the rule rather than the exception as people realize that their social networks tell them what's going on, recommend what they should do, answer their questions, and even help curate and filter the incredible volume of information they have access to. People will realize that a team is nothing more than a mini social network.

The blame cultures of the past will recede as workstreaming gains momentum. People will share what they are doing, how they did it, and what they'd like to do. And their networks will respond, rating them, curating them, but no longer berating them.

This sense of team will pervade the work environment and beyond.

Firms will have to work hard to attract talent: talent in the form of staff, talent in the form of partners, talent in the form of customers.

A firm's values and ethics and track record will become its brand, alive and vulnerable in the social networks. This brand will be what attracts, retains, and develops the talent. People will migrate to the workplaces where they share the same values and ethics. Staff, partners, and customers will all migrate that way. The talent war will be won and lost on the field of corporate values and ethics.

Information flows will also change as collaboration transcends selfishness. Collective intelligence techniques will become more important: prediction markets, crowdsourcing, folksonomies, the lot. As the volumes of data grow, visualization and filtering techniques will also gain in importance. The semantic web will have arrived as Big Data engenders Big Analytics.

As the barriers of the enterprise come down, as companies learn to become more "social," as networks connect companies with their customers and partners, security concepts will also evolve, moving away from the perimeter firewall models of today into a data- and entitlement-driven approach at individual, application, and device levels.

Inspirational leadership will become more important, not just at the enterprise level, but at the team level. When all other things are equal in terms of values and ethics, people will join companies just to be able to work with a particular leader, just to be inspired. To learn. And to teach.

And we will slowly see the establishment of the economics of abundance replacing the poverty implied in the economics of scarcity. As George Bernard Shaw said, "If I have an apple and I give you that apple, you have the apple and I don't. If I have an idea and I give you that idea, we both have that idea." Information will be seen to be the extreme nonrival good that it is; knowledge will be there for all to gain; and the wisdom that comes from the learning of experience will form the difference.

sixteen

Bonus Chapter with Andrew McAfee

Andrew McAfee, the author of *Enterprise 2.0*, is a principal research scientist at MIT, where he continues to explore how emergent social and collaborative technologies are affecting the ways organizations conduct business. He is credited with coining the term *Enterprise 2.0* five years ago, and it has garnered attention and momentum since.

I had the opportunity to speak with Andrew and decided to add our conversation as a bonus chapter as I believe there were a lot of interesting and valuable insights. Below is the transcript of our discussion.

Do you regret coming up with the term Enterprise 2.0*?*
New phenomena need new names. I was the first one to hang a label on companies' use of emergent social software platforms for their business purposes. I chose *Enterprise 2.0* to play off the term *Web 2.0*.

You have defined Enterprise 2.0 a few times over the past few years. Can you define what it is? Previously it has been used to include customers, partners, and employees.
Enterprise 2.0 is the use of emergent social software platforms by businesses in pursuit of their goals regardless of whether it is inside or outside the firewall. I personally have spent more time researching and working with organizations inside the firewall mainly because there

are a lot of people doing a good job focusing on the customer- and external-facing side of things.

What about social CRM, now being used as a way to describe customer-facing initiatives via emergent social software platforms?

One of the problems we technologists have is that we keep using different labels to talk about the same phenomena. This is an old debate and harmful instead of helpful. I would flip this on its head and ask why people feel they need to come up with new terms when a useful term already exists. I think it's a unique kink of the IT industry, which turns out new jargon more often than it turns out new products.

If organizations don't invest in Enterprise 2.0, what do you think will happen to them?

If they own a diamond mine or an oil well, I think nothing serious will happen to them. There are lots of ways to get competitive advantage as a business, and some businesses are kind of immune to Enterprise 2.0 or other things. Most of us are not sitting on those types of businesses. It's clear that the pace of change, the pace of business, and the pace of competition are increasing. In that world, sitting on top of a complicated situation and being able to apply ways to share information, find relevant expertise, and bring more minds to collaborate on a problem is important and getting more important over time. However, does this mean that every organization needs to adopt Enterprise 2.0 or it won't be here in a few years? That's way too strong a statement.

The longer we look at the history of the IT industry and the way they try to market and sell their products, the less surprising this type of "do or die" mentality becomes. In fact, this type of thinking is losing a lot of its power, and executives are tired of hearing this message since they have heard it from the ERP days. It is more helpful to say that there is a set of business opportunities, challenges, and needs that can be addressed by 2.0, and if these things are important for a particular business, they should probably pay attention to and invest in them.

What's happened with E2.0 that you least expected?

I am surprised on two fronts. On the technology side of things it is clear that we don't have the final form of the solution and still don't understand all the possibilities of emergent social software platforms. Google+ is a good example and is legitimately different from most other forms of emergent social software. Smart technologists are still figuring things out and tinkering to find the best solutions for how people actually want to share things and collaborate. There is still a large amount of innovation taking place here. I am constantly pleasantly surprised at the innovation in the space.

The second thing I am surprised about is a bit paradoxical: It is the speed and the slowness of adoption. The fact that there is an Enterprise 2.0 conference on both coasts and that there is this active debate over what the terms should be is due to the fact that the ideas have a lot of traction and interest. There is a strong community behind all of this. It's rare now to find an organization that isn't doing something on this front.

However, the idea has been slow to change fundamentally how organizations operate and make use of these things. I still get asked the same questions I did years ago about security, risks, and business benefits. I'm surprised at the speed and the inertia on the organizational front.

Why do you think so many vendors look alike in terms of features, functionality, and user interface?

Why should we be surprised by that? Spreadsheet programs all look the same, and so do word processing programs. These technologies tend to converge rather quickly to things that appear to be working. However, I think there is still a lot of innovation that is coming our way, so even though vendors may have settled down, it's only a temporary thing. Tools will change and integrate more tightly as things evolve.

What are some of the macroeconomic factors affecting E2.0?

The pace of business, the pace of change, and the pace of competition are all increasing and affecting Enterprise 2.0. Teams are now becoming more virtual, and the telecommuting revolution is actually happening. Organizations are spreading around the world, and the need for coordination and knowledge sharing is greater than ever. I have to struggle to see how it can be done any other way except by deploying these emergent social and collaborative tools that give people a voice and that make it easy to share information, find subject matter experts, and collaborate.

What role does mobile play in E2.0?

It's clearly going to play a huge role as the world of work is changing in all the ways I talked about. Devices are always on and always on us, making it easy to share, participate, collaborate, and narrate your work anywhere you are.

How do you bridge the gap between Gen X and Gen Y and Gen Z? How do you accommodate everyone regardless of age or technological fluency?

You're not going to bridge the gap. Those two communities have totally different technology preferences and patterns. There is no silver bullet that will fix that. I believe that the technology that will be used in collaboration will be determined by the most powerful person in that group. If the partner at a law firm wants to use e-mail or if the CEO at a large organization wants to use messaging, those will be the technologies used. I also think that the millennials entering the workforce are a large and vocal demographic, and this is one of the reasons organizations are exploring these types of tools.

Lead by example, and if you believe Enterprise 2.0 is powerful, get out there and do it yourself. Share documents, send status updates, post links; do what you need to do to show and encourage your peers. Organizations also need to be careful not to buy into the fantasy that the fact that people want things to be egalitarian means that they will be. We aren't just going to get rid of hierarchies.

I know you say this often, but I have to ask: Have you heard any Enterprise 2.0 horror stories yet?

No; I still have no Enterprise 2.0 horror stories to share.

How can organizations stay up to date with new tools and technologies? It seems as though things are changing and evolving at a pace that organizations can't keep up with.

That is just the nature of the technology industry, and things aren't going to change. It is hard and is frustrating, but it is a reality. What organizations can do is keep their eyes on what they are trying to do as a business instead of focusing on trying to grab the latest gizmo that comes out. Focusing on the business drivers first will dictate the tools that an organization should be using. I call this an inside-out approach. It's always going to be important to have some resources to scan the technology landscape to see what exists.

When do you think E2.0 will become prevalent in organizations? What does the business landscape look like in the future?

Ten years is an eternity in this world. If you think about it, nothing we know about today was around 10 years ago. There was no Facebook, no Twitter, and no Foursquare and many other vendors and platforms didn't exist, so it's really hard to predict. What I can say with some confidence is that innovation will continue. I don't think that the last 10 years were the peak of innovation for the technology space. There will be deeper and broader change; that is what makes this world so fascinating and hard to predict.

What are your favorite E2.0 examples or success stories?

Tata Consultancy Services, Best Buy, and the movement we are seeing toward Government 2.0.

What is your take on governance and policies regulating the use of emergent social software in organizations?

For organizations that really restrict and try to regulate how employees use tools, this is not just a detriment; it is the kiss of death. The more rules you have trying to regulate and control how employees use these tools, the greater a detriment it is. I realize that some organizations are regulated and more heavily controlled, but that doesn't mean they should act as the thought police to regulate digital expression; that doesn't make any sense to me. I would also question whether organizations have the same type of rules and regulations for employees using e-mail as they do for employees using emergent social software.

What indicators predict the success of an Enterprise 2.0 initiative?

I believe the sincerity of management in letting employees use emergent social software in their organizations and the enthusiasm conveyed by management are the key predictors. Management needs to put trust in the employees to use the tools and technologies.

Who is your ideal Enterprise 2.0 team composed of?

I would want a couple of technologists who are user experience professionals who can design simple and intuitive tools. I would also want a curator or two to keep the content looking good. Finally, I would want a few informal evangelists and champions and formal leaders (executives or decision makers) of the organization. In a regulated industry it is also important to include HR and legal/compliance.

How do you get people involved?

Assuming that I was a senior person at an organization, I would designate some and cajole and convince others. I would try to get as many people as I could to narrate their work and/or their ignorance. This is one of the quickest ways to show momentum and success. I also recommend that organizations not start the conversation by telling people about the platform or about the technology. Instead, the conversation needs to start by conveying the value to the employees and the benefits of using the tools and technologies.

Any closing thoughts?

Let's not kid ourselves that organizations are going to walk away from existing hierarchies, routines, and the like, just because a new set of technologies is available and because people want them to. Instead, we will see a complement of this with a much more peer-based collaborative way to do things. This is good news.

Afterword

Reflecting on *The Collaborative Organization*, I'm reminded of my aphorism that this is not an information age. Traditional media—print, radio, television, management information systems, and the first era of the web—gave us better access to information. However, today we have access to the intelligence contained in the craniums of other people.

Rather than an information age, it's more appropriate to speak of an age of networked intelligence in which we can collaborate with others on a global basis at the speed of light. This is why collaboration has become probably the hottest topic in business today.

A recent study by McKenzie that was much hyped at the 2011 World Economic Forum in Davos indicates that collaboration in the office can demonstrably increase not only profits but also market share. The most profound change in vertically integrated corporations is rapidly occurring, driven by a technology push, a demand pull, and a demographic kick that collectively are enabling an organizational transformation.

Standing back for a bit, why is all this happening?

Technology Push

The web originally was about connectivity and information sharing. Fiber optics facilitated exponentially increasing bandwidth at much lower cost, making access to the Web nearly ubiquitous, some would even argue a human right. The evolution of the web coined by O'Reilly as Web 2.0 is how the new web is used for collaboration, changing the way we orchestrate capability to innovate, create goods and services, and engage with the world.

The exponential growth of collaborative technologies in the consumer market is well demonstrated with the adoption of cell phones. Of the 7 billion people on the planet, 60 percent have cell phones, with 1.4 billion cell phones sold in 2010 alone. Social networking facilities have seen some of the fastest growth in history, reaching 10 percent of the world's population in just eight years. On Facebook over 100 million people are tagged in pictures each day.

This platform for interaction has given rise to content-sharing technologies such as Google Docs and YouTube, blogging technologies for sharing ideas, microblogging technologies for broadcasting notifications, and wikis for the collaborative development of content.

These technology enablers have enjoyed remarkable growth in social revolutions, as demonstrated in the changing course of governments, exposure of corruption, and an unprecedented volume of shared data. However, it's only recently that these capabilities have created a demand for collaborative technologies in business.

Demand Pull

The new business environment demands a new corporate architecture that is based on networks. Old vertically integrated hierarchies are morphing into business webs—horizontally integrated ecosystems—that allow companies to focus on what they do best and partner to do the rest. Business webs demand greater levels of collaboration than did their vertically integrated predecessors. Though plagued by miscommunications, time zone delays, and outdated e-mails, these new business webs are typically more efficient than old ERP-enabled hierarchical companies because the pressures of the marketplace are brought to bear on every business function. Moreover, the input from various business web partners is essential to a successful operation. Firms that collaborate more effectively and build better business webs with lower transaction costs will achieve important competitive advantages.

With these new business webs, the way we make decisions is changing. Historically, we have assumed that business decisions are based solely on facts, information, and evidence provided to executives by the most senior knowledge workers. But cognitive science now shows that the strongest influence on decisions is emotion—our gut feelings. When there are several people making a decision, the problem is compounded. Some people do not disclose important information because they're not sure that they understand it fully or can articulate it properly. Others don't want to rock the boat. If the business culture is hierarchical, people will be afraid to speak up and contradict the boss even if they have crucial information. It is better to support the boss with a marginal fact than contradict him with an important truth.

Businesses were structured as hierarchies in which information was distilled toward the top executives, who made the decisions and issued commands that flowed back down to the front lines. A whole industry of executive information systems redefined as business intelligence was created to give the people at the top summarized, analyzed, and sliced and diced views of vast quantities of information so that they could more intelligently command and control their resources and the company.

These tools were effective at providing information content but failed to deliver significant business value. What was missing was the context—the insights into the data and what the data meant to the company. Decision makers were drowning in data with limited understanding of what it all meant. Seeing that sales were up in a certain demographic in Utah yet down in the same demographic in Wyoming was once defined as intelligence. But without knowing the why, that intelligence has little value. Collaboration with the stakeholders in the business web is what creates insights and context that are actionable.

What investments in information management of the 1990s and 2000s defined as business intelligence did was share and make visible data and content through different perspectives. That's it. Any intelligence was left to the viewer. The current investments in collaboration, properly implemented, will take the next necessary step for creating and sharing actionable insights in the right context.

Most important, the new collaborative suites are replacing traditional primitive technologies such as electronic mail. They combine industrial-strength social networking, ideation capabilities, new generation document tools such as wikis, blogging and microblogging, collaborative decision management, and next generation knowledge management and analytics to create nothing less than a new operating system for the enterprise. I have a conflict of interest discussing these tools as I've been deeply involved in building one: Moxie Software's Employee Spaces.

Demographic Kick

Accelerating the trend toward more collaborative business models is the new generation of young employees. In my 1997 book *Growing Up Digital* I dubbed them the Net Generation. They've grown up digital, and their knowledge and use of a multidirectional, if not a multidimensional, Internet has influenced their cultural attitudes. It's made them natural team members who expect back-and-forth interaction rather than command-and-control discipline. The baby boomers were satisfied with knowing what decision was made, but today's young employees want to know why. They're not insubordinate; they just recognize that understanding the reasons behind the decision can make the difference between success and failure in implementation.

This emerging generation has from childhood had access to interactive games that require both team building and strategic skills. Learning a game and having died (virtually) a hundred times before winning makes them far more determined and more likely to try new ideas and take calculated risks. Unlike boomers, who absorbed unidirectional TV programs, their echo grew up with interactive technology. They collaborated constantly through online chats, multiuser video games, and, more recently, text messages and Facebook. For teenagers today, doing their homework is a social and collaborative event involving text messages, instant messages, and Facebook walls to discuss problems while the iPod plays in the background.

In the workplace, Net Geners are a powerful force for change. My research shows that companies that selectively and effectively embrace Net Gen beliefs and philosophy perform better than do those which don't. In fact, I'm convinced that the Net Gen culture is the new culture of work. Net Generation employees are ideally suited for today's new corporation. They are savvy, confident, upbeat, open-minded, creative, and independent, which makes them a challenge to manage. To meet their demands for more learning opportunities and responsibility ownership, instant feedback, greater work-life balance, and stronger workplace relationships, companies must alter their culture and management approaches while continuing to respect the needs of older employees. Properly cultivated, this generation's attributes will be a critical source of innovation and competitive advantage to the organization.

This generation will demand collaborative decision making in the workplace, and old-style managers who resist will soon find themselves isolated. The old guard is no longer leading; now it's playing defense.

Organizational Transformation

It is clear that a new decentralized taxonomy of collaboration for the enterprise is emerging as the dominant paradigm. It will speed up the metabolism, lower the costs, and enable previously unimagined innovation in and between firms based on previously unimagined levels of collaboration. This will require a new openness and transparency and ultimately a new sense of trust.

Hundreds of years ago, businesses were small groups of individuals, artisans, and apprentices. They produced a high-quality custom product at low volumes. But the industrial age created demands for much higher volume at much lower costs. The business model of the artisans needed to evolve.

The hierarchical structure and the vertically integrated organization were born, resulting in a dramatic change in the business environment of the time. It evolved over the last century, capable of mass production at much lower costs. During this period, the first world markets and their superior schools had the advantage as knowledge entered the office or plant during the day to create capacity and then left the facility for the night.

With today's mature transportation and communications systems, labor no longer goes to work. Quite the opposite; work now goes to labor. Companies are now finding regions in the global economy that can mass-produce the same products at much lower costs. Unfortunately, reducing our cost structures to compete has become a race to the bottom as plants first moved from the U.S. Northeast to the South (when nonunion air-conditioned factories became more cost-effective), then to Mexico, to China, and now to Vietnam. Nevertheless, as costs are dropping quickly, so are the margins.

Logistics and lower-cost transportation through the simple but disruptive concept of containerization ensured that the advantage of proximity to first world markets is now gone. This is even more the case for digital products and services that have next to zero cost for delivery.

The first world response to this digital commoditization is to look for new ways to innovate from its rich collective intelligence by providing high-value solutions to more complex business problems and rapidly changing consumer demands. But clearly the challenge is far beyond what any single person can know or, for that matter, what any single bureaucracy can filter to the top. We have entered an age of collaboration, driven by the need for innovation.

Just as the business world changed for the artisans in the Industrial Revolution, the business world is changing again. Last time it was a demand for mass production and lower costs. Now it's a demand for innovation.

Don Tapscott

Don Tapscott is the author of 14 books, including (with Anthony D. Williams) *Macrowikinomics: Rebooting Business and the World*. He is an adjunct professor at the Rotman School of Management, University of Toronto. Twitter: @dtapscott.

INDEX